THE IMAGINARY PHOTO MUSEUM

THE IMAGINARY PHOTO MUSEUM

With 457 Photographs from 1836 to the Present

Renate and L. Fritz Gruber

With texts by Helmut Gernsheim, L. Fritz Gruber,
Beaumont Newhall, and Jeane von Oppenheim

English Translation by Michael Rollof

Penguin Books

Penguin Books Ltd, Harmondsworth,
Middlesex, England
Penguin Books, 625 Madison Avenue,
New York, New York 10022, U.S.A.
Penguin Books Australia Ltd, Ringwood,
Victoria, Australia
Penguin Books Canada Ltd, 2801 John Street,
Markham, Ontario, Canada L3R 1B4
Penguin Books (N.Z.) Ltd, 182-190 Wairau Road,
Auckland 10, New Zealand
First published in Germany as *Das imaginäre Photo-Museum* by DuMont
Buchverlag 1981

This translation first published in Great Britain in Penguin Books 1982
Published simultaneously in the U.S.A. by Harmony Books

Made and printed in Germany

Contents

THE IMAGINARY PHOTO MUSEUM: FICTION AND REALIZATION

L. Fritz Gruber

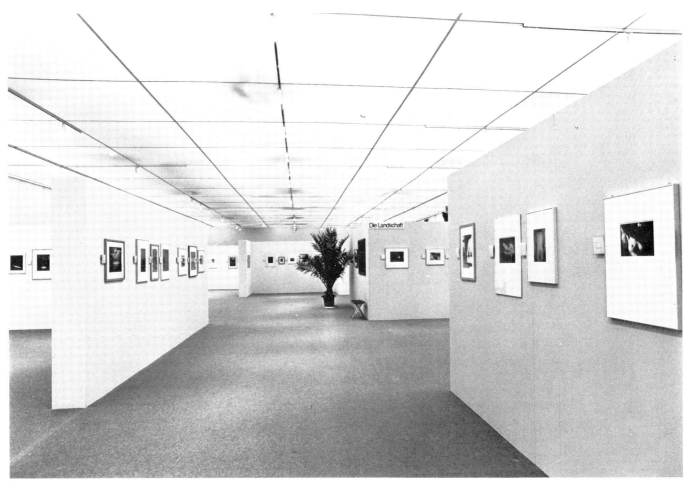

The Imaginary Photo Museum—a view of the exhibition.

Photokina, the photography trade fair and exhibit that takes place in Cologne every year, has demonstrated over a period of thirty years the importance of the documentary and creative aspects of photography with more than three hundred exhibits. Doubtless, it has also provided numerous impulses for the collection and exhibition of photographs, and new writings on photography.

Photokina is aware that it was neither the first to do any of this nor alone in its efforts. Beaumont Newhall's remarks in this volume delineate the historical development of these photographic exhibitions.

But whatever that development might have been, in 1900, it seemed to Photokina that the time had come to show its respect to those museums, public galleries, and libraries that hold photography in the same high esteem that they hold the more tradi-

tional art forms. Therefore, we made up a representative list of these institutions and made every effort to borrow for our exhibit only vintage prints. The Imaginary Photo Museum was shown from September 12 until September 28, 1980, at the Kunsthalle in Cologne. It was not conceived as a traveling exhibit and therefore remained unique—loans of the kind we received are made only rarely nowadays.

We have discovered, in the meantime, what a valuable and often fragile pictorial and cultural property photographs can be. Many of them were taken for their day and not meant to last. Least of all were they designed for museum status, and in contrast to graphic art whose rank was always recognized, photographs were not treated as *objets d'art* from the very start. And so, many of the earliest photographs are extremely rare and exceedingly fragile.

So much the more, Photokina feels indebted to lenders whose generosity was, one assumes, facilitated by the fact that the exhibit would not travel. It was a lengthy and strenuous undertaking but also unique for the organizer of the Imaginary Photo Museum to pore over the representative list of the important collections in Europe, America, and Japan, and to ask for selected single pieces as loans. But it was a joy to discover with what love and care, with what understanding the photographs are safeguarded. It was also a pleasure to find some photos which otherwise only crop up at auctions in a well-preserved state at these institutions.

As much as we sought to create an objective selection, it inevitably bears subjective traits. This holds true as much for the list of museums as for the actual works chosen. During the two years spent organizing the exhibition we were joined by seasoned curators, so that the selection changed and began to fill out. Still, we could only show what was actually available from these collections and what they were willing to make available to us. One could certainly select any number of exhibits of equal importance from the existing material.

The purpose of the exhibit was to realize a fiction, a dream—and at the same time provide a delight to the eyes. The Imaginary Photo Museum had to exist for its own sake and not to construct tangential connections with something outside itself.

The exhibit was arranged chronologically on the ground floor and into a cross section of seven basic photographic themes on the second floor. The chronology section, with four text tablets, which are also in this book, detailed the sequence of photographic styles from 1840 to ca. 1980. The analogy section provided comparison, similarities, and differences regardless of the periods of the photographs. Here the purpose was to intensify and enrich the observers' visual experience by means of otherwise unusual juxtapositions. In every other respect the pictures and legends were to speak for themselves.

And they evidently did so with great success. During the seventeen days of the show, nearly fifty thousand visitors attended; the international press responded positively; and Helmut Gernsheim provided a factual and critical assessment of the show (see page 237). Two days after the show all works of art were on their way back to their home museums. There remains only the memory of an exhibition that has been called unique and a once-in-a-lifetime event.

What was the Imaginary Photo Museum has now become this book that corresponds to the idea set forth in André Malraux's classic essay that the works of art scattered about the world should be brought together by means of the modern techniques of reproduction and printing. Thus, this book perpetuates the brief life of this "ideal museum" in another form. While photography, of course, also knows the concept of the "original," still, more than any other medium, it lends itself to the duplicating process and can be served by it as here.

Of course, the presentation of the photographs has changed. The spacious magic of the exhibition halls has been transformed by a publication that is governed by the laws of typography and printing. Here the photographs are presented and paired in a similar but sometimes different order and are moved much closer together. Color photographs, which seemed to appear only occasionally in an exhibition primarily devoted to black-and-white, have been collected in one section here. In this way the printed *Imaginary Photo Museum* has acquired a life of its own. Ideally, it will provide new thought impulses and, by means of biographical data, afford the reader additional information.

As is inevitably the case with large collective undertakings of this kind, thanks must be extended in many directions: first of all to the institutions, photographers, and their heirs who entrusted to us their photographs; then to the Cologne Fair and the Photoindustrieverband; and, last, to our closest associates: Renate Gruber, Bettina Gruber, Jeane von Oppenheim, and Christoph Heidelauf—and to many others who are mentioned elsewhere.

MUSEUMS AND PHOTOGRAPHY

Beaumont Newhall

It is a surprising historical fact that although photography was accepted by the art community soon after its invention, art museums were most reluctant to include photography in their programs until recent times. One of the great nineteenth-century exhibitions, the Art Treasures Exhibition of 1857, included a separate gallery for photography in the vast building erected for the purpose in Manchester, England. But this was a temporary museum, a showplace. The first established art museum to feature photography on a permanent basis appears to be the Kunsthalle in Hamburg. Under the directorship of the art historian Alfred Lichtwark, a mammoth show of amateur photography was organized in 1893 by Ernst Juhl, an enthusiastic amateur who promoted and collected photographs as works of art. Over six thousand prints filled all of the museum's galleries. There was an historical section, including many of the earliest daguerreotypes made in Hamburg—perhaps the first recognition by an art museum of photography's past.

The first museum in America to collect photographs in a systematic way was the Smithsonian Institution in Washington, D.C. Although not an art museum, pictorial photographs were included in its collecting in addition to photographs chosen specifically for their scientific and technical interest. To Alfred Stieglitz, the American photographer who did so much promotion of photography as a fine art, this was a minor triumph. He was overjoyed when, in 1910, the trustees of the Albright Art Gallery in Buffalo, New York, not only put on a large exhibition of international pictorial photography, but made an extraordinary commitment to the medium. Stieglitz wrote about it in a letter to Ernst Juhl: "The exhibition made such a deep artistic impression that the trustees bought twelve pictures for very good prices, and even set apart a gallery for them. This space will remain a permanent home for pictorial photography. The dream I had in Berlin in 1885 has finally become a reality."

Alas the museum—now styled the Albright-Knox Art Gallery—did not fulfill its commitment. In 1937 there was no "permanent gallery of pictorial photography." The director at that time and I searched for the photographs that had been purchased: original prints by Stieglitz's contemporaries Eduard J. Steichen, Clarence H. White, Gertrude Käsebier, Heinrich Kühn, and other less well-known names, as well as modern prints from the original paper negatives taken in the 1840s by the Scottish photographers David Octavius Hill and Robert Adamson. We found them all, happily in good condition, in dead storage in the basement.

I was then librarian of The Museum of Modern Art in New York. The museum was young, the staff was young, and we were considered intelligent even though we were iconoclastic. Besides showing modern painting and sculpture we put on display architectural renderings and models, furniture, household utensils, and even machine parts as art objects. A film library had already been established—the first in any art museum in the world. And now, in 1937, it had been decided by the trustees and the director, Alfred H. Barr, Jr., to mount a large, comprehensive exhibition of photography, embracing its entire history. I was appointed director of the exhibition, which filled all of the galleries. The Photo Secession group was beautifully represented by what I had found in Buffalo. In retrospect, the exhibition was the most important of its kind to be held in an art museum in America. It attracted huge crowds and much criticism. The *New York Herald-Tribune* headed a leader on its editorial page with "Camera Obscura" and gave a glowing account of the show. But the art critic of the *New York Sun* wrote in despair: "How struggle against an ocean? Your only chance, they say, when caught far off from shore by the tide, is to swim with it, trusting to be carried in to some safe landing place. . . . So I suppose I shall have to swim with the modern museum and give up painting until this second edition of the dark ages has passed. . . . Painting was grand while it lasted." Despite the controversy—or perhaps because of it—the exhibition was shown in twelve museums, from Boston to San Francisco, in its entirety.

The happy outcome was the formation of the Department of Photography at The Museum of Modern Art—a museum within a museum, with a permanent collection, a library, an exhibition program, and the publication of catalogs and books, the first of which was my *History of Photography*.

With the opening of George Eastman House in Rochester, New York, in 1949, America had its first museum dedicated solely to photography in all branches, including film. I was appointed curator, and I followed the pattern established by The Museum of Modern Art, but expanded beyond the artistic contributions of the medium.

Museums specializing in photography now exist in England, France, Germany, Austria, Czechoslovakia, and Italy.

Major art museums the world over are now avidly collecting photographs of the past and present, and regularly schedule major exhibitions of them.

Every photography curator dreams of an ideal museum containing the finest examples of the masters of all time, fully representative of every style and every technique. Such an ideal is, of course, impossible—even with an unlimited budget. For, paradoxically, the ability of the negative-positive process to yield unlimited numbers of prints has seldom been taken advantage of by art photographers. Furthermore, such printing methods as gum bichromate paper depend on the hand of man to bring out the image. Each such print is unique. The photographic print is a fragile object: if unprotected its surface can be scratched and the emulsion cracked. Improperly processed negatives and prints can be destroyed by the very light that brought them into being, or by contamination with sulfur compounds present in the atmosphere. Thousands upon thousands of photographs have been deliberately destroyed as valueless. The American poet Joaquin Miller bought twenty thousand negatives from the San Francisco studio of Bradley and Rulofson after it became defunct. He bought not for the love of photography, but for his love of flowers. He needed glass for his vast conservatory. "One by one they passed away in the bath of chemicals," he told an interviewer. "And now they're all gone—just plain panes of glass letting God's sunshine in on my roses. . . ."

Were a count possible, it is likely that it would show that fewer photographs taken since 1836 have survived than pictures made by other media—simply because of neglect. The physical, chemical, and wanton destruction of photographs makes the supply rare.

But happily, quantities are now well cared for and preserved by museums and the growing number of individuals. With great generosity many of these collectors have shared their treasures for the duration of Photokina to permit thousands to enjoy, for once, an ideal museum of photography.

1 Carl Ferdinand Stelzner, *Burned-out Ruin and the Nicolai Church*, 1842 Museum für Kunst und Gewerbe, Hamburg

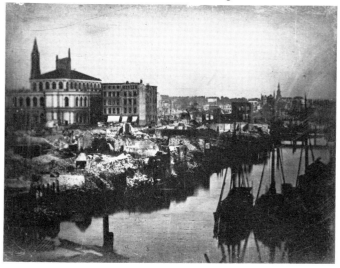

2 Carl Ferdinand Stelzner, *Burned-out Ruin with the New Stock Exchange*, 1842 Museum für Kunst und Gewerbe, Hamburg

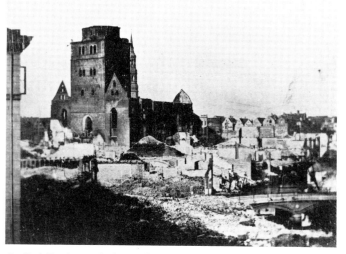

CHRONOLOGY

In the beginning, there was the sheer pleasure in the technical achievement of "the picture from the machine." What for thousands of years had solely been achieved by human hands—to fix and interpret three-dimensional perception two dimensionally—was now accomplished through the collaboration of physics (lens and camera) and chemistry (light-sensitive substances).

The daguerreotype process, established in August 1839, only produced unique images on metal plates and was merely a precursor of what we now call photography. *The Imaginary Photo Museum* contains only two examples of this process, by Stelzner and Babbitt. But a number of other inventors, working independently of each other, were busy improving on the daguerreotype. For example, in 1839 Hippolyte Bayard showed

3   Platt D. Babbitt, *Group at Niagara Falls*, ca. 1855
George Eastman House, Rochester

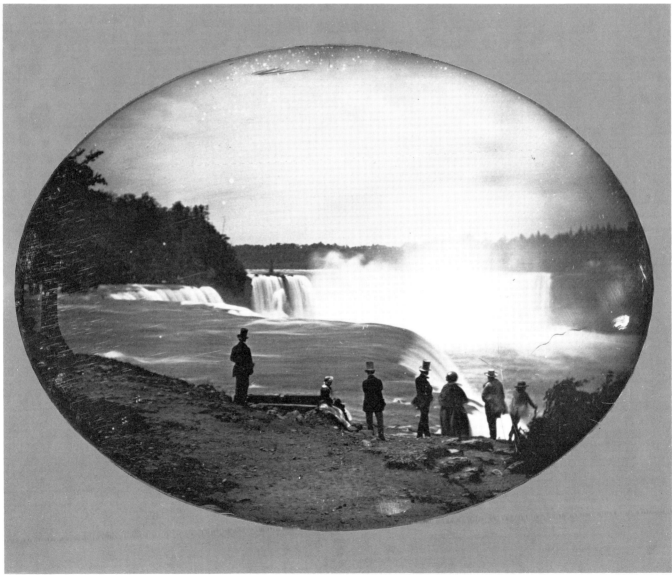

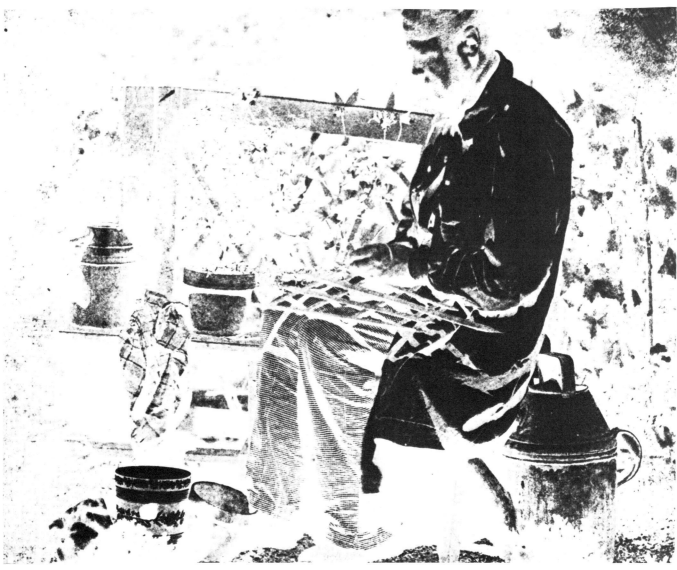

4 Hippolyte Bayard, *Hippolyte Bayard in His Garden*, 1845–1847
Société Française de Photographie, Paris

his latest results in the first photographic exhibit ever to take place.

Henry Fox Talbot, an Englishman, brought photography to the stage where one could make as many positives as desired from a single negative. *The Imaginary Photo Museum* includes several of his valuable vintage prints that show some of the subjects that have remained central to photography ever since: objects, still lifes, portraits, scenes, cityscapes, and landscapes.

The central subject of photography since its inception has been man himself. David Octavius Hill must be regarded as the first artistic portrait photographer. With his partner, Robert Adamson, he carefully posed his models to keep them as still as possible—at a time when photographs required a long exposure period. Soon thereafter came the first closeups, by the masterful Julia Margaret Cameron, the first important woman photographer.

During the early period of photography, photographers such as Eduard Baldus, Felice A. Beato, Robert Bedford, Bisson Frères, Francis Frith, Gustave Le Gray, Charles Nègre,

Carlo Ponti, and Félix Teynard took their large awkward equipment to capture the fabled and distant sights of antiquity, such as pyramids or the Temple of Baalbeck, which until then were known only from verbal accounts or from engravings. Opposed to the beauties of nature and imposing architecture was the ugliness and destructiveness of war. This was captured by the universally gifted Roger Fenton in Europe, and in America, by Mathew Brady, Alexander Gardner, and Timothy O'Sullivan, who provided the first photographic accounts of war and its consequences with graphic directness.

By way of contrast, other photographers used photography to transmit a pseudo-reality by creating sentimental scenes. Examples of this direction are the work of Gustave Rejlander and Henry Peach Robinson; the latter also produced large allegorical collages.

Etienne Carjat, Antoine Samuel Adam-Salomon, Franz Hanfstaengl, and Nadar made their mark on the history of photography with superior portrait work. These self-made masters of the early camera were succeeded by professionals who con-

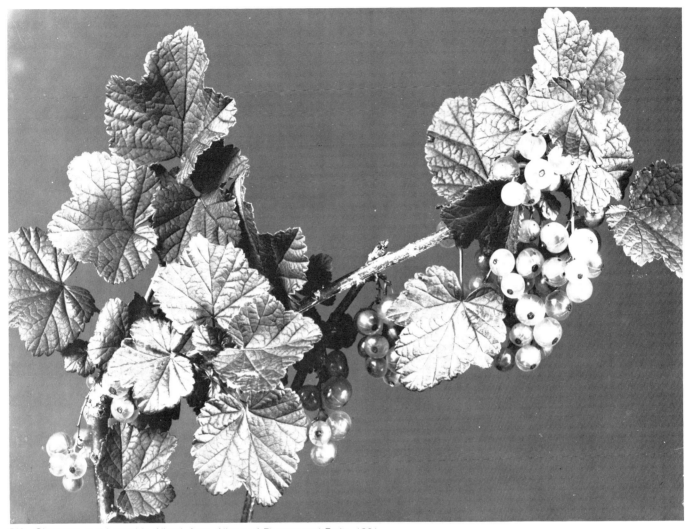

5/6 Giuseppe and Leopoldo Alinari, from *Album of Flowers and Fruits*, 1861
Fondazione Fratelli Alinari, Florence

ducted their calling as a business. The price for this democratization of the medium became an increasing shallowness. Falsification of photography occurred not only by the use of artificial props and drapes but also through the retouching process. Accordingly, even human beings became little more than interchangeable parts of photography's moveable scenery in an age characterized by long established bourgeois values.

It was an outsider and amateur, Dr. Peter Henry Emerson, who moved a step beyond the atrophied style of this kind of picture making and pointed the way to photography's next future.

Talented and ambitious turn-of-the-century amateur photographers sought and found their own individual styles. Initially, many of them tried to emulate painting techniques to conceal the photographic origin of their work by means of special printing and graphic methods, and their results should, therefore, be regarded as aspects of graphics. Yet these photographers regarded themselves as an elite group that had risen above the lowlands of professional photography. They not only used upper-middle-class living rooms and gardens for their "ambience," they even took their models—generally wives

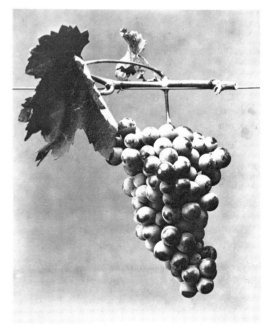

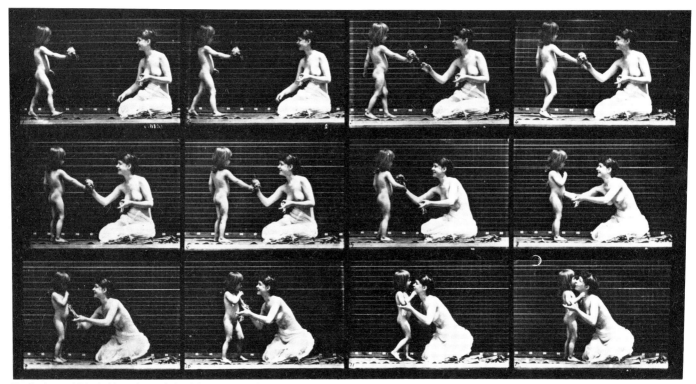

7 Eadweard Muybridge, from *Animal Locomotion*, Philadelphia, 1887
Fotografiska Museet, Stockholm

and friends—out into the open and arranged pleasant scenes or scenes of "deep significance" with appropriately suggestive titles. Still lifes, landscapes, and city sights were imbued with a romanticized flair. Nudes seemed to rise out of a mysterious darkness and unrecognizable surroundings. All this was called "art" photography.

European art photographers such as Oskar and Theodor Hofmeister, Rudolf Dührkoop, Heinrich Kühn, Hans Watzek, Hugo Henneberg, Robert Demachy, and Léonard Misonne were in the habit of exchanging photographs with each other and of arranging for exhibitions. In England, under the leadership of George Davison, a group of photographers formed the Linked Ring. They also invited foreign photographers with a similar style to join them. The manner in which they composed their space and details bears the imprint of the then current style of art nouveau.

Photo Secession was founded in the United States in 1902. Its moving spirit and undisputed leader was Alfred Stieglitz, a photographer and publicist who, from 1903 until 1917, published *Camera Work*, in which he presented photographers he had discovered, such as Alvin Langdon Coburn, Gertrude Käsebier, Edward Steichen, Paul Strand, and others.

The photographs in *Camera Work* were generally presented in the form of tipped-in gravures and were accompanied by essays from well-known authors, among them one particular champion of photography: George Bernard Shaw. Simultaneously Stieglitz maintained a small gallery where he exhibited vintage prints and also the work of avant-garde European painters and graphic artists.

Gradually, the style of most photographers changed from the romantic to the more realistic. Stieglitz's *The Steerage* must be regarded as the turning point. Jacob Riis, who photographed slums and was more interested in the content of photographs for their realism and truth than in art, became a new kind of social critic—one with a camera rather than a pen. Later, Lewis Hine photographed the horrors of child labor and effected reforms in the child labor laws.

Those who were creatively ambitious turned toward subjects with strict yet elegant forms. For example, there was Frederick H. Evans with his quiet records of church interiors and sweeping stairways, or E. O. Hoppé with representations of early technical constructions. Others, such as Paul Strand, discovered graphic lines and planes in their surroundings and shaped these into abstract patterns. Alvin Langdon Coburn created approximations of cubism with his kaleidoscopic "vortographs," and Christian Schad exposed light-sensitive paper without the use of a lens. His "Schadographies" are pioneer achievements in the margins of photography's history.

These new experiments marked the beginning of a new age in photography and manifested themselves in very different documentation and formal directions.

World War I destroyed many traditions but simultaneously created an atmosphere which provided photographers with far greater freedom to test ideas previously unknown.

Aside from certain early photographic experiments by Man Ray and Moholy-Nagy, photography experienced its most fundamental and fruitful era of picture taking in the 1920s and 1930s. The spectrum of photography was extraordinarily extended and deepened, with many new ideas and theories about content and composition.

During this time, man was the central subject of photography. There were the surrealistic scenes of Cecil Beaton, the cool objectified people of August Sander, Edward Steichen's *Vanity Fair* personages flooded in light, the frontally lighted stylish pictures by Hugo Erfurth, Helmar Lerski's focus on workers' faces, the facial expressions of unemployed country people by Dorothea Lange, and Bill Brandt's willful black-and-white interpretations so rich in contrasts. All of them expressed their individuality as photographers and, as we know today, guaranteed a lasting authenticity to their work.

At the same time a broad segment of the public expressed great interest in contemporary events, which was then satisfied by pictorial reports in the major illustrated journals of the day. In Germany, journals such as the *Berliner Illustrirten Zeitung* and the magazine *Uhu* stand out in this field, as did their star photographers Dr. Erich Salomon and Felix H. Man, who were the early pioneers in photojournalism showing unvarnished moments in the lives of their important contemporaries.

The Bauhaus principles of concentrating on fidelity and objectification when approaching a subject also had their effect on photography by directing it to capture the surface with great precision so as to penetrate to the substance of an object.

A forerunner of this trend of sober lighting was Eugène Atget, who photographed numerous vanishing Paris sights, though not without nostalgia.

In Germany, Albert Renger-Patzsch was the representative of this visual perception and this photographic profession of faith. In the United States, Paul Weston with his carefully developed positives was followed by Ansel Adams's heroic and monumental landscapes, while Paul Outerbridge, Jr., used small formats to emphasize the esthetic and fashionable. As successors to the Bauhaus tradition, Americans Aaron Siskind and Harry Callahan worked with highly reduced abstractions while the youngest teacher at that famous institute, the multitalented Austrian Herbert Bayer, created surprisingly concrete photo-collages.

Some photographers took to the streets or to out-of-the-way places where they discovered a kind of witty and revealing poetry in the episodic—for example, André Kertész, who had become famous for his classic photo of a fork, now turned toward the charmingly anecdotal. Brassaï captured Paris nightlife and that city's underworld, while Cartier-Bresson created almost musically brilliant snapshots that captured the right moment forever. And in America, as if directed by pure chance, Walker Evans made astonishing discoveries by merely photographing traffic or passersby.

These photographers seemed to create their work only for themselves, following an inner mission even when an outer one was also provided. Their photographs communicated a new way of seeing and knowing what occurs around and probably also inside us.

In Europe in the meantime, World War II had broken out, which meant the end of one kind of photography. In America, *Life* magazine, which was modeled on the German illustrateds, succeeded with unadorned reports of battle scenes. W. Eugene Smith and Robert Capa, in particular, became famous for their realistic accounts of action in the war zones. Capa's most famous picture of D-Day and the dead on Normandy Beach, captured the end of a horrendous dictatorship and the prospect of peace.

The photography of the postwar period was first of all determined by the printed page, and by extension, photojournalism. *Life* magazine's prestige and printruns kept increasing and its editor-in-chief, Wilson Hicks, was considered the great discoverer who gave talent its first chance. In Paris, Magnum Photos was formed by Cartier-Bresson, Capa, and "Chim" Seymour and provided the illustrated magazines of the world with a library of photos.

Fashion magazines such as *Vogue* and *Harper's Bazaar* developed new young talents like Irving Penn and Richard Avedon. Color was added as a new dimension and inspired individual creativity with its improved reproductive and printing techniques.

Two names stand out: Irving Penn and Ernst Haas. Penn created dramatic black-and-white portraits and fashion photographs and also became a master of color photography. Ernst Haas transmitted new visual experiences with magic pictures of New York, Paris, and Venice. A third, Eliot Porter, who must be regarded as belonging to the preceding generation, with a spartan and pure use of color was able to heighten his primarily scientific photographs of nature and of the flights of birds.

In Germany, six photographers formed the group fotoform around Wolfgang Reisewitz, and one of its members, Otto Steinert, eventually acquired international renown with his subjective photography (*Subjektive Fotografie*).

In the 1950s and 1960s photojournalists Margaret Bourke-White and Philippe Halsman, who took more *Life* magazine covers than anyone else, won worldwide recognition. An unusual night reporter named Weegee roamed the streets of New York taking photos with flashbulbs of accidents and crimes. William Klein acquired his reputation with unconventional and dynamic photography albums of New York, Tokyo, Rome, and Moscow. The Swiss, Robert Frank, in the style of Walker Evans, had a revolutionary effect with his seemingly accidental shots of North American everyday life, which he entitled The Americans, while Hiroshi Hamaya perceived America from his own particular national perspective. Bill Owens, with an interest in middle-class life, documented its manifestations in suburbia.

The large magazines were forced to retrench under the impact of television and the soaring cost of printing. Nonetheless, strong individual talents asserted themselves confronting reality with highly individual perspectives. Diane Arbus became famous for her melancholy photographs. Chargesheimer possessed a seemingly uncanny ability to capture the personalities of prominent people, and to capture events, landscapes, and buildings as well as the life and emptiness of cities with precise verisimilitude. Lee Friedlander explored usually neglected and marginal areas of existence, and Minor White sought to create a kind of religion from what seemed immaterial conceptions.

Since photography had already revealed so many facets of itself, it seemed difficult to discover new ones. Three Americans, however, did succeed—in their own way. Duane Michals with his psychological portraits and his discovery of the series of sequential photographs, which are arranged scenes that elicited astonishingly mysterious associations and initiated an oft-imitated pictorial questioning of our existence; Les Krim produced scandals with absurdities—nude persons among grotesque household utensils; and Ralph Gibson with his highly cultivated and intellectualized photographs of fragments of people and objects that he placed in odd surrealistic surroundings. In Germany, Hilla and Bernhard Becher won entry into the art scene with conceptual serial photographs of industry, technology, and half-timbered houses.

In recent years the creative and documentary sides of photography have been alternating between an emphasis on the banal and undefined self-reflections. This kind of photography means to point out paltry conditions or seeks to communicate itself from the inside to the outside, tries to bring the photographer's thoughts and feelings close to the viewer by means of frequently mysterious subjects. Not everything still speaks to everyone comprehensibly. Still, a demanding and frequently vain gallery art has developed from both directions.

In color photography, where a decade-long search for beauty is nearing its end, it achieved its highest form with two Italian representatives: Franco Fontana's captivatingly brilliant interpretations which consist of lines and geometrical patterns, and Luigi Ghirri's wittily ambiguous muted inventions.

In America the creative side of photography has turned toward the affirmation of topographic and architectural themes. Photographers like William Eggleston, Joel Meyerowitz, and Stephen Shore have won museum recognition with work along these lines.

They and others also employ the new instamatic method with large format cameras that allow them a leisurely focus with both eyes on their subject on the screen. In contrast to the speed of the method, however, one can sense the time the photographers have taken in selecting the structure of their pictorial projects. Marie Cosindas explored the uniqueness of the technique and material, and produced still lifes and portraits that have the tonal quality of old masters.

The amateurish small instamatic camera, when used by experts, has also penetrated into demanding realms. This miniature technique has been able to capture the fleeting and intimate, and when used in series this method has frequently become the means of expression of serious professionals.

In any event, the unique monochrome of Monsieur Louis Jacques Mandé Daguerre has in wondrous ways found its completion in the unique process of Dr. Edwin H. Land and his Polaroid cameras, realizing the early dream of the first inventors: to produce individual photographs, without effort and delay, in full color. Between these two demarcation lines photography has become the most frequently used medium of our time. Museums and collections have made it their duty to protect the most valuable examples.

L. Fritz Gruber

CHRONOLOGY

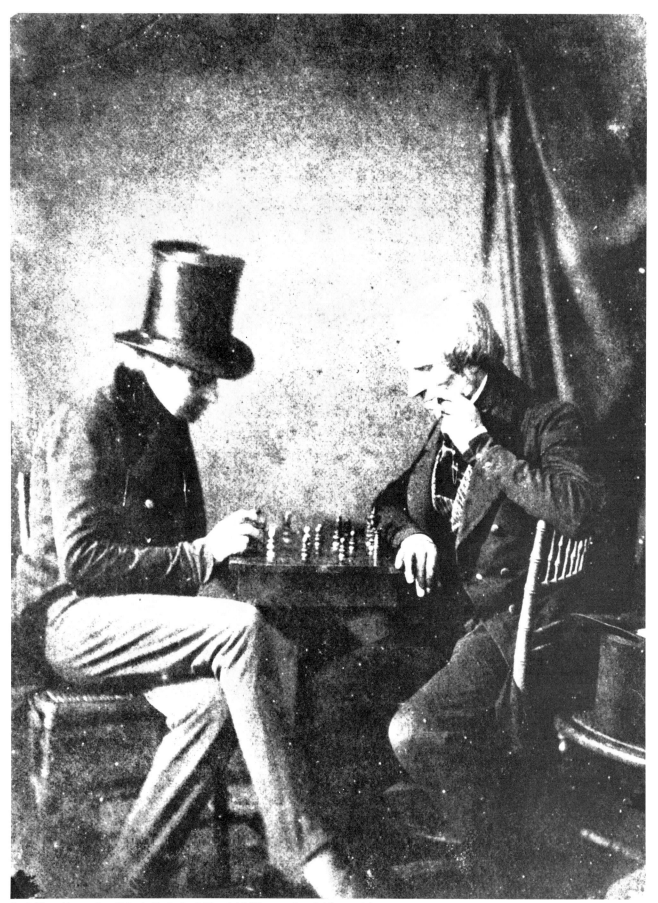

8 William Henry Fox Talbot, *Portrait of Claudet* (sitting on the right), no date
The Fox Talbot Museum, Lacock

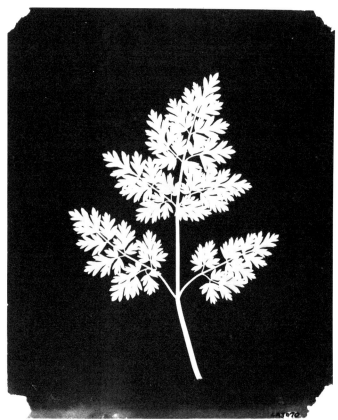

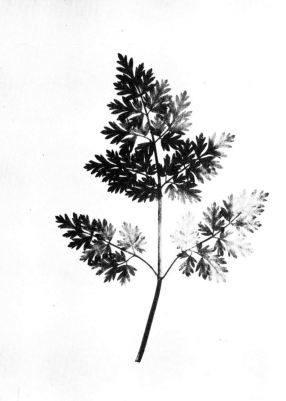

9 William Henry Fox Talbot, *Photogenic Drawing of a Leaf,*
   negative, ca. 1836–1839
   The Fox Talbot Museum, Lacock

10 William Henry Fox Talbot, *Photogenic Drawing of a Leaf,*
    positive, ca. 1836–1839
    The Fox Talbot Museum, Lacock

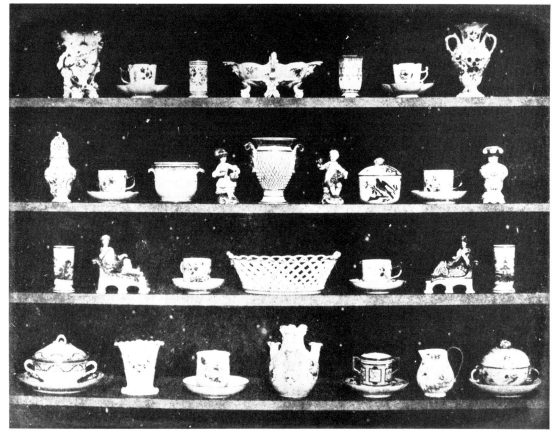

11 William Henry Fox Talbot, *Articles of China*, Plate 3 from *The Pencil of Nature,* no date
    The Fox Talbot Museum, Lacock

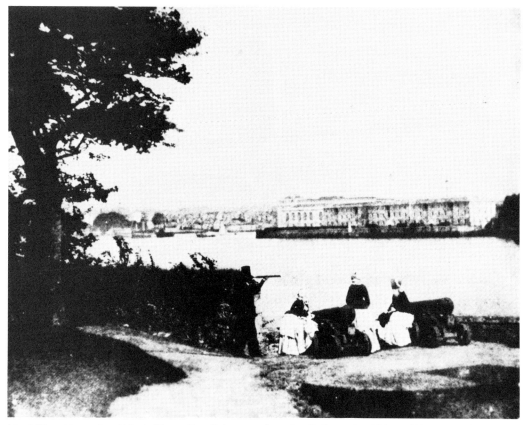

12 William Henry Fox Talbot, *Man with a Telescope from the Battlements of Mount Edgecomb, Plymouth,*
no date
The Fox Talbot Museum, Lacock

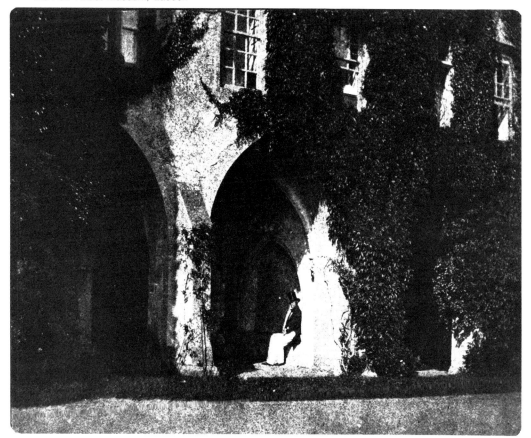

13 William Henry Fox Talbot, *The Reverend Calvert Jones Sitting in the Cloisters at Lacock Abbey,*
no date
The Fox Talbot Museum, Lacock

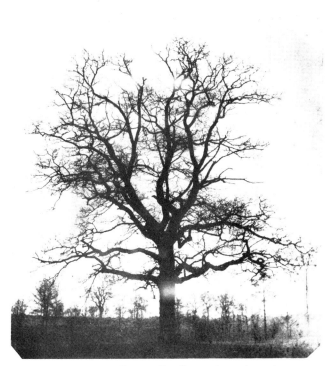

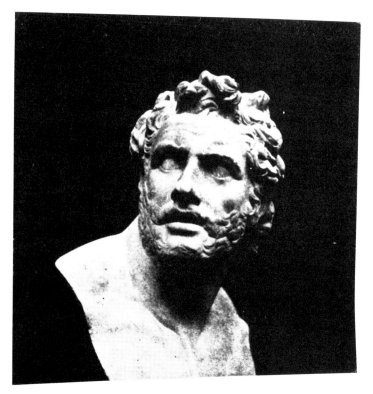

14 William Henry Fox Talbot, *Elm Tree at Lacock*, no date
The Fox Talbot Museum, Lacock

15 William Henry Fox Talbot, *The Bust of Patroclus*, Plate 5 from
The Pencil of Nature, August 9, 1843
The Fox Talbot Museum, Lacock

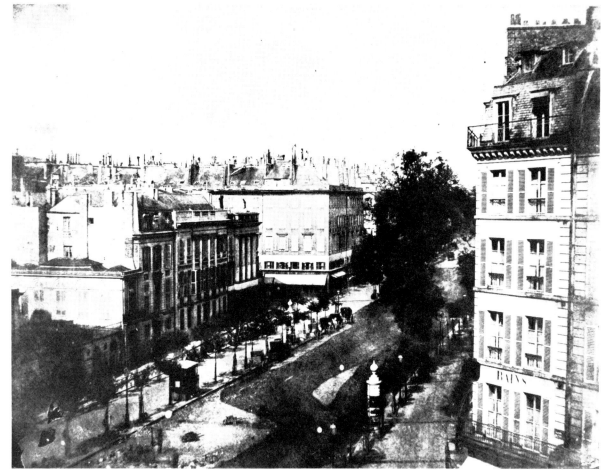

16 William Henry Fox Talbot, *Avenue des Capucines*, ca. 1843
The Fox Talbot Museum, Lacock

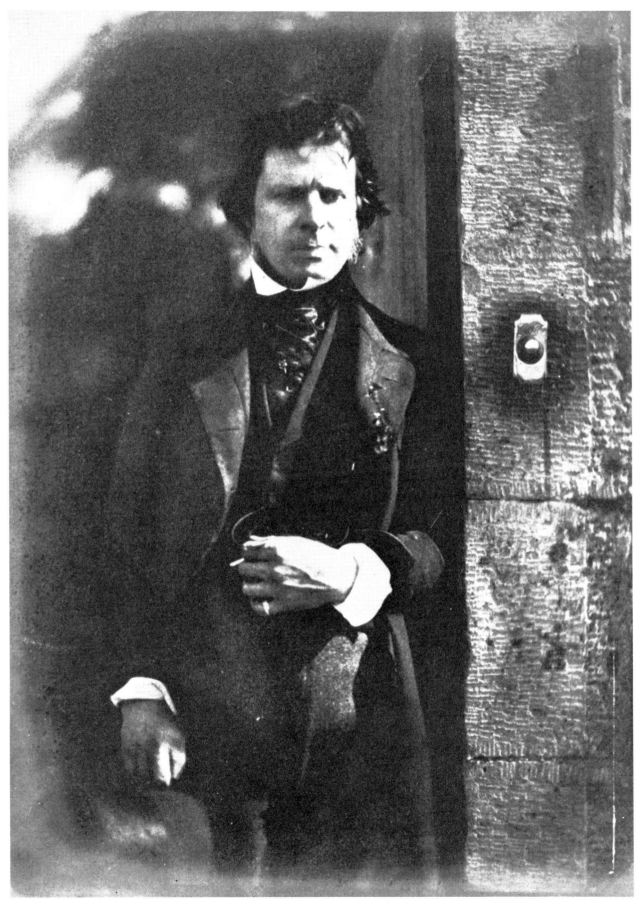

17 David Octavius Hill and Robert Adamson, *Self-portrait (D.O. Hill)*, ca. 1843
    Museum Ludwig, Cologne

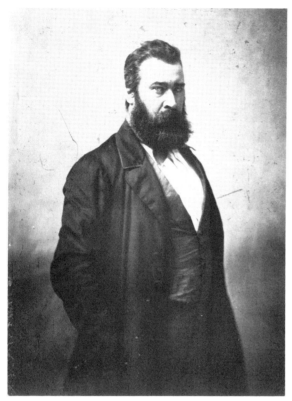

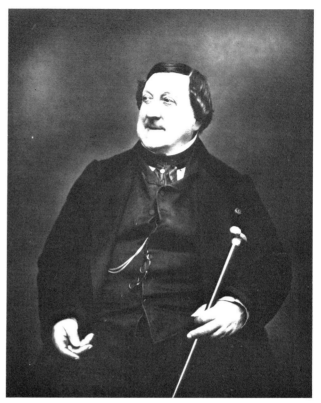

18 Nadar, *Jean-François Millet,* 1858
Agfa-Gevaert Foto-Historama, Leverkusen

19 Etienne Carjat, *Giacomo Rossini,* ca. 1870
Münchner Stadtmuseum, Munich

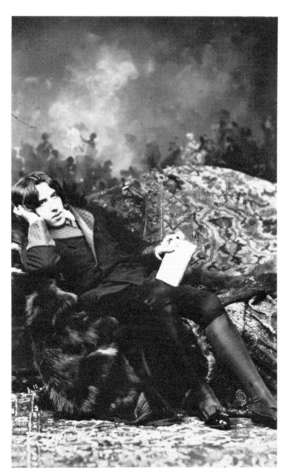

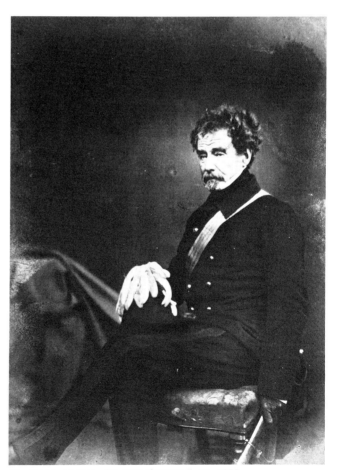

20 Napoleon Sarony, *Oscar Wilde,* ca. 1892
National Portrait Gallery, London

21 Roger Fenton, *Sir John Campbell,* ca. 1855
Det kongelige Bibliotek, Copenhagen

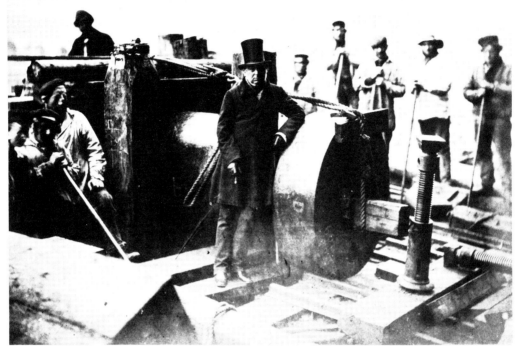

22 Robert Howlett, *J. Stevenson,* 1857
Victoria and Albert Museum, London

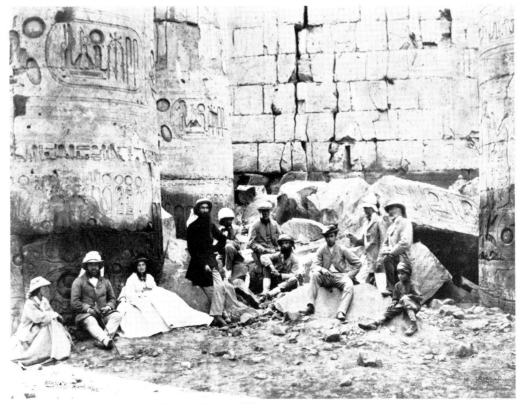

23 Francis Bedford, *Prince of Wales, Carnak,* 1862
Det kongelige Bibliotek, Copenhagen

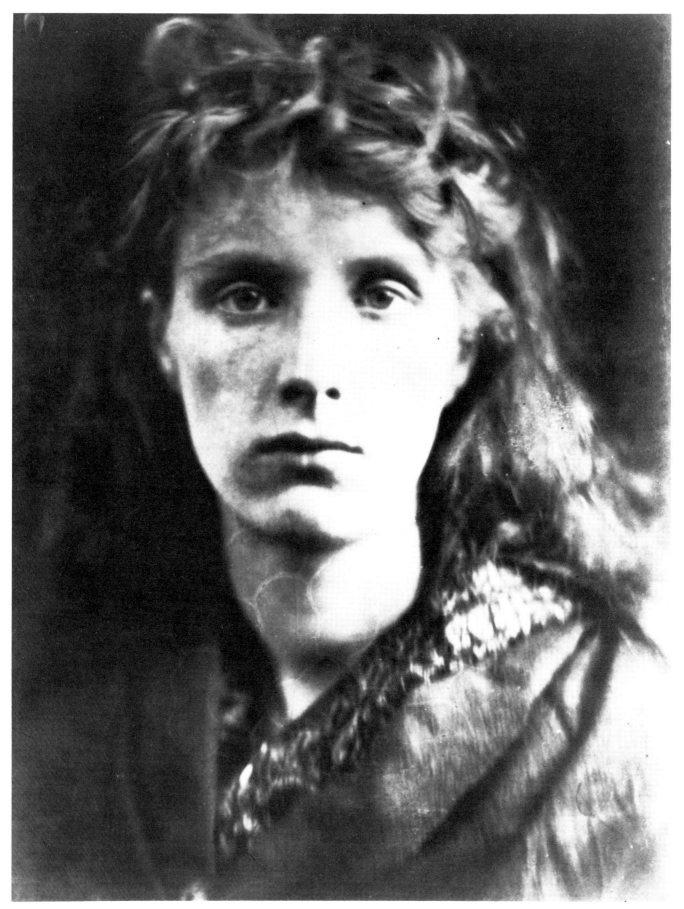

24   Julia Margaret Cameron, *The Mountain Nymph, Sweet Liberty*, 1870
The Royal Photographic Society of Great Britain, Bath

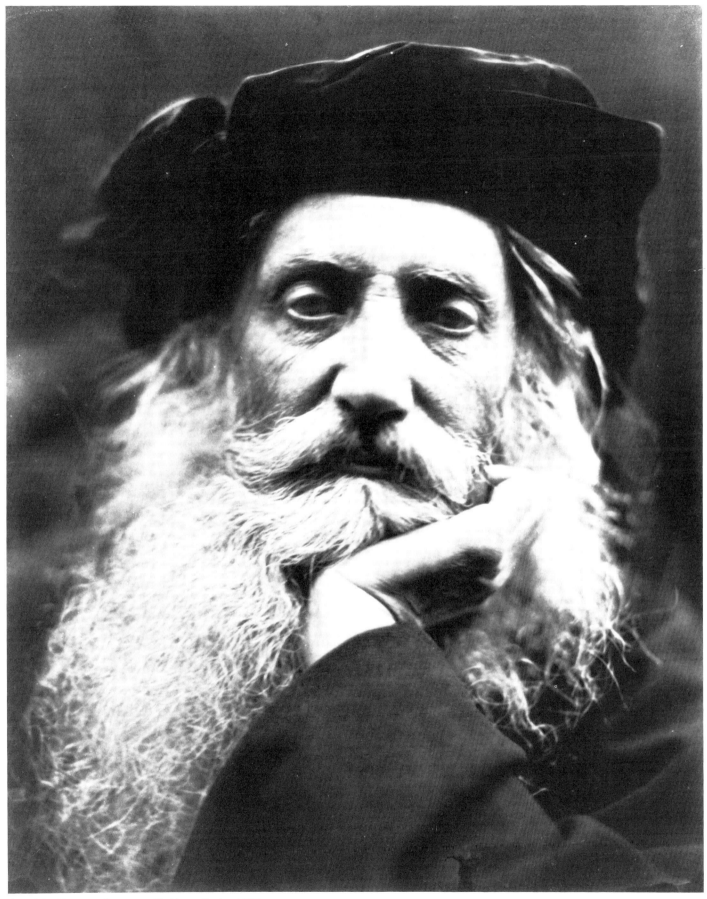

25 Julia Margaret Cameron, *Sir Henry Taylor*, 1867
Gernsheim Collection, Austin

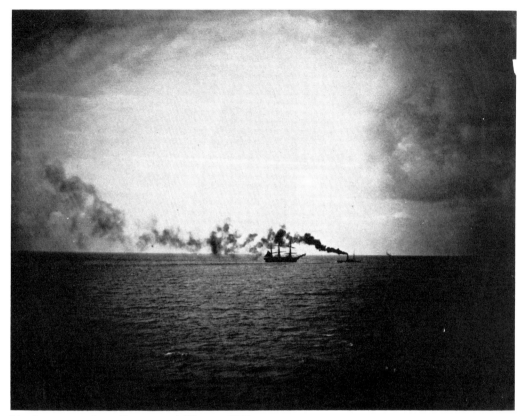

26   Gustave Le Gray, *Seascape of Sète*, ca. 1857
Victoria and Albert Museum, London

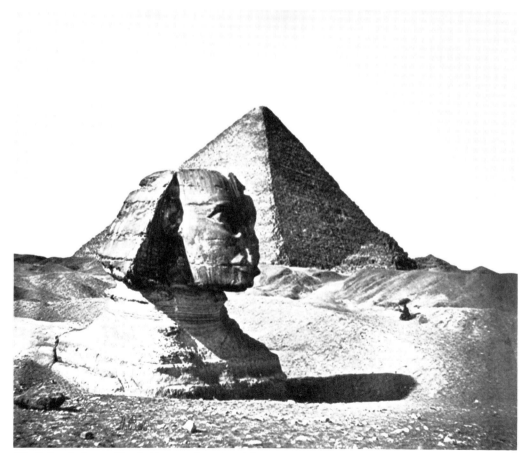

27   Felice A. Beato, *The Sphinx and Pyramid of Cheops in Distance*, 1865
Gernsheim Collection, Austin

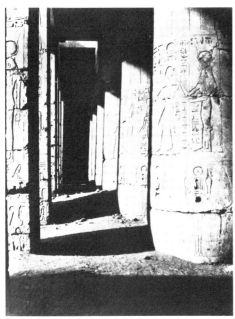

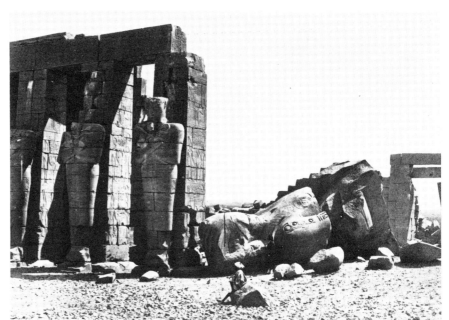

28 Félix Teynard, *Thebes, Medînet-Habou,*
    2nd. Courtyard, Southeast Gallery, ca. 1851
    Det kongelige Bibliotek, Copenhagen

29 Francis Frith, *Osiride Pillars and Great Fallen Colossos,* 1858
    The Art Institute of Chicago

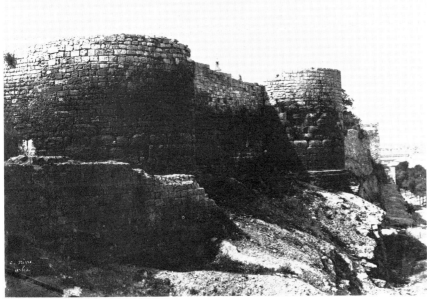

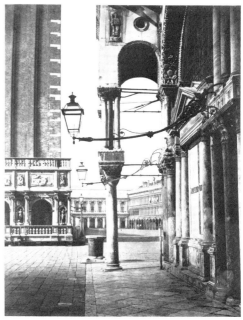

30 Charles Nègre, *Arles, the Ramparts,* 1852
    Het Sterckshof Museum, Antwerp

31 Carlo Ponti, *Piazza San Marco, Belltower,*
    Venice, ca. 1860
    Gernsheim Collection, Austin

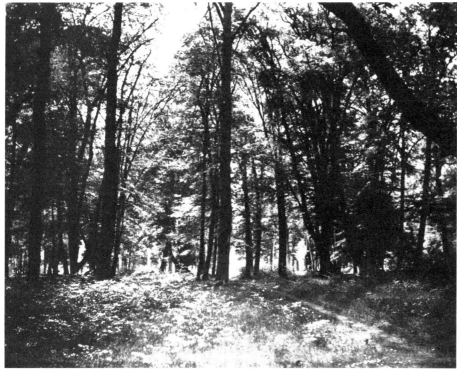

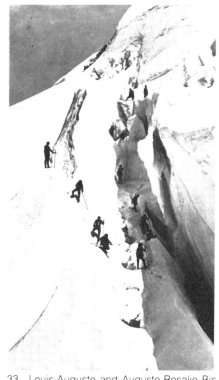

32 Gustave Le Gray, *Study of Trees*, no date
Victoria and Albert Museum, London

33 Louis-Auguste and Auguste-Rosalie Bisson, *Savoy 44, the Crevice*, ca. 1860
Bibliothèque Nationale, Paris

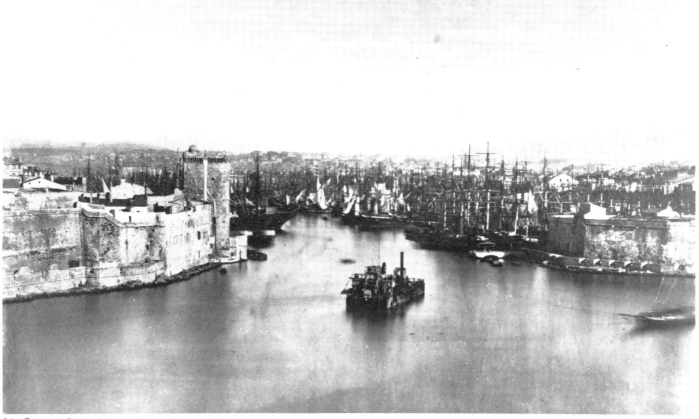

34 Edouard-Denis Baldus, *Marseille*, ca. 1858
Gernsheim Collection, Austin

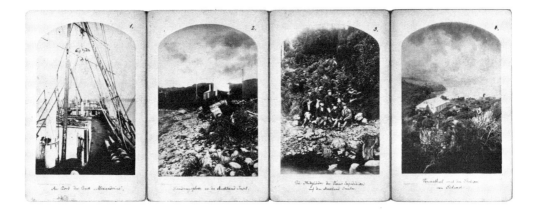

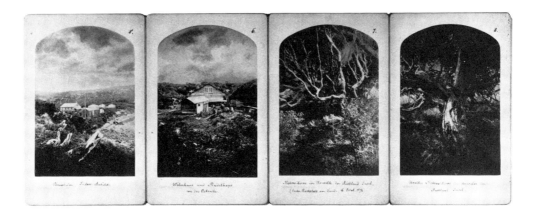

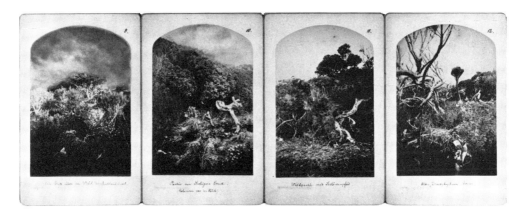

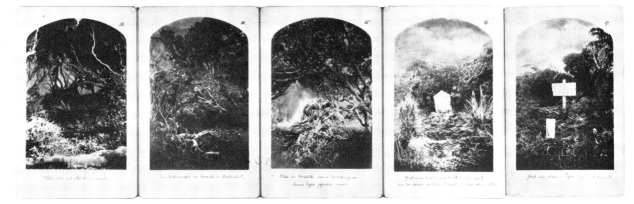

35   Hermann Krone, *Album,* 1874
Museum Folkwang, Essen

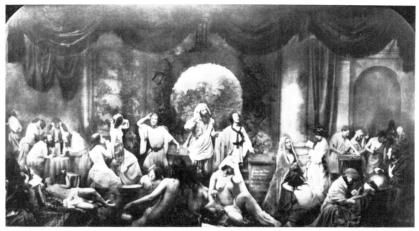

36   Oscar Gustave Rejlander, *The Two Ways of Life*, 1858
The Royal Photographic Society of Great Britain, Bath

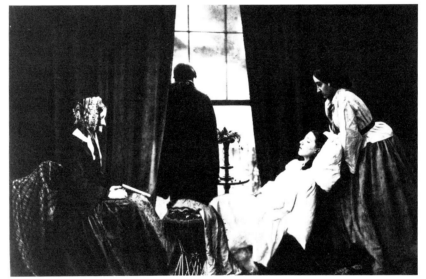

37   Henry Peach Robinson, *Fading Away*, 1858
The Royal Photographic Society of Great Britain, Bath

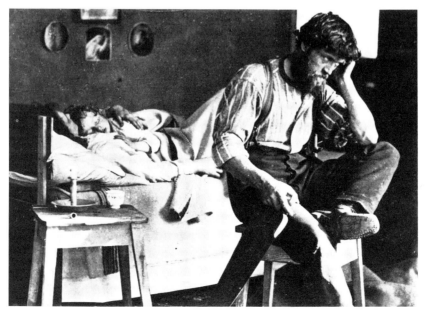

38   Oscar Gustave Rejlander, *Out of Work*, ca. 1860
The Royal Photographic Society of Great Britain, Bath

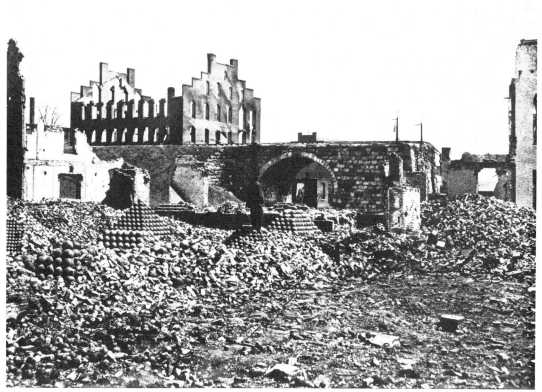

39 Alexander Gardner, *Ruins of Paper Mill, Richmond, Virginia*, 1865
    Museum of Fine Arts, Boston

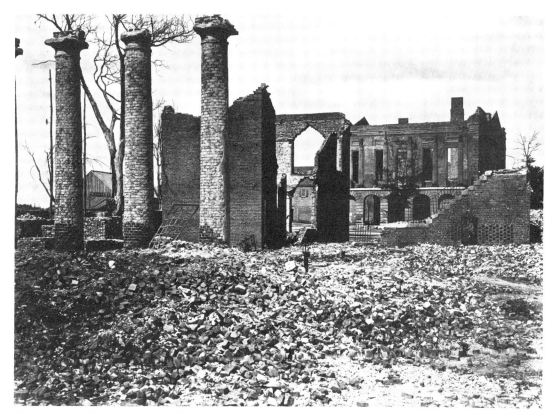

40 George N. Barnard, *Ruins in Columbia, South Carolina*, 1865
    The Library of Congress, Washington, D.C.

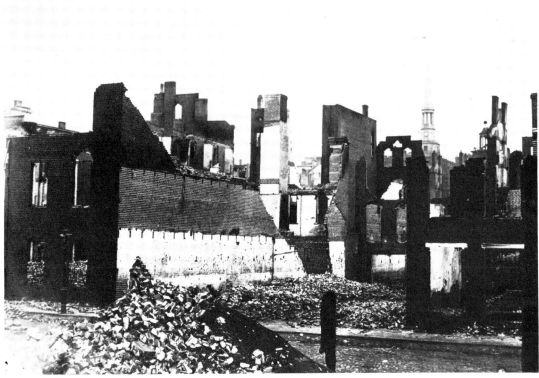

41 Mathew B. Brady, *Ruins of Richmond*, 1865
The Museum of Modern Art, New York

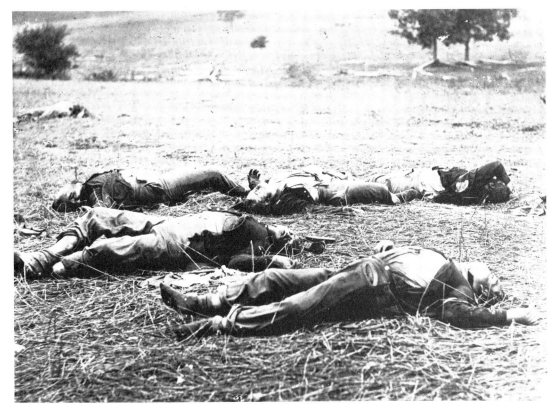

42 Timothy H. O'Sullivan, *Battlefield of Gettysburg, Bodies of Dead Federal Soldiers on the Field of the First Day's Battle*, July 1863
The Library of Congress, Washington, D.C.

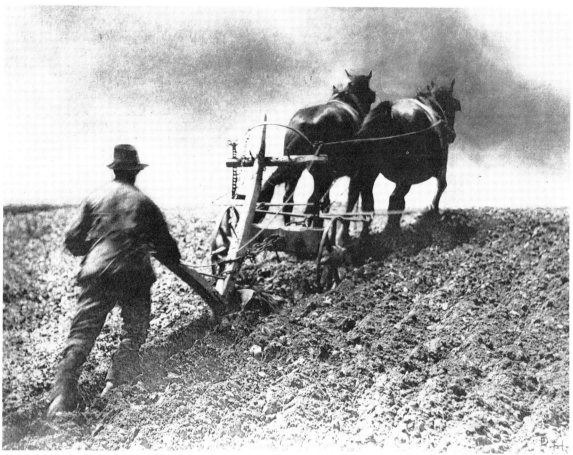

43 Peter Henry Emerson, *A Stiff Pull*, 1890
    Kodak Museum, Harrow

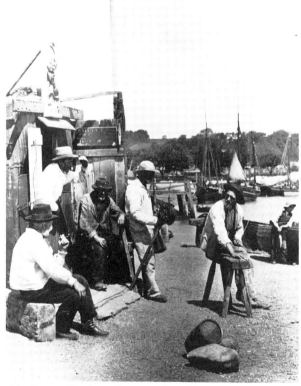

44 George Davison, *Group at Ferry House*, 1888
    Kodak Museum, Harrow

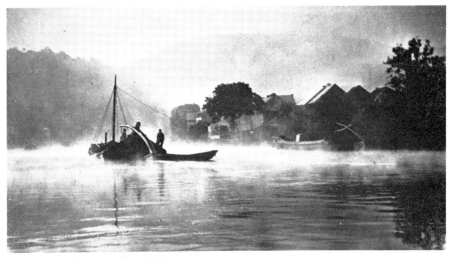

45 Léonard Misonne, *Gilly*, 1898
Agfa-Gevaert Foto-Historama, Leverkusen

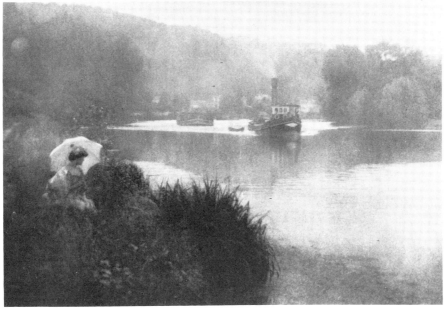

46 Emile Joachim Constant Puyo, *Woman with Sunshade by the Waterside*, ca. 1896
Société Française de Photographie, Paris

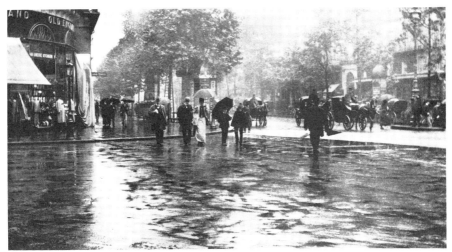

47 Alfred Stieglitz, *A Wet Day, Paris*, 1897
The Art Institute of Chicago

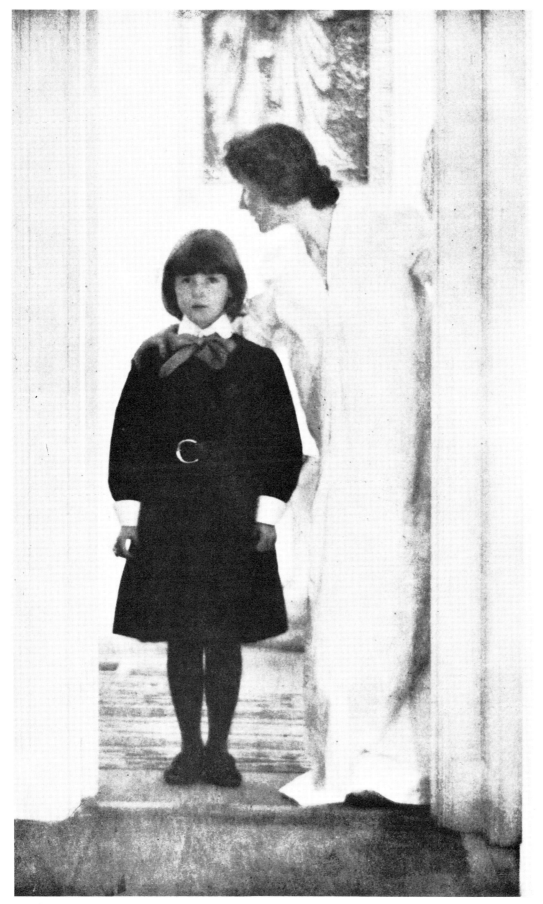

48 Gertrude Käsebier, *Blessed Art Thou among Women*, 1899
The Museum of Modern Art, New York

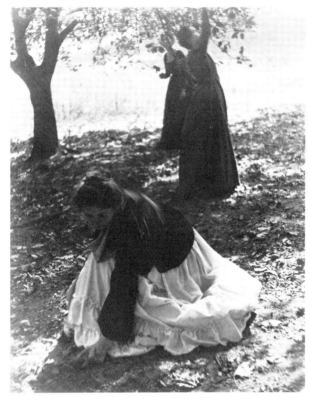

49 Clarence H. White, *In the Orchard*, 1900
    The Library of Congress, Washington, D.C.

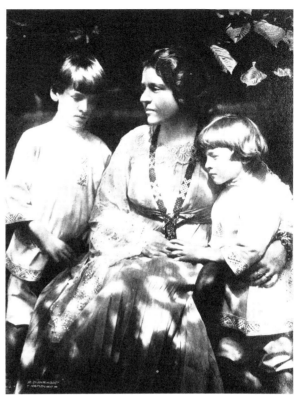

50 Rudolf Dührkoop, *Ilena Luksch-Makowsky with Her
    Children, Peter and Andreas*, ca. 1910
    Museum für Kunst und Gewerbe, Hamburg

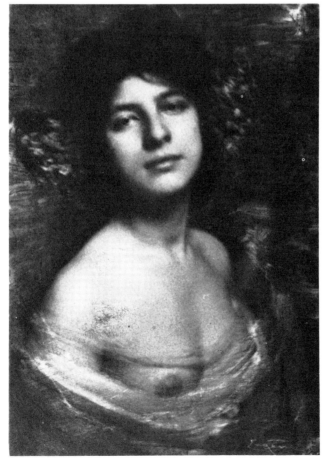

51 Frank Eugene, *Hortense*, no date
    The Art Institute of Chicago

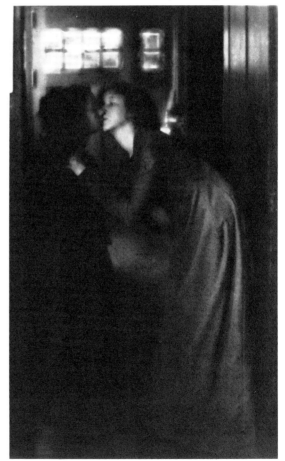

52 Clarence H. White, *The Kiss*, 1904
    The Library of Congress, Washington, D.C.

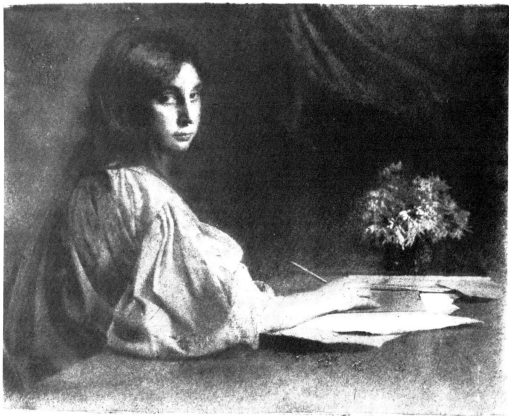

53 Robert Demachy, *Study (The Letter)*, no date
The Royal Photographic Society of Great Britain, Bath

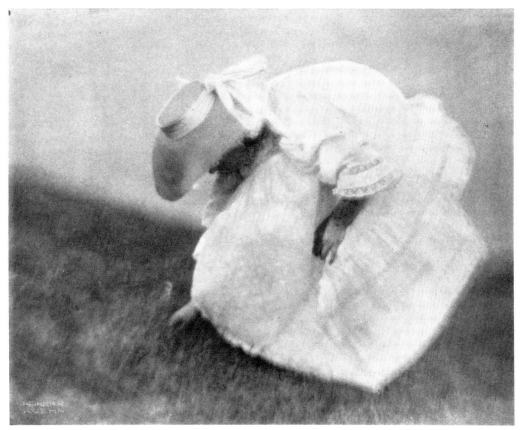

54 Heinrich Kühn, *Portrait of a Girl*, 1905–1906
Museum Folkwang, Essen

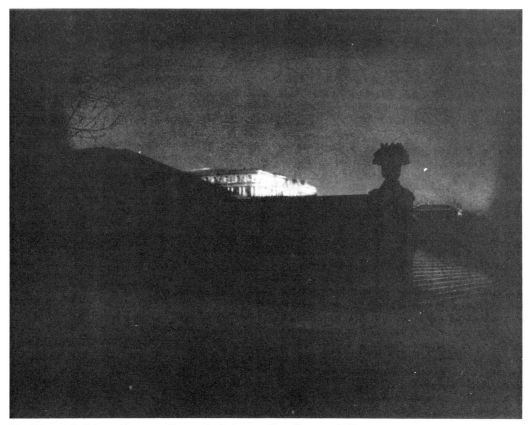

55 Edward Steichen, *Nocturne, Orangerie Staircase, Versailles,* ca. 1910
    The Museum of Modern Art, New York

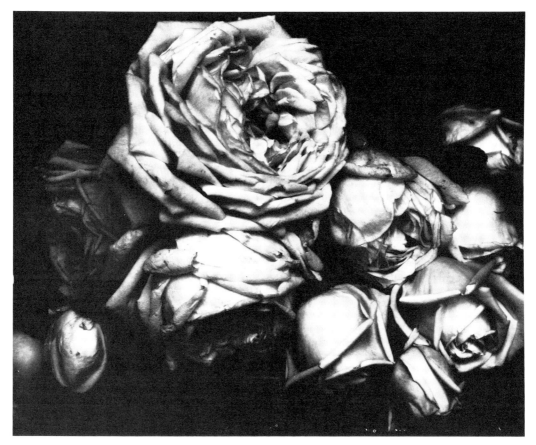

56 Edward Steichen, *Heavy Roses, Voulangis, France,* 1914
    The Museum of Modern Art, New York

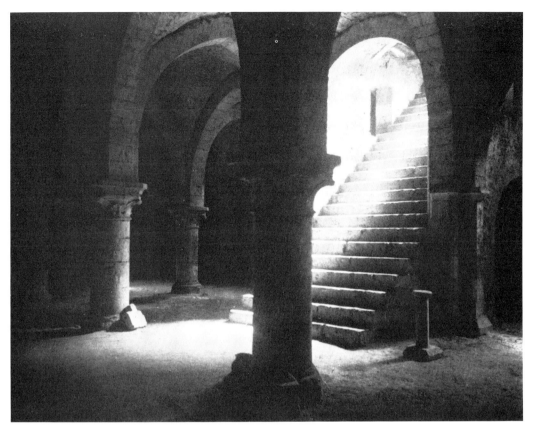

57   Frederick H. Evans, *Ancient Crypt Cellars in Provins, France*, 1910
     The Library of Congress, Washington, D.C.

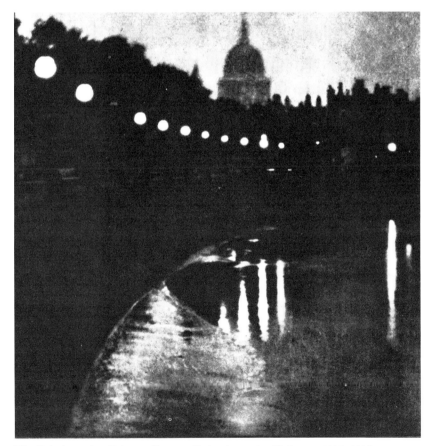

58   Alvin Langdon Coburn, *Thames Embankment by Night*, ca. 1905–1910
     The Royal Photographic Society of Great Britain, Bath

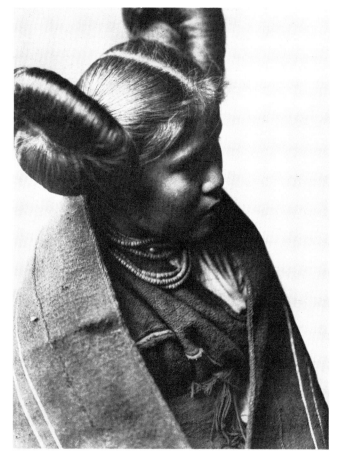

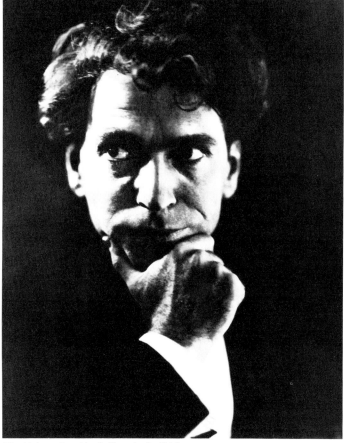

59   Edward Sheriff Curtis, *Chaiwa-Tewa-Profile*, 1921
     Art Museum, University of New Mexico, Albuquerque

60   Helmar Lerski, *Self-portrait*, 1912
     Museum für Kunst und Gewerbe, Hamburg

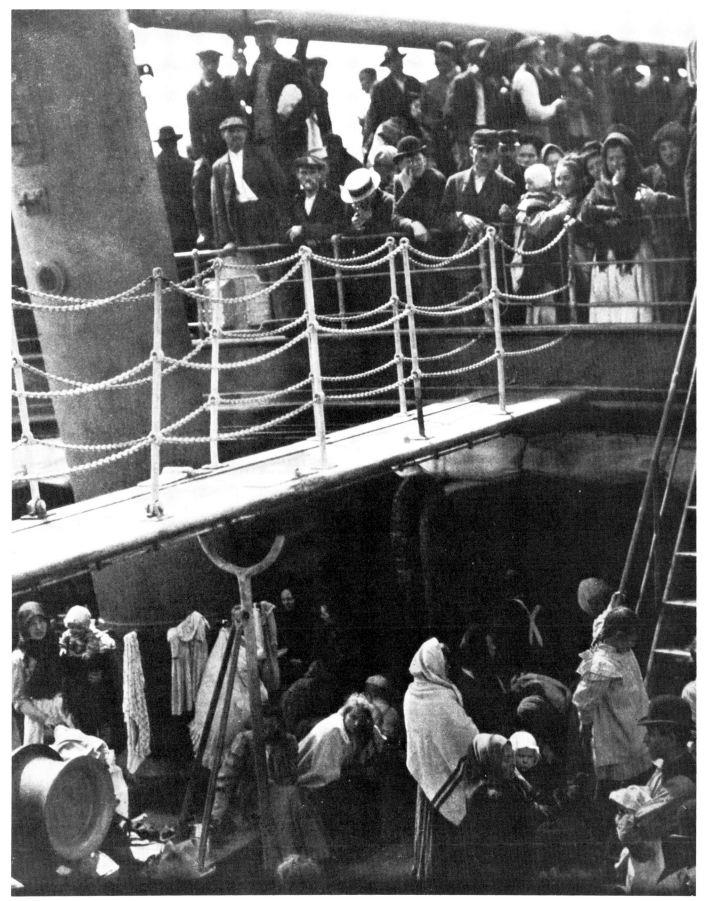

61   Alfred Stieglitz, *The Steerage*, 1907
George Eastman House, Rochester

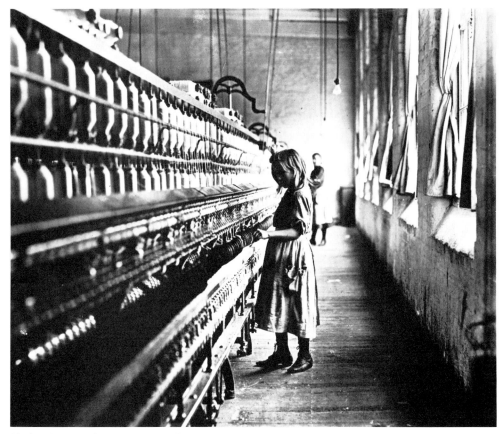

62 Lewis Hine, *Girl Working in a Cotton Mill*, 1908
    The Art Institute of Chicago

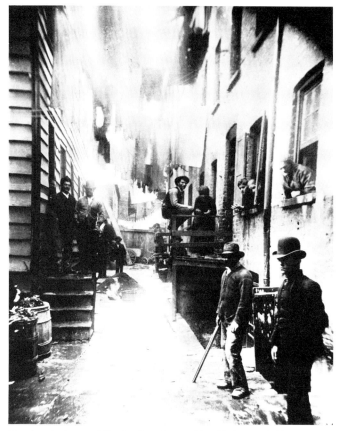

63 Jacob August Riis, *Ludlow Street*, *New York*, ca. 1890
    Münchner Stadtmuseum, Munich

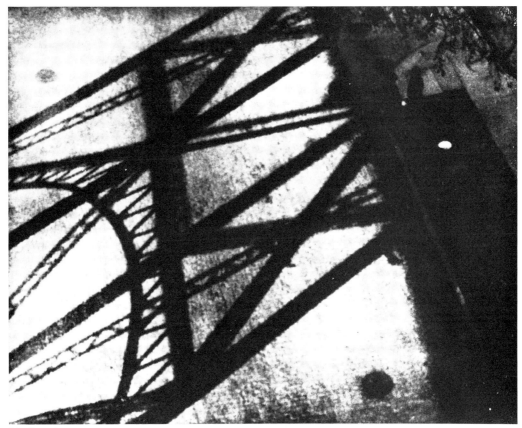

64   Paul Strand, *New York*, 1916
     Gernsheim Collection, Austin

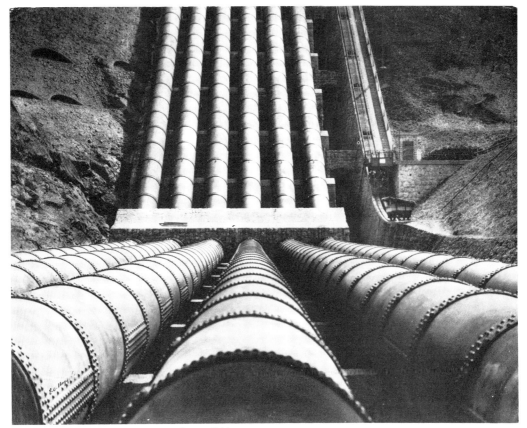

65   Emil Otto Hoppé, *Romance of Steel*, 1911
     Bibliothèque Nationale, Paris

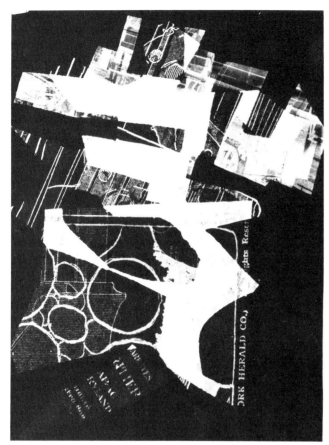

66 Christian Schad, *Schadography*, 1918
The Museum of Modern Art, New York

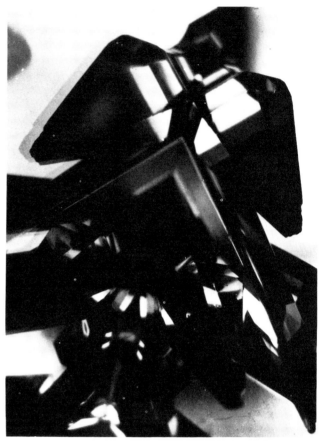

67 Alvin Langdon Coburn, *Vortograph*, 1917
George Eastman House, Rochester

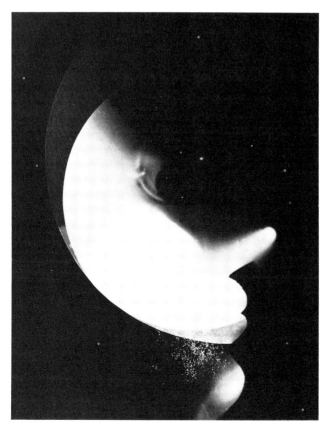

68 László Moholy-Nagy, *Self-portrait*, ca. 1922
Museum Folkwang, Essen

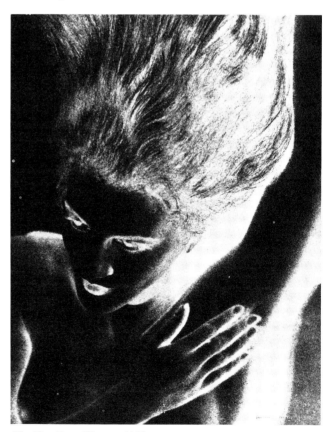

69 Man Ray, *Woman,* 1929
Bibliothèque Nationale, Paris

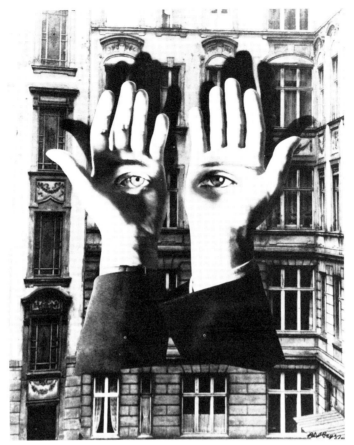

70 Herbert Bayer, *Lonely City Dweller*, 1932
    Museum Folkwang, Essen

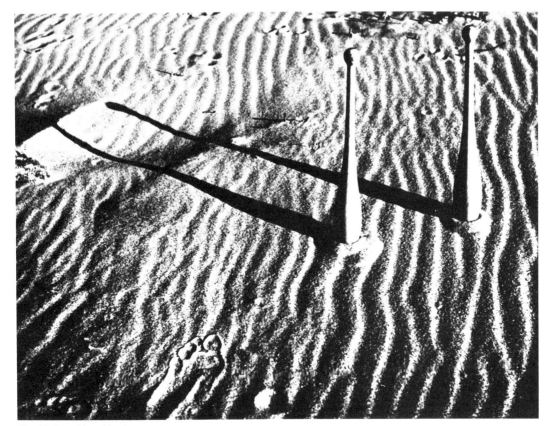

71 Herbert List, *Hamburg*, 1931
    Museum Folkwang, Essen

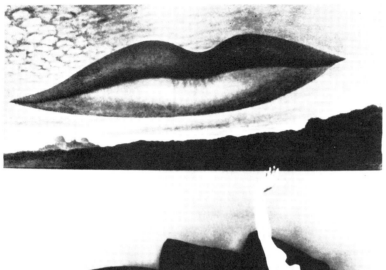

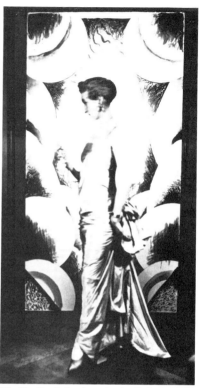

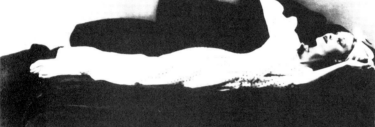

72 Man Ray, *The Lovers*, no date
    Museum Ludwig, Cologne

73 Sir Cecil Beaton, *Lady Oxford*, 1927
    Victoria and Albert Museum, London

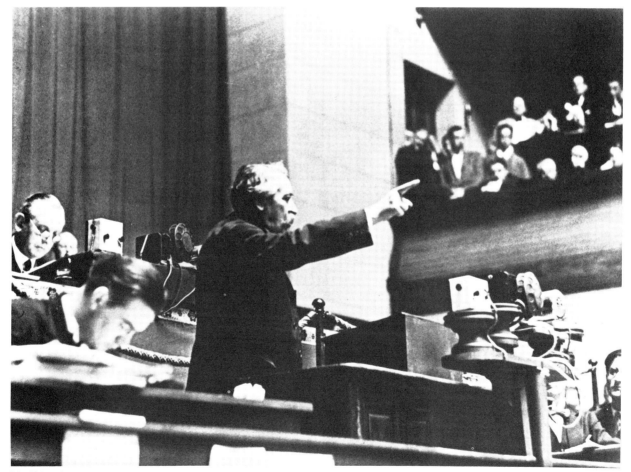

74 Erich Salomon, *Aristide Briand*, 1929
    Stiftung für die Photographie, Kunsthaus, Zürich

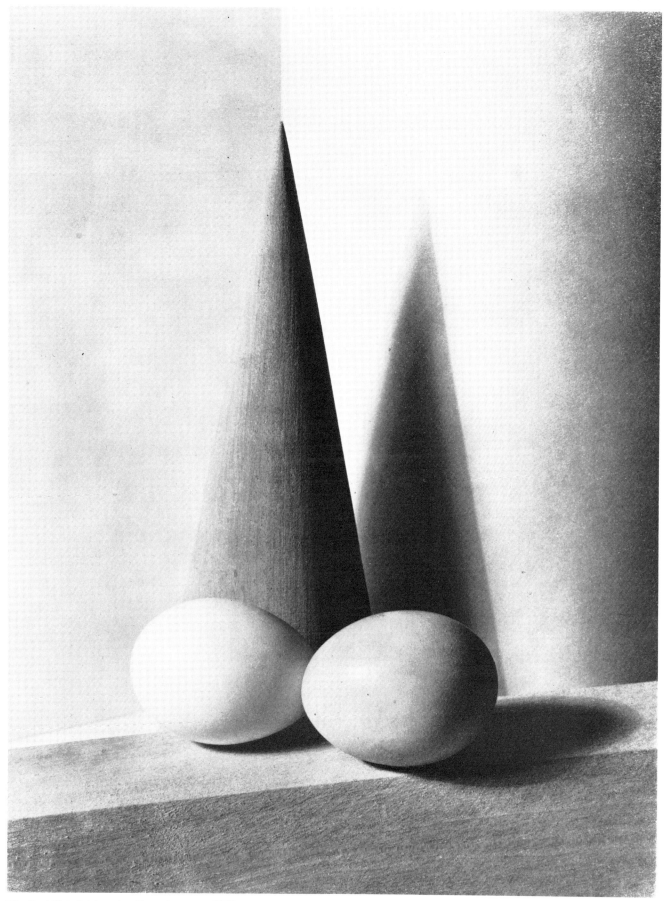

75 Paul Outerbridge, Jr., *Consciousness*, 1931
The Art Institute of Chicago

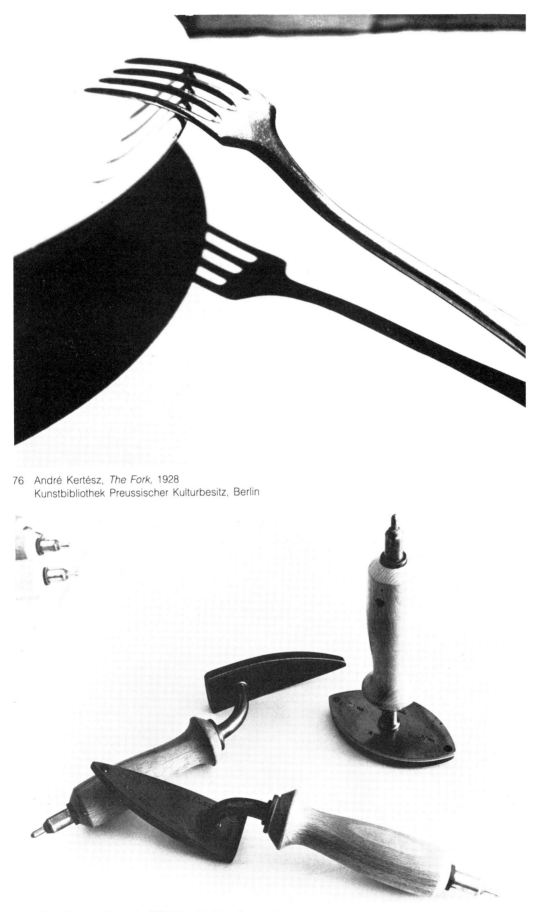

76 André Kertész, *The Fork*, 1928
Kunstbibliothek Preussischer Kulturbesitz, Berlin

77 Albert Renger-Patzsch, *Still Life with Utensils*, no date
Kunstbibliothek Preussischer Kulturbesitz, Berlin

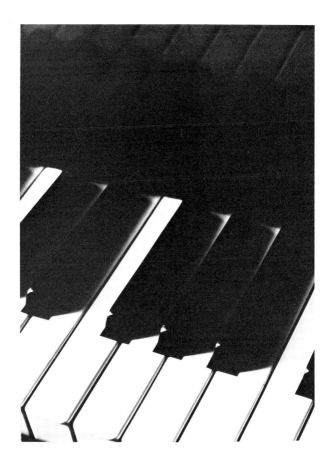

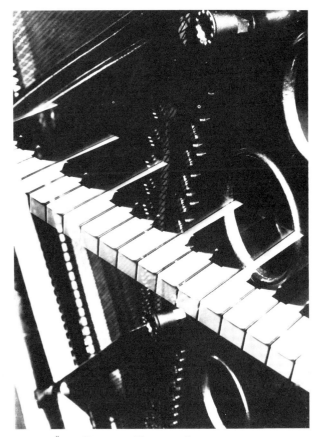

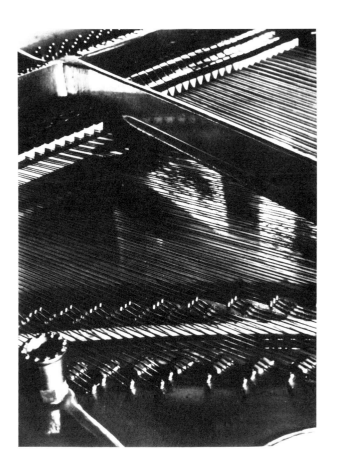

78a–c Änne Biermann, *Piano*, no date
Kunstbibliothek Preussischer Kulturbesitz, Berlin

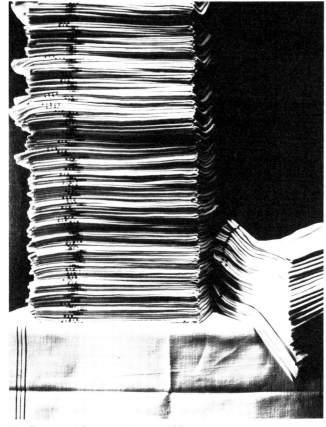

79 Emmanuel Sougez, *Linens*, 1935
Bibliothèque Nationale, Paris

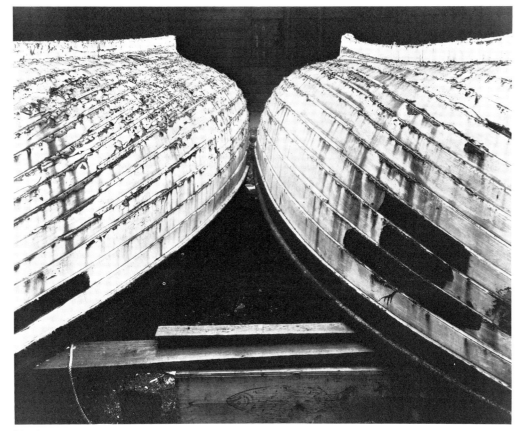

80 Ansel Adams, *Hulls*, 1933
San Francisco Museum of Modern Art

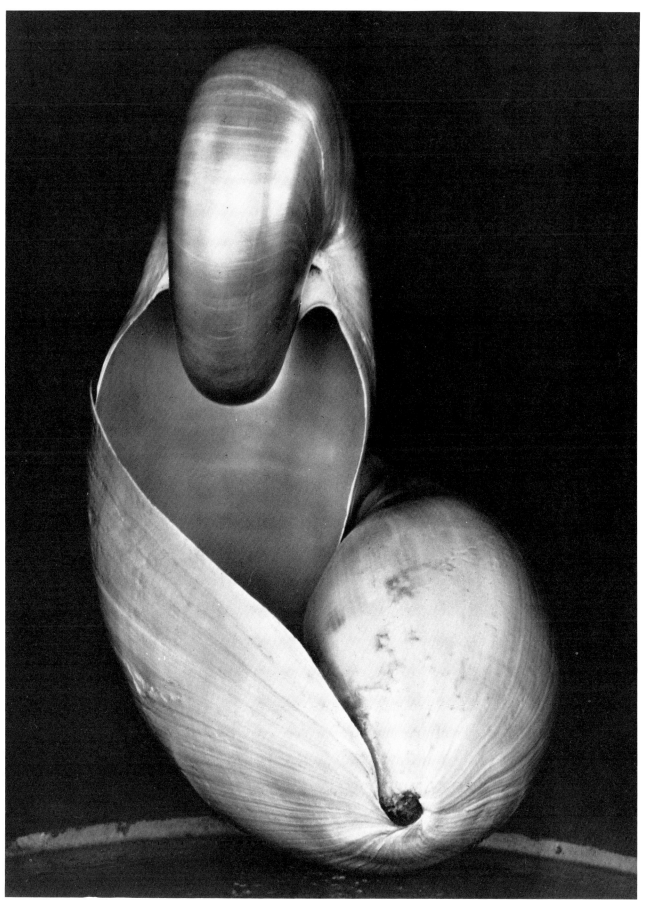

81 Edward Weston, *Shell,* 1927
San Francisco Museum of Modern Art

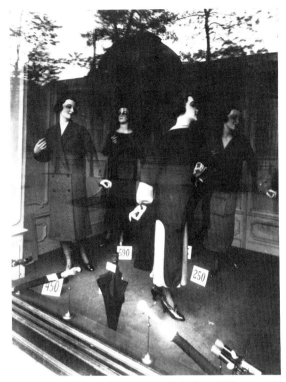

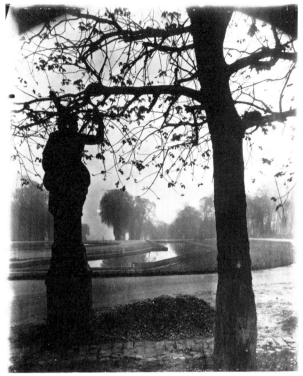

82 Eugène Atget, *Avenue des Gobelins*, 1925
The Museum of Modern Art, New York

83 Eugène Atget, *Saint Cloud*, 1926
The Museum of Modern Art, New York

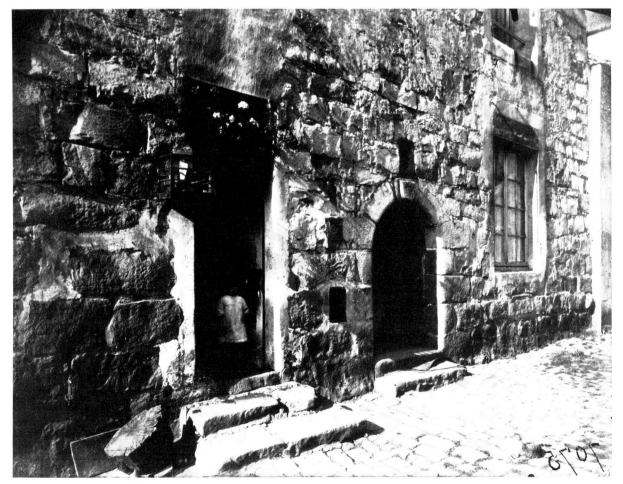

84 Eugène Atget, *Gif—Old Farmhouse*, 1924
The Museum of Modern Art, New York

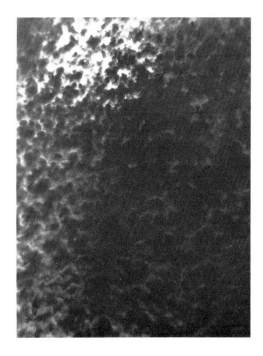

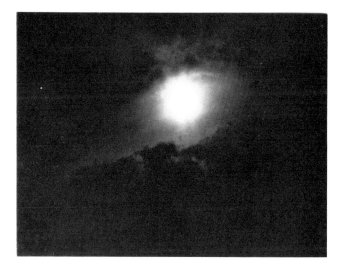

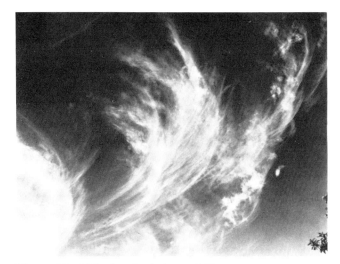

85a–c   Alfred Stieglitz, *Equivalents*, 1930
The Art Institute of Chicago

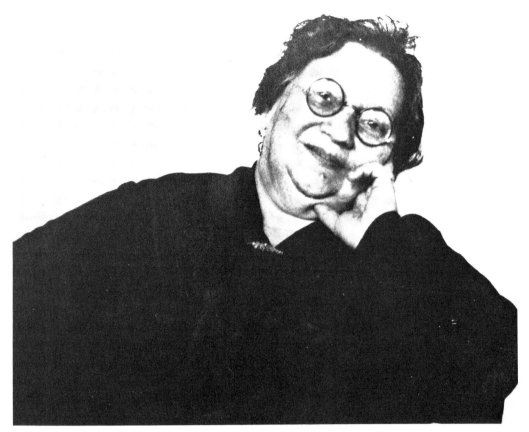

86 Hugo Erfurth, *Mother Ey*, 1934
    Agfa-Gevaert Foto-Historama, Leverkusen

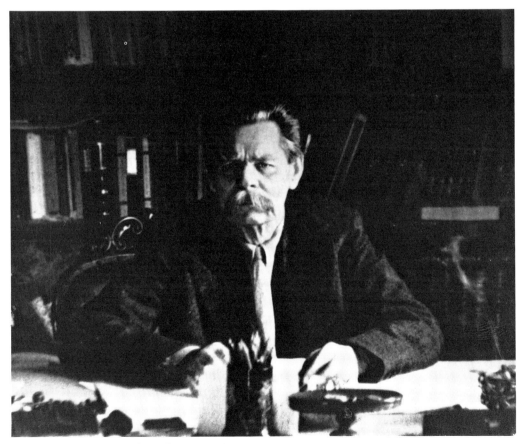

87 Felix H. Man, *Maxim Gorki, Sorrento*, 1932
    Fotografiska Museet, Stockholm

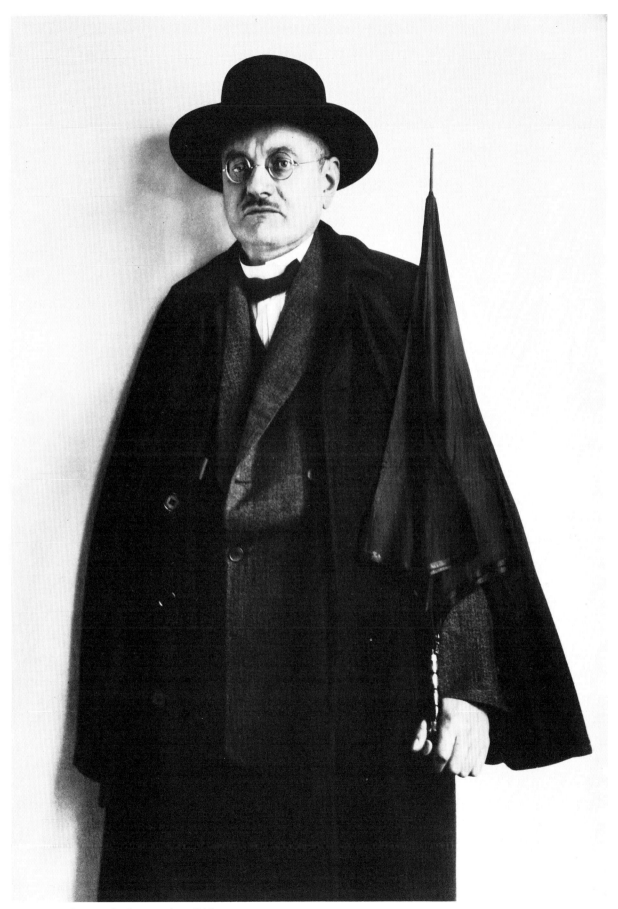

88   August Sander, *Parliamentarian*, 1928
Museum Ludwig, Cologne

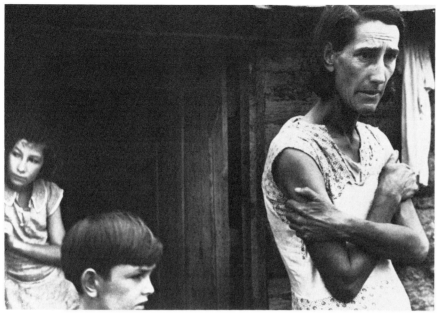

89 Ben Shahn, *Destitute*, 1935
    San Francisco Museum of Modern Art

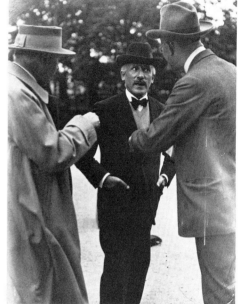

90 Alfred Eisenstaedt, *Toscanini in Bayreuth,*
    1932
    Münchner Stadtmuseum, Munich

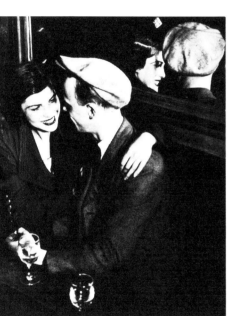

91 Brassaï, *In Paris*, 1933
    Museum Ludwig, Cologne

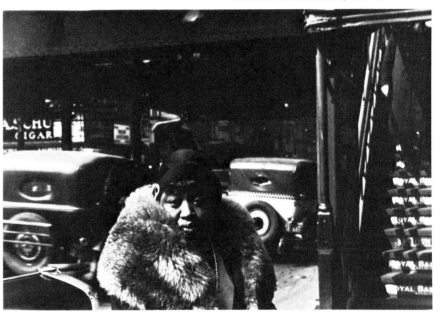

92 Walker Evans, *42nd Street*, 1929
    The Art Institute of Chicago

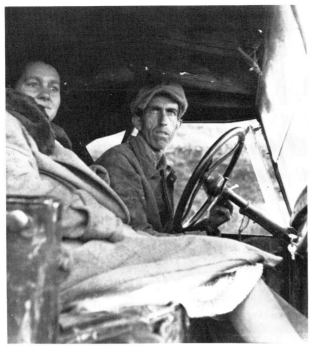

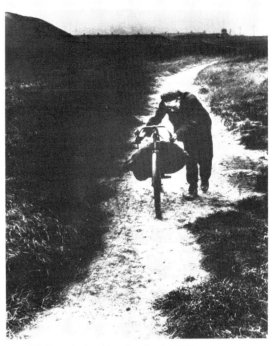

93　Dorothea Lange, *Ex-tenant Farmer on Relief Grant in the Imperial Valley, California*, 1937
The Library of Congress, Washington, D.C.

94　Bill Brandt, *Looking for Coal*, 1936
Museum Ludwig, Cologne

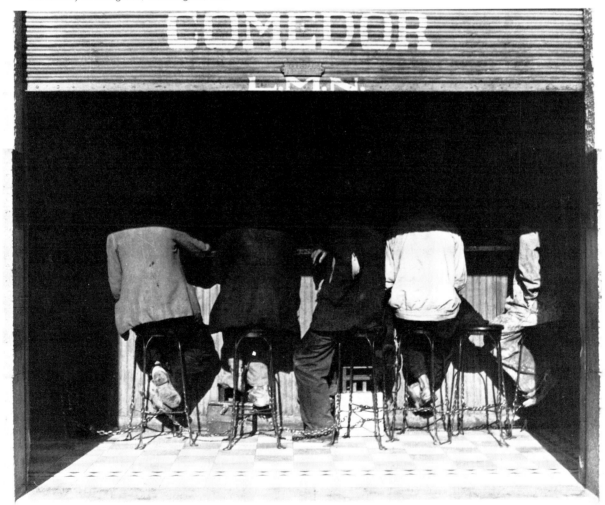

95　Manuel Alvarez Bravo, *The Stooped*, 1934
The Art Institute of Chicago

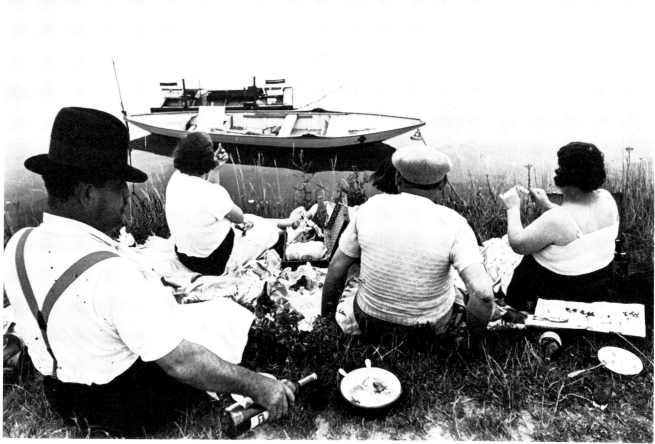

96   Henri Cartier-Bresson, *Lunch by the Marne*, 1938
     Museum Ludwig, Cologne

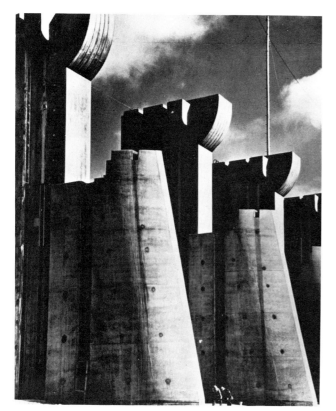

97   Margaret Bourke-White, *Life* magazine's first cover,
     Fort Peck Dam, Montana, 1936
     The Art Institute of Chicago

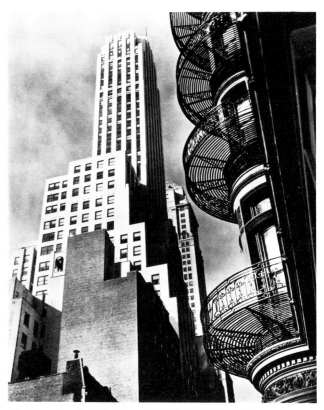

98   Berenice Abbott, *Murray Hill Hotel Spiral*, 1935
     The Art Institute of Chicago

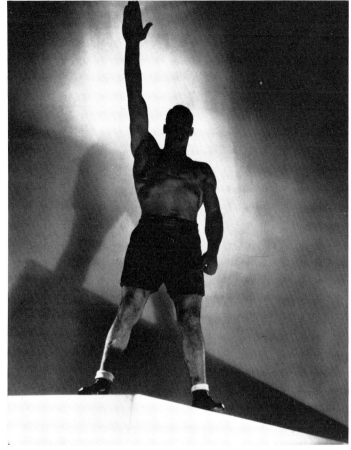

99 Edward Steichen, *Primo Carnera*, 1933
George Eastman House, Rochester

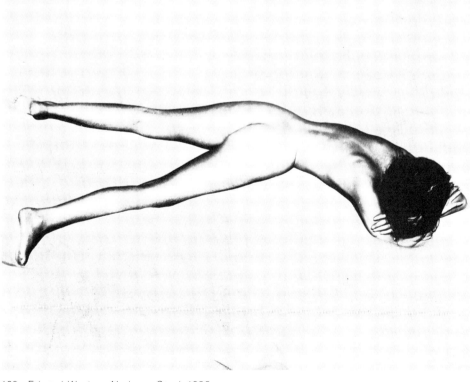

100 Edward Weston, *Nude on Sand*, 1936
The Royal Photographic Society of Great Britain, Bath

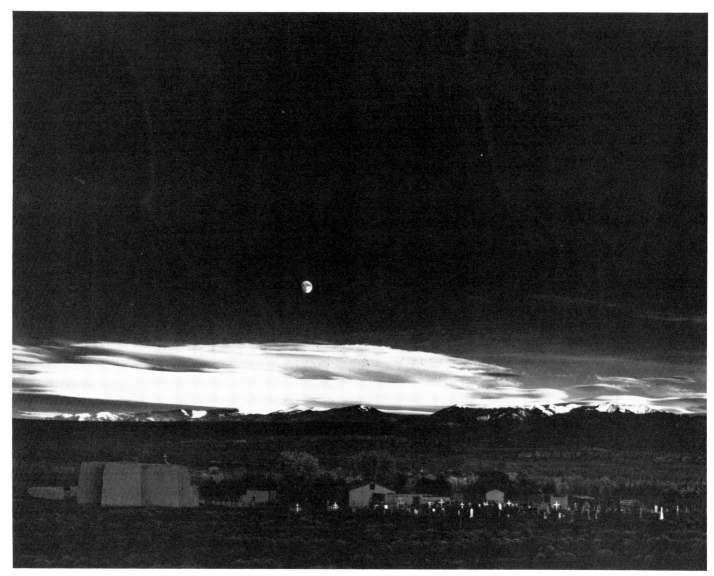

101   Ansel Adams, *Moonrise over Hernandez*, 1944
George Eastman House, Rochester

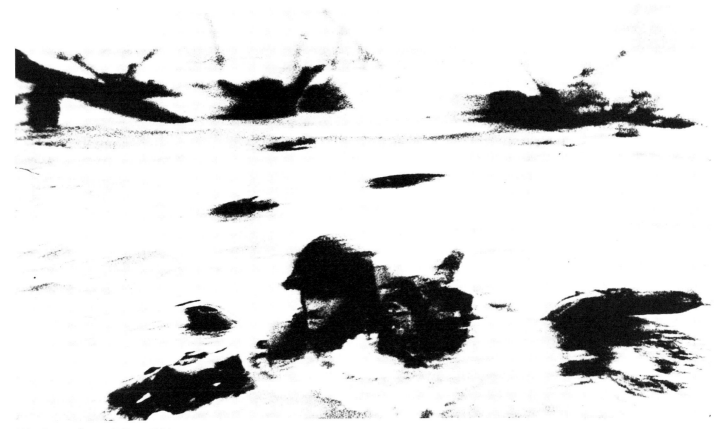

102 Robert Capa, *D-Day*, 1944
Stedelijk Museum, Amsterdam

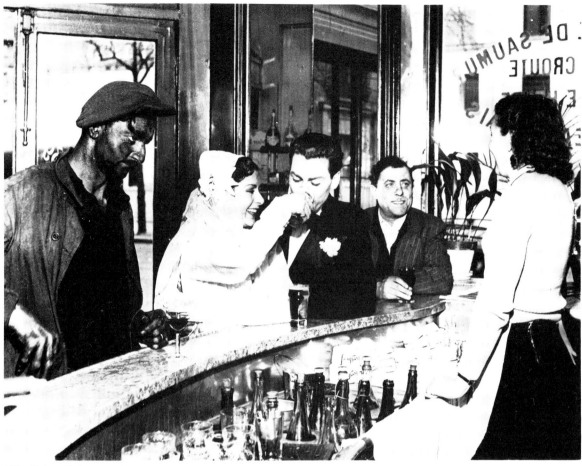

103 Robert Doisneau, *Coalman and Newlyweds*, 1948
Bibliothèque Nationale, Paris

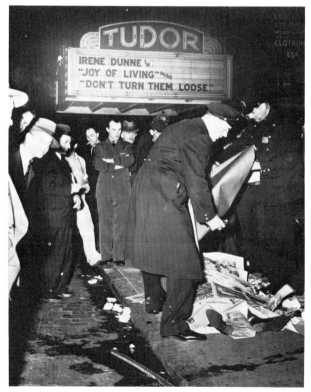

104 Weegee, *Man Killed in an Accident*, 1945
Bibliothèque Nationale, Paris

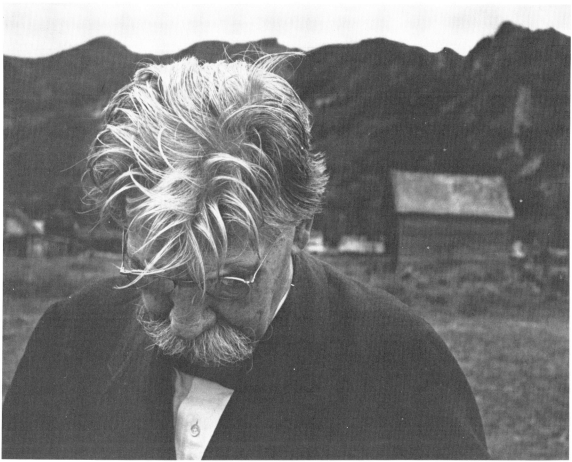

105   W. Eugene Smith, *Albert Schweitzer*, 1949
Museum Ludwig, Cologne

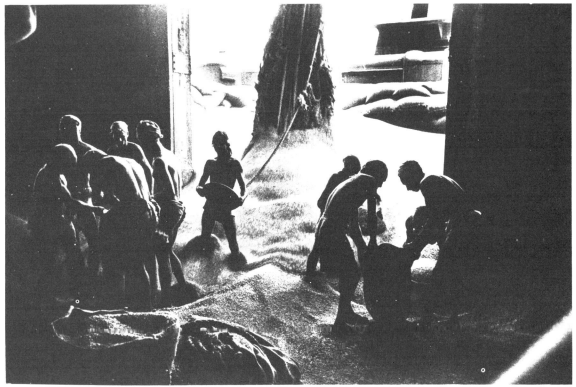

106   Werner Bischof, *Bihar, India*, 1951
Stiftung für die Photographie, Kunsthaus Zürich

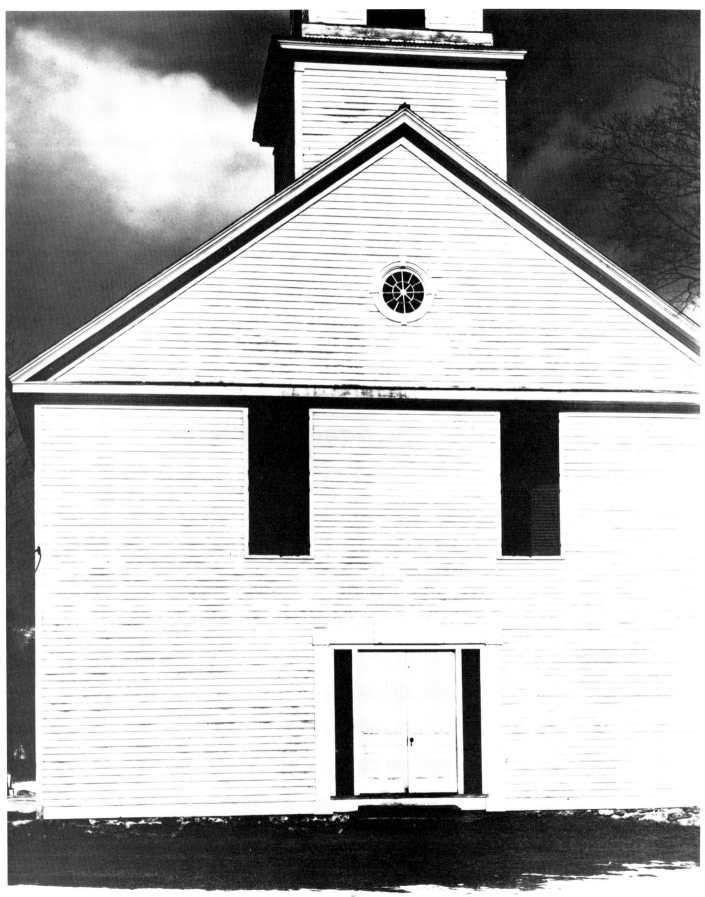

107   Paul Strand, *Vermont Church,* 1944
      Museum of Fine Arts, Boston

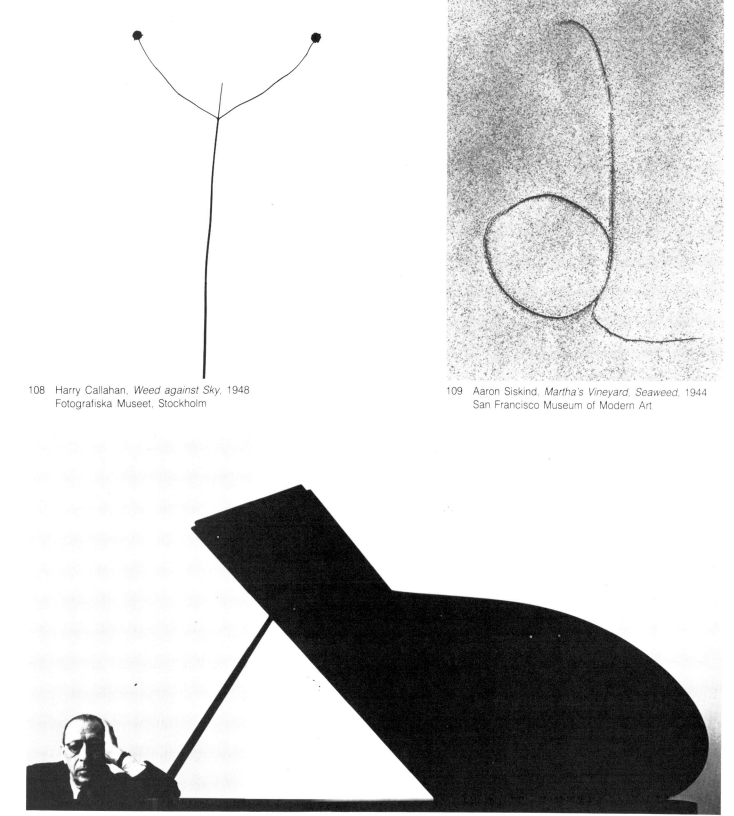

108 Harry Callahan, *Weed against Sky,* 1948
Fotografiska Museet, Stockholm

109 Aaron Siskind, *Martha's Vineyard, Seaweed,* 1944
San Francisco Museum of Modern Art

110 Arnold Newman, *Igor Stravinsky,* 1946
Fotografiska Museet, Stockholm

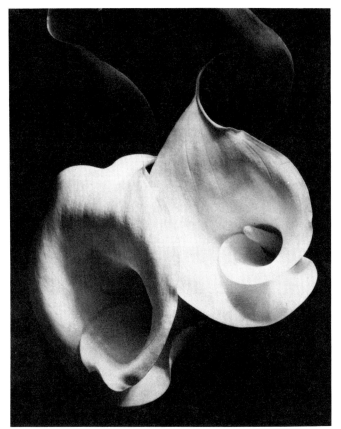

111 Imogen Cunningham, *Two Callas*, ca. 1948
The Art Institute of Chicago

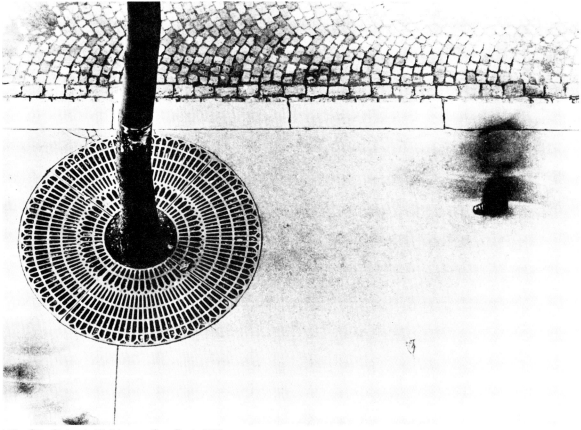

112 Otto Steinert, *Walking on One Foot*, 1950
Museum Folkwang, Essen

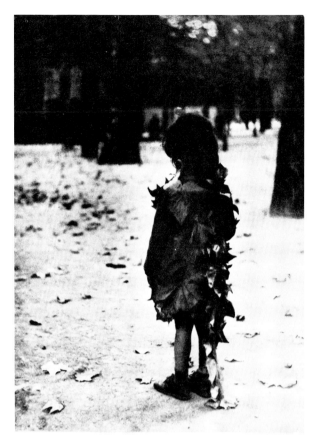

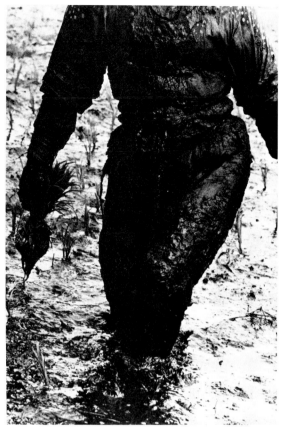

113   Edouard Boubat, *Child with Coat of Leaves*, 1947
Museum Folkwang, Essen

114   Hiroshi Hamaya, *Toyama, Japan*, 1955
Museum Ludwig, Cologne

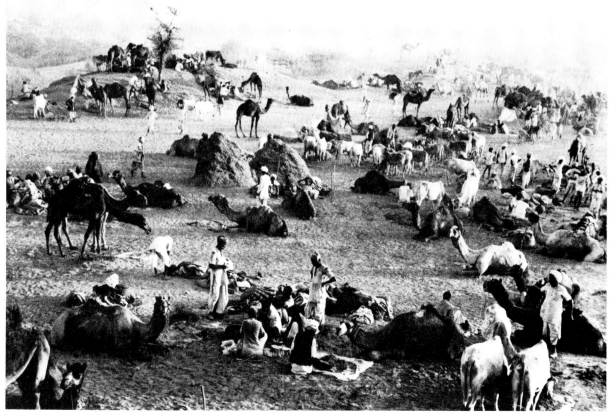

115   Marc Riboud, *Radjastan, India*, 1956
Bibliothèque Nationale, Paris

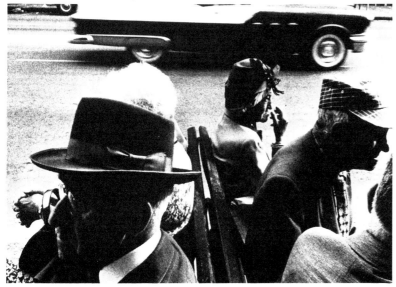

116 Robert Frank, *St. Petersburg, Florida*, 1958
The Art Institute of Chicago

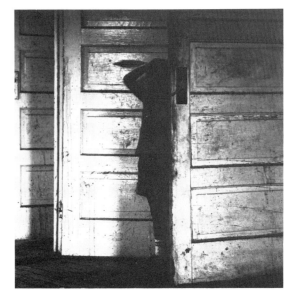

117 Ralph Eugene Meatyard, *Untitled*, no date
Art Museum, University of New Mexico,
Albuquerque

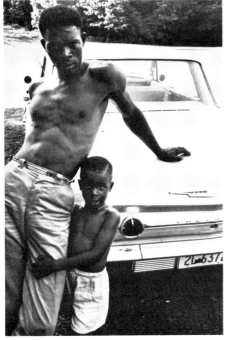

118 Bruce Davidson, *Untitled (Man and Boy)*,
no date
The Art Institute of Chicago

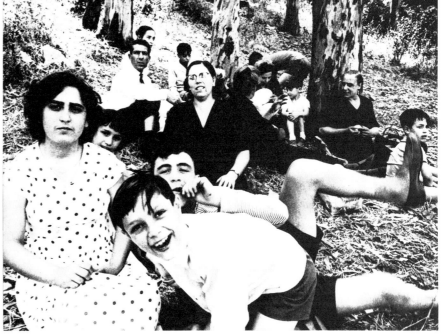

119 William Klein, *Lunch on the Grass, Rome*, 1956
Museum Ludwig, Cologne

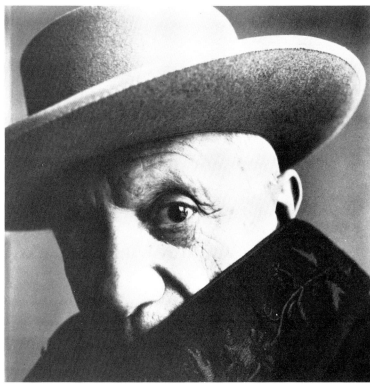

120 Irving Penn, *Pablo Picasso*, 1957
Museum Ludwig, Cologne

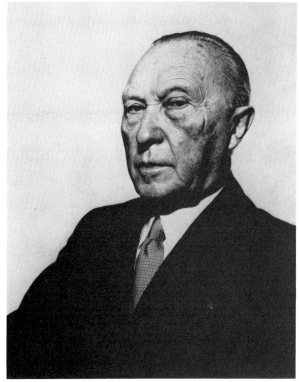

121 Chargesheimer, *Konrad Adenauer*, 1956
Museum Ludwig, Cologne

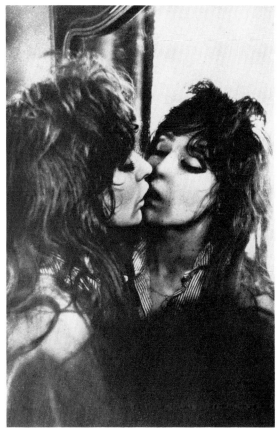

122 Ed van der Elsken, *St. Germain*, ca. 1952
Stedelijk Museum, Amsterdam

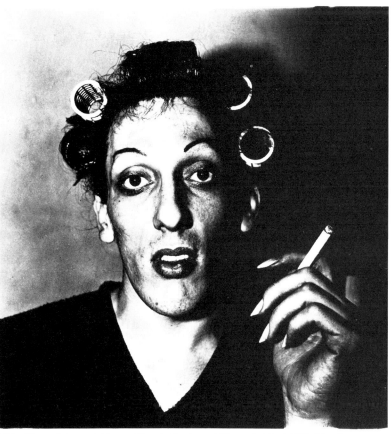

123 Diane Arbus, *A Young Man in Curlers at Home in West 20th Street, New York*, 1956
San Francisco Museum of Modern Art

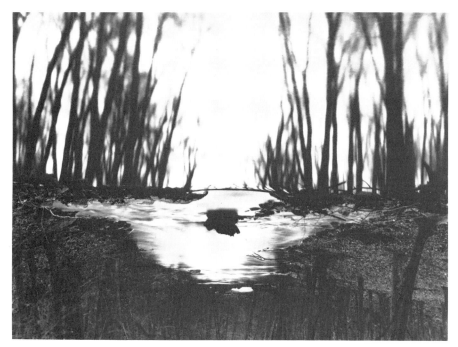

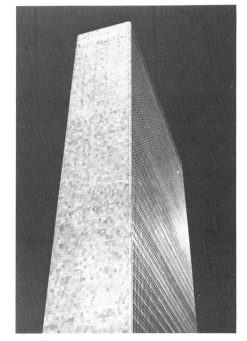

124 Paul Caponigro, *Creek and Trees*, 1968
San Francisco Museum of Modern Art

125 Charles Sheeler, *United Nations Building*,
ca. 1950, The Library of Congress,
Washington, D.C.

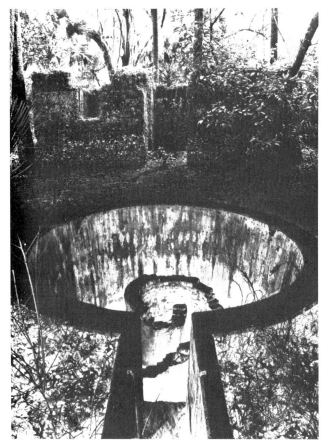

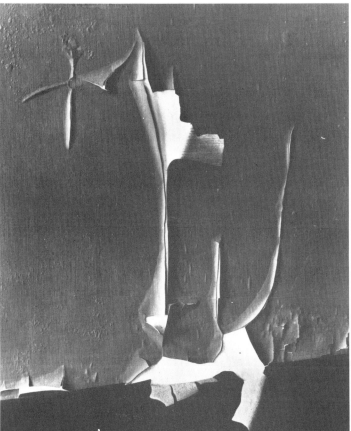

126 Jerry Uelsmann, *Ritual Ground*, 1964
The Royal Photographic Society of Great Britain, Bath

127 Minor White, *Peeled Paint*, 1959
San Francisco Museum of Modern Art

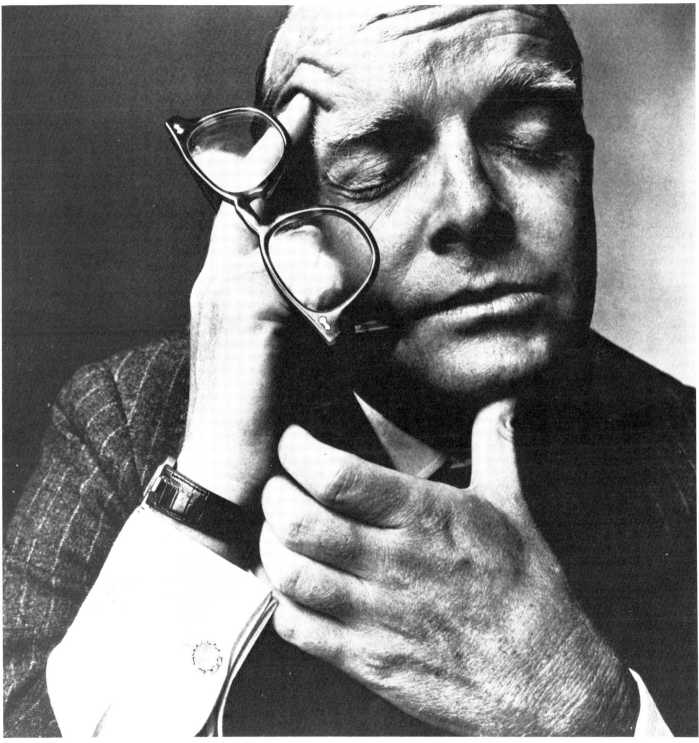

128 Irving Penn, *Truman Capote,* 1965
Fotografiska Museet, Stockholm

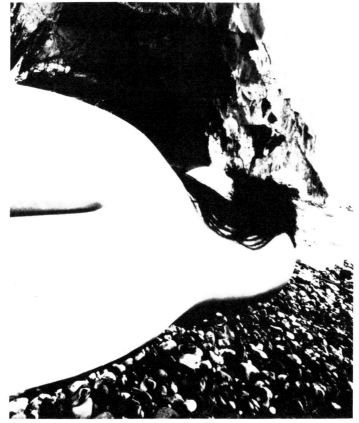

129　Bill Brandt, *Nude*, 1953
Fotografiska Museet, Stockholm

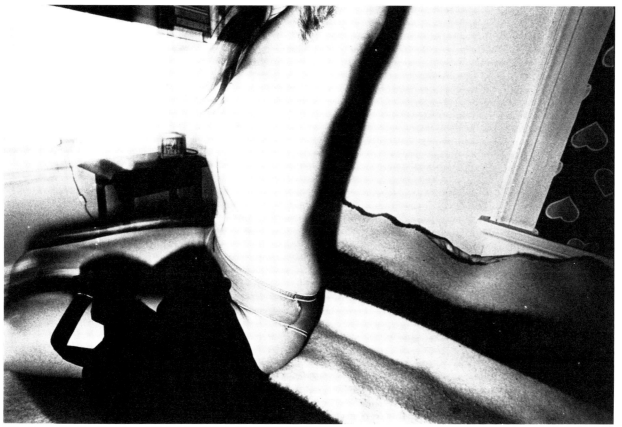

130　Roger Mertin, *Breast and Hair (after E.W.), Rochester*, 1973
Art Museum, University of New Mexico, Albuquerque

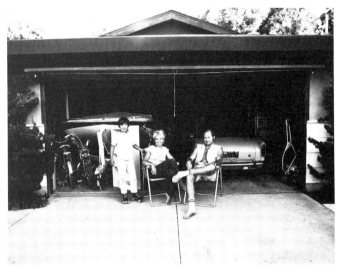

131 Bill Owens, *"Our house is built with the living room in back, so in the evenings we sit out front of the garage and watch the traffic go by,"* 1972
Fotografiska Museet, Stockholm

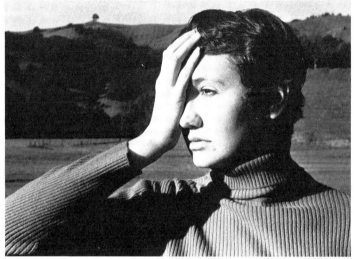

132 Ralph Gibson, *Maurine,* ca. 1972
Stedelijk Museum, Amsterdam

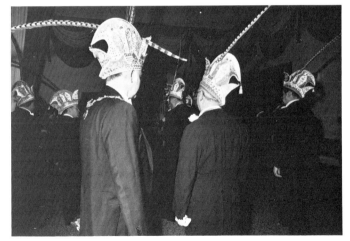

133 André Gelpke, *Carnival,* 1978
Museum Folkwang, Essen

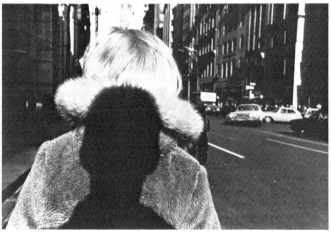

134 Lee Friedlander, *Self-portrait, Woman with Shadow,* 1973
San Francisco Museum of Modern Art

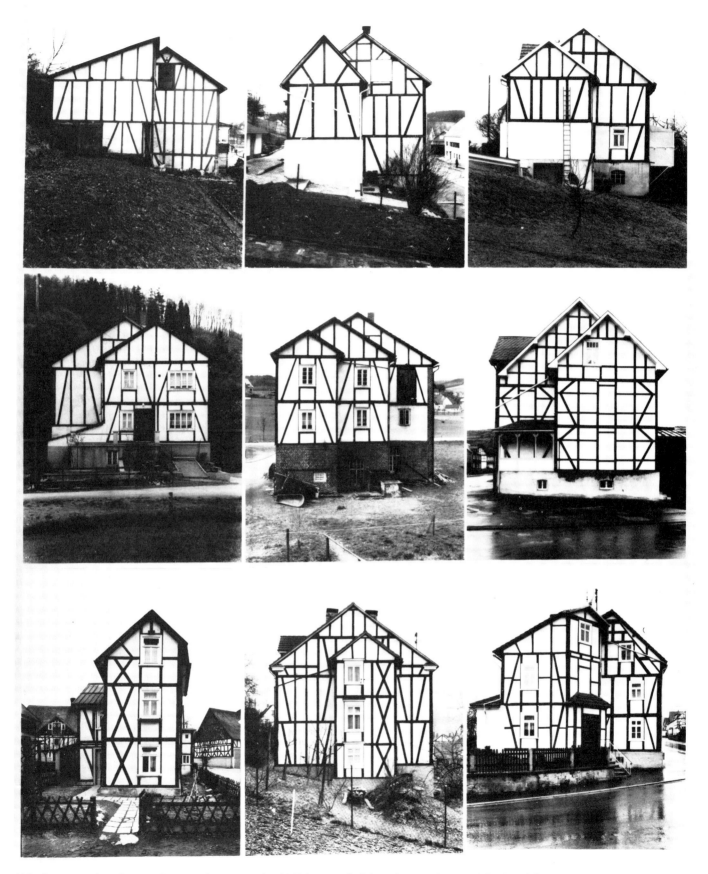

135 Bernd and Hilla Becher, Typology from the series *Half-timbered Buildings from the Industrial Region of Siegen*, 1959–1974
Museum Ludwig, Cologne

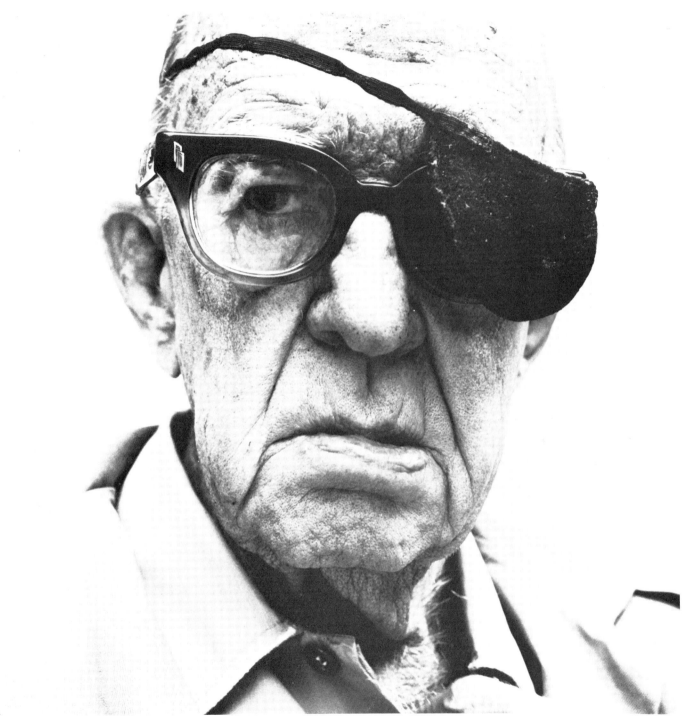

136 Richard Avedon, *John Ford*, 1972
Museum für Kunst und Gewerbe, Hamburg

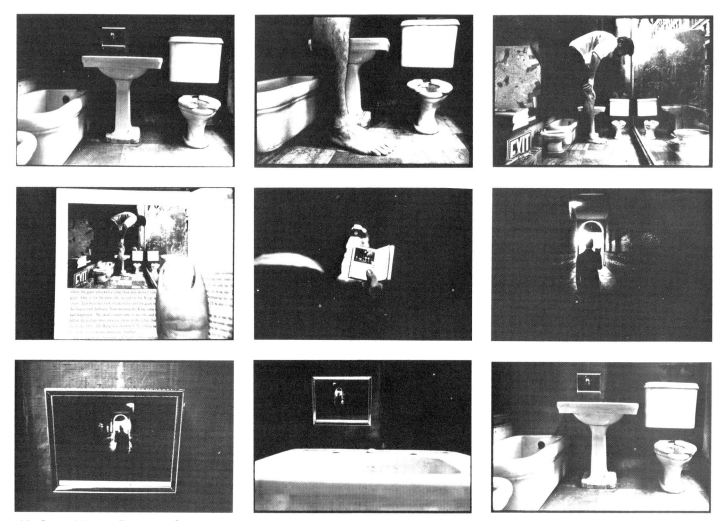

137 Duane Michals, *Things are Queer*, no date
Stedelijk Museum, Amsterdam

COLOR PHOTOGRAPHY

A Problem for Collections

In sheer numbers, color photography has far outstripped black-and-white photography in every domain—among amateurs, professionals, and scientists. The photo industry, itself, declares that 90 percent of all photographs taken are in color. Yet color photography makes up only a small part of the photography collections in museums, galleries, and libraries. Why is that the case?

A Hundred Years' Catching Up

Black-and-white photography has more than a hundred-year gain over color photography, both as a documentary and as a creative medium—and has proved its artistic worth from the very beginning. Compared to this achievement the early color photographs have something of an experimental and odd look about them. When you come upon an early color photograph that has been preserved, you feel pride in the mere fact of the technical achievement. Color photographs often seem to have been colored by hand. In short, you tend to detect the mere joy in having been able to make them at all instead of an ambition for artistic achievement. If one discounts a few painterly examples from the turn of the century, it is only with the introduction of color film—in the middle 1930s—that ambitious photographers have devoted themselves to a creative use of color—and successfully, too.

The Extra Dimension

Compared to black-and-white photography, color demands of the artist a mastery over another dimension. The accustomed reduction of a subject to the monochrome, aside from forcing him to deal with form and composition, had absolved the photographer from having to deal with how an image might appear in color. Color, however, requires a talent of its own—to clarify, through the surface glow, also the meaning of a subject. The esthetic charm of color photographs tends to sway its producers as well as its observers more in the direction of uncontrollable feelings than that of exercising sober reason, and therefore color photography is more dependent on imponderables than is black-and-white. While millions who take snapshots delight in results that seem true to nature (the more colorful the better), committed photographers are forced to use color sparingly as a determining element of visual expression and visual pleasure.

The Question of Expense

Producing color photographs is more expensive and more complicated than black-and-white. The serious photographer must either acquire special darkroom equipment or entrust his work to the filter of strange influence in a laboratory where the results will no longer reflect his own uncompromising control. Instamatic photography, however, allows him to compare the result with the subject at once without having to depend on middlemen. Additional takes enable him to come closer to his original concept whether through different lighting or different exposure time, even if they add to the expense. At the same time, he must be aware that every color film, as soon as it leaves the manufacturer, begins to deteriorate, so that even more so than with black-and-white, he must make numerous new proof sheets.

Permanence: The Main Problem

Whereas we possess black-and-white photographs from the earliest stages of the art that retain the tonal quality and intensity "as on the first day," the life-expectancy of color photographs must be regarded as extremely endangered. Not only can the light that initially produced them also diminish or destroy color photographs, but the color elements themselves contain the germs of their own decomposition, and can change by becoming disarranged or by disappearing altogether. Even well-preserved photographs from the past century have often suffered such alteration and devaluation. While color permanence may not be of such great importance to the consumer, it remains a decisive criterion for the creative photographer and for the collections. The recommendation of one color film manufacturer to seal and freeze color originals cannot be the solution. Manufacturers know this, which is why they are still seeking to make improvements. One only hopes that they will succeed. Only when the process of color photography has been perfected will the invention have been completed. The best creations of color photography belong as much in libraries, museums, and galleries as those of black-and-white have for years.

Color as the Consummation

The above-mentioned reasons explain the reservations that collectors and curators continue to express regarding color photography even today. Luckily, however, their abstinence is not total. We succeeded in obtaining an excellent selection of color photographs for the Imaginary Photo Museum. It confirms the mastery with which they were created. Concentrating them in one section of the book and separating them from the black-and-white plates may grant them the showcasing they deserve.

L.F.G.

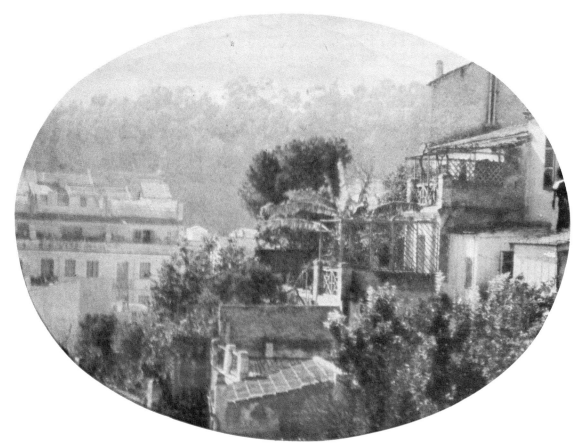

138   Louis Ducos du Hauron, *Tekmni District: Algiers*, 1884
Société Française de Photographie, Paris

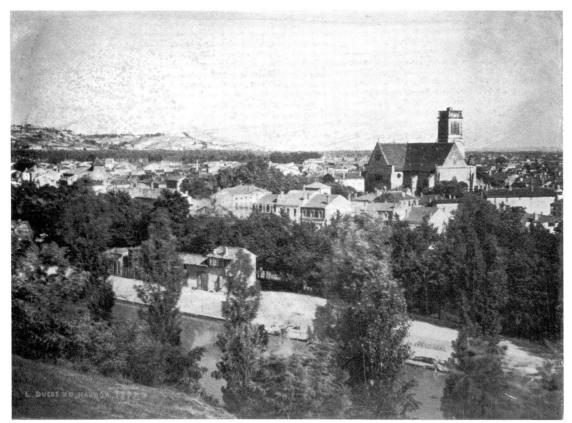

139   Louis Ducos du Hauron, *The Angoulème Countryside*, 1877
Société Française de Photographie, Paris

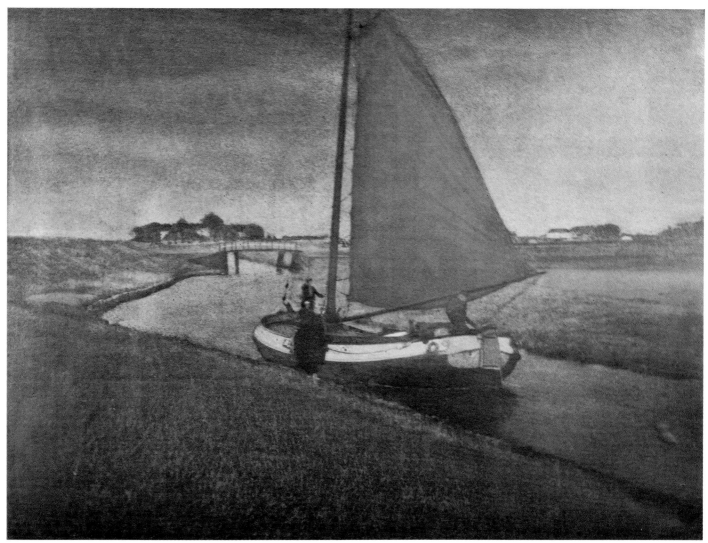

140 Theodor and Oskar Hofmeister, *Dutch Canal*, 1909
Museum für Kunst und Gewerbe, Hamburg

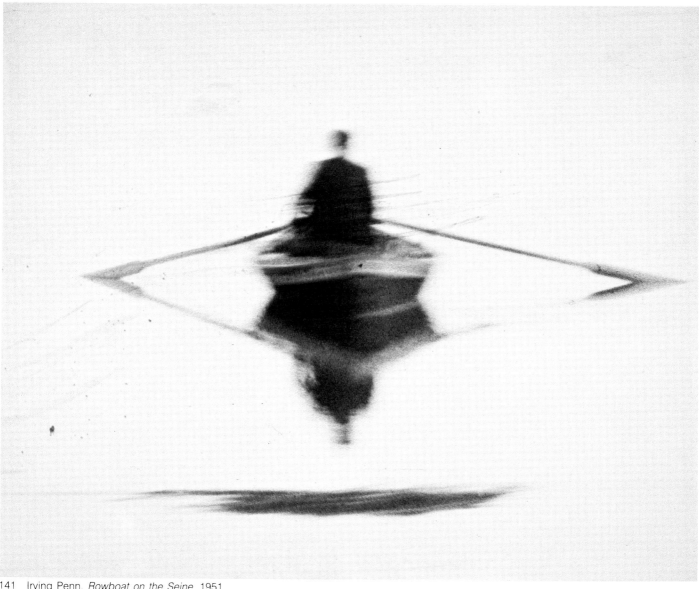

141 Irving Penn, *Rowboat on the Seine,* 1951
Museum Ludwig, Cologne

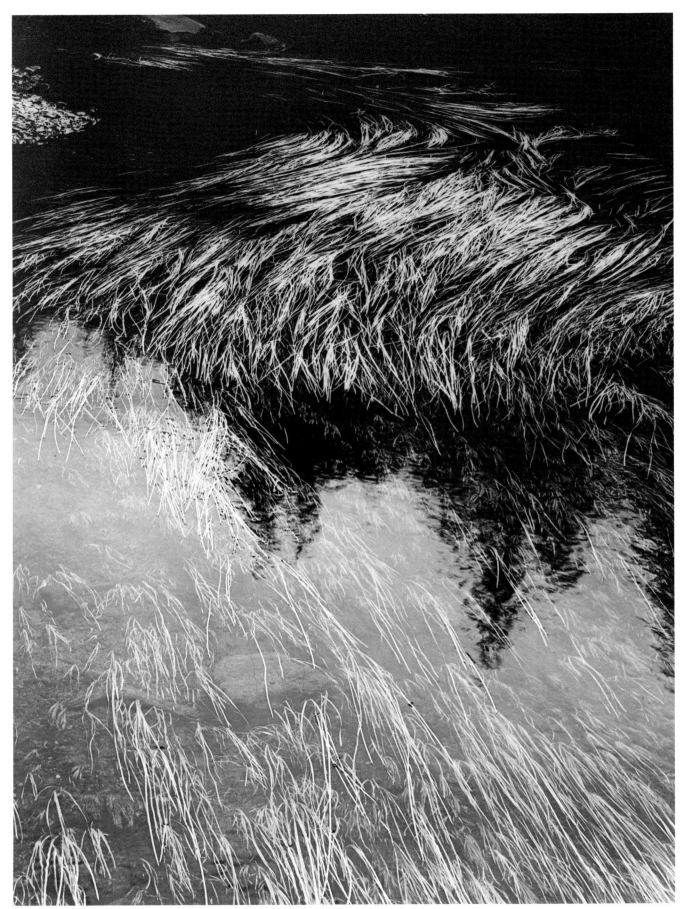

144   Eliot Porter, *Woodland Stream, Pittsburgh, New Hampshire*, 1965
      Art Museum, University of New Mexico, Albuquerque

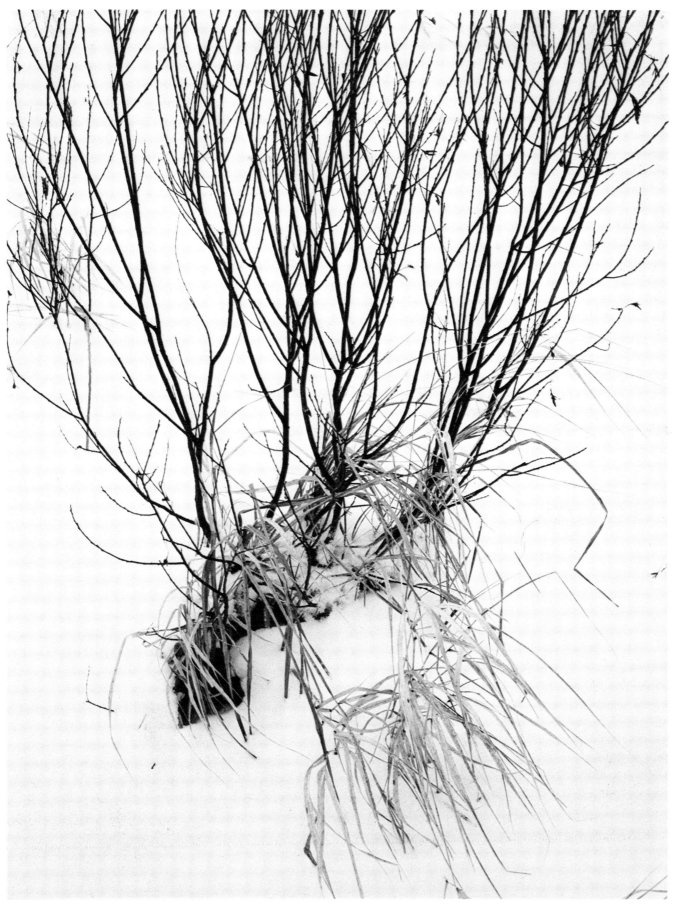

145 Eliot Porter, *Bush and Yellow Grass, Adirondacks,* 1965
Art Museum, University of New Mexico, Albuquerque

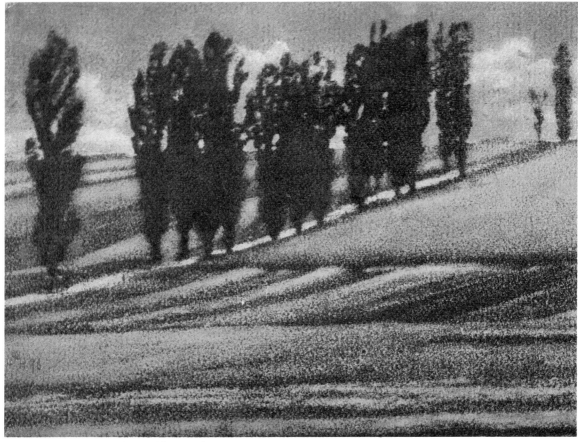

146 Hugo Henneberg, *Poplar Alley*, no date
     Kunstbibliothek Preussischer Kulturbesitz, Berlin

147 Franco Fontana, *Landscape*, 1974
     Stedelijk Museum, Amsterdam

148　Franco Fontana, *Landscape*, 1974
　　Stedelijk Museum, Amsterdam

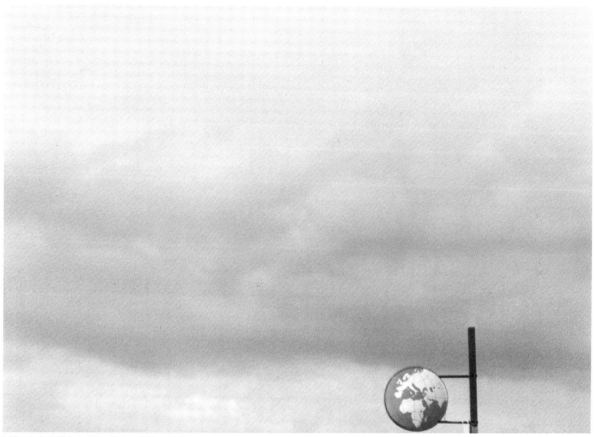

149 Luigi Ghirri, *The Spina Lido*, 1978
Università di Parma

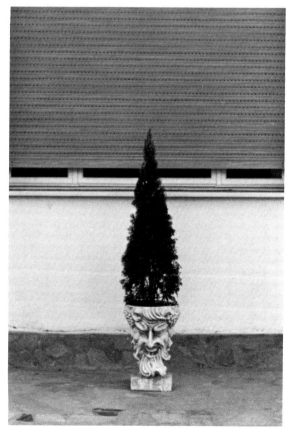

150 Luigi Ghirri, *Modena*, 1973
Università di Parma

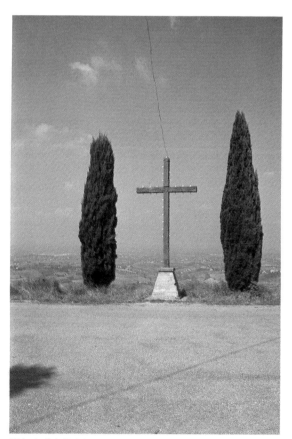

151 Luigi Ghirri, *Vignola*, 1974
Università di Parma

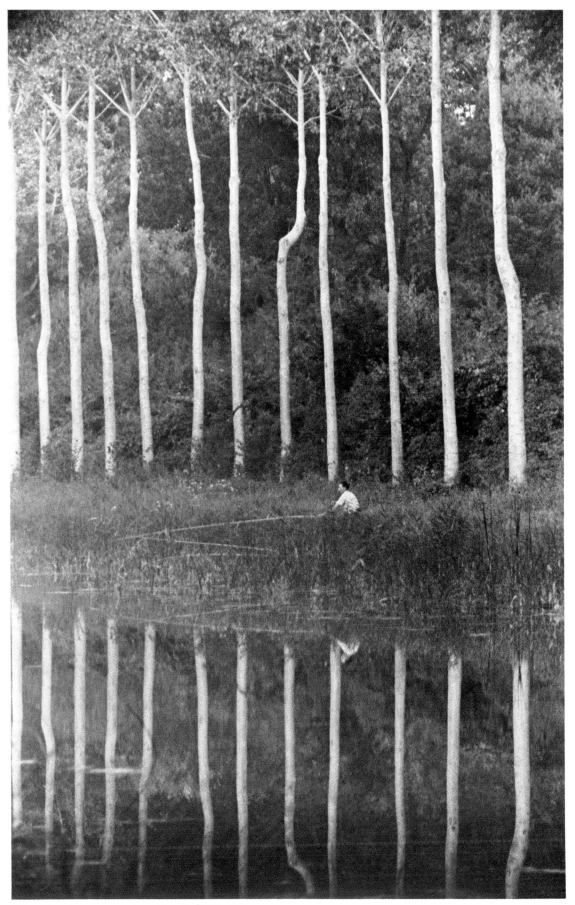

152   Irving Penn, *Trees along French Canal*, 1951
The Museum of Modern Art, New York

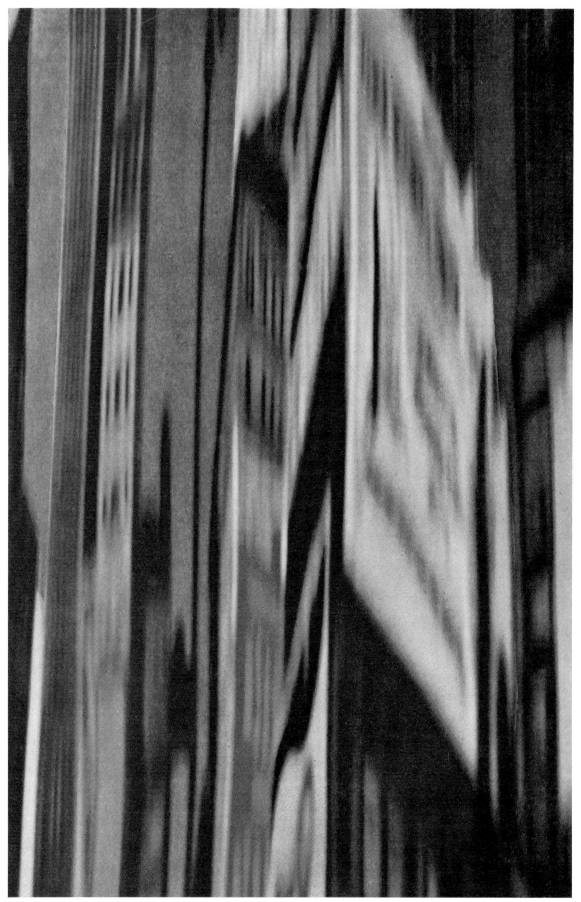

153 Ernst Haas, *New York (Blurred Skyscrapers)*, 1952
The Museum of Modern Art, New York

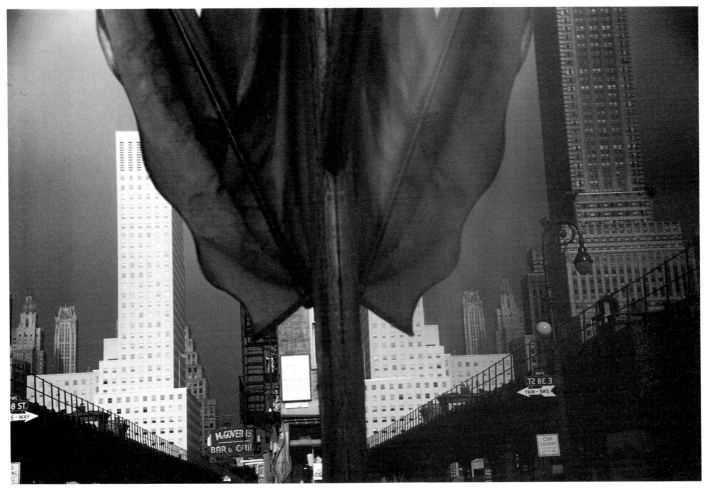

154   Ernst Haas, *Corner of 38th Street, New York*, 1952
The Museum of Modern Art, New York

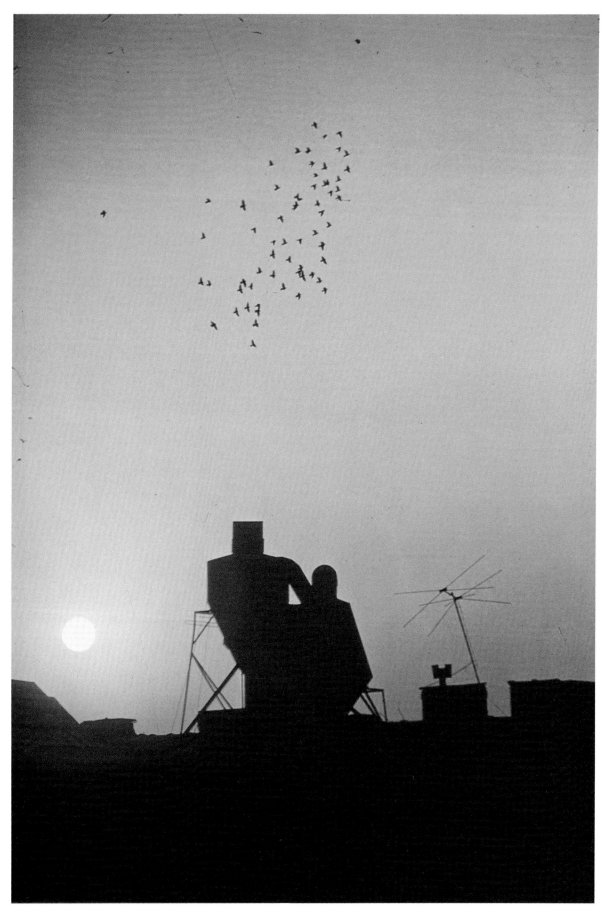

155 Ernst Haas, *New York (Sunset Silhouette)*, 1952
The Museum of Modern Art, New York

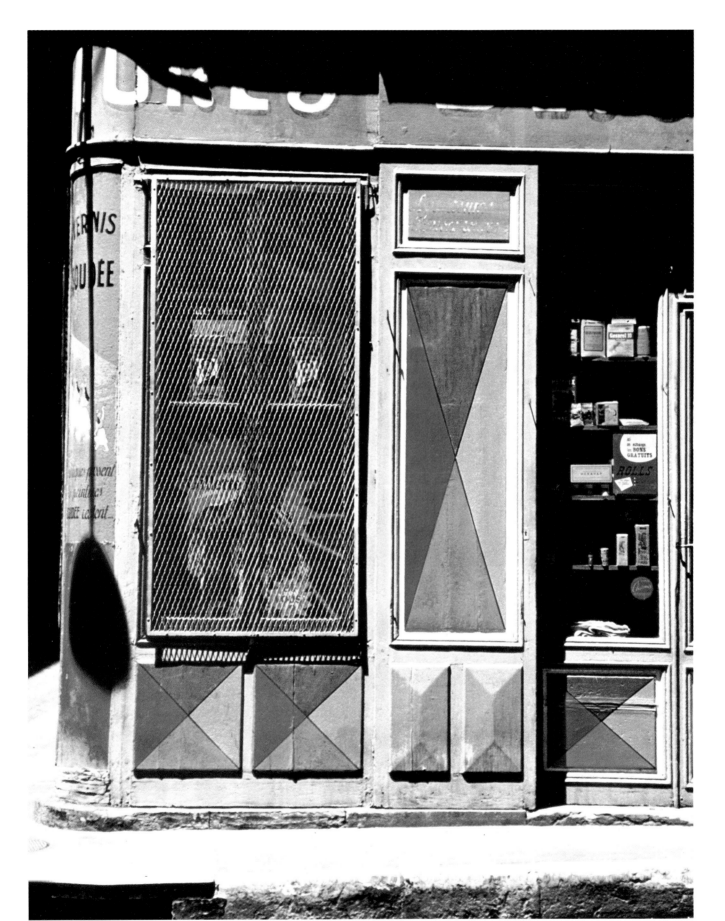

156   Arthur Siegel, *France,* 1953
The Art Institute of Chicago

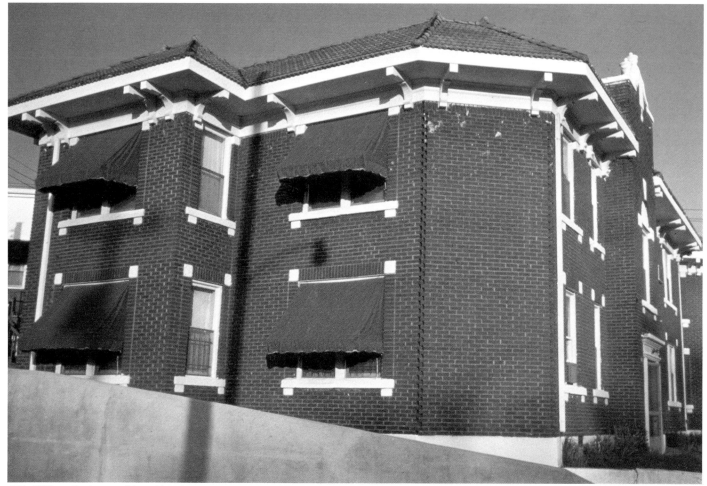

157 William Eggleston, *Memphis*, 1969–1970
The Museum of Modern Art, New York

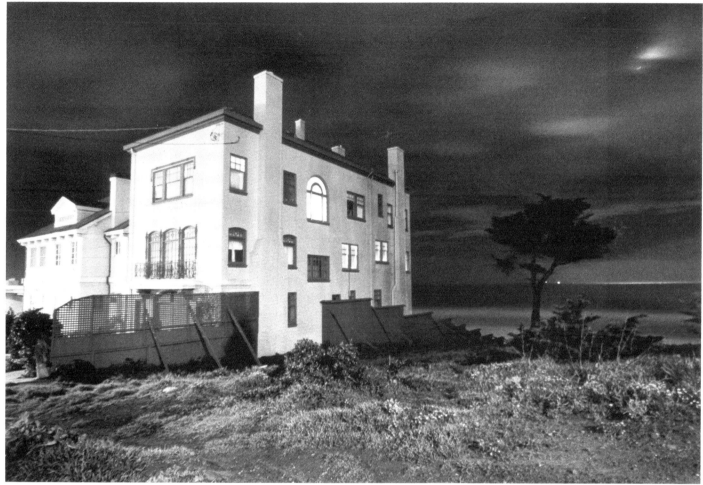

158   Arthur Ollman, *Untitled,* 1976
San Francisco Museum of Modern Art

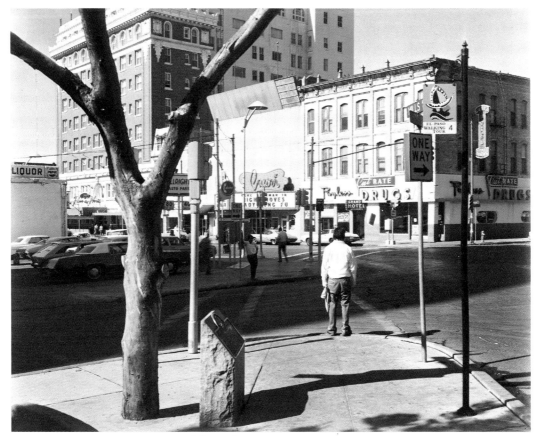

159   Stephen Shore, *El Paso Street, El Paso, Texas*, 1975
The Museum of Modern Art, New York

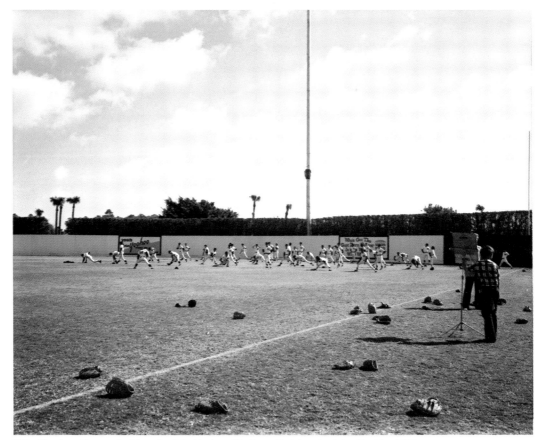

160   Stephen Shore, *Fort Lauderdale Yankee Stadium, Fort Lauderdale, Florida*, 1978
The Museum of Modern Art, New York

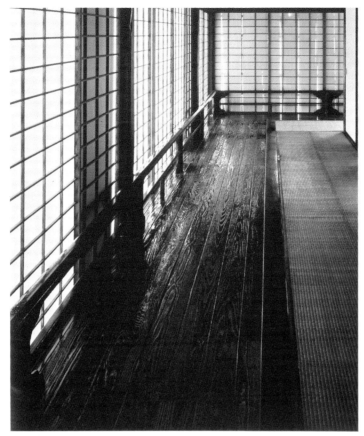

161 Ken Domon, *Katsura Rikyu, Kyoto*, 1974
Shadai Gallery, Tokyo

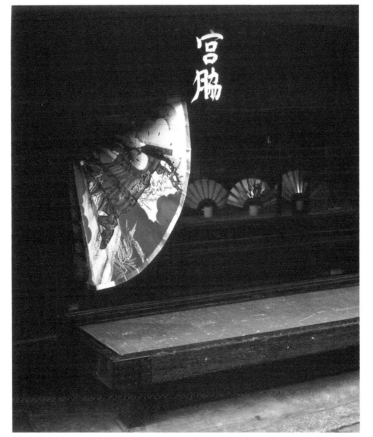

162 Ken Domon, *Miyawaki Fan Shop*, 1960
Shadai Gallery, Tokyo

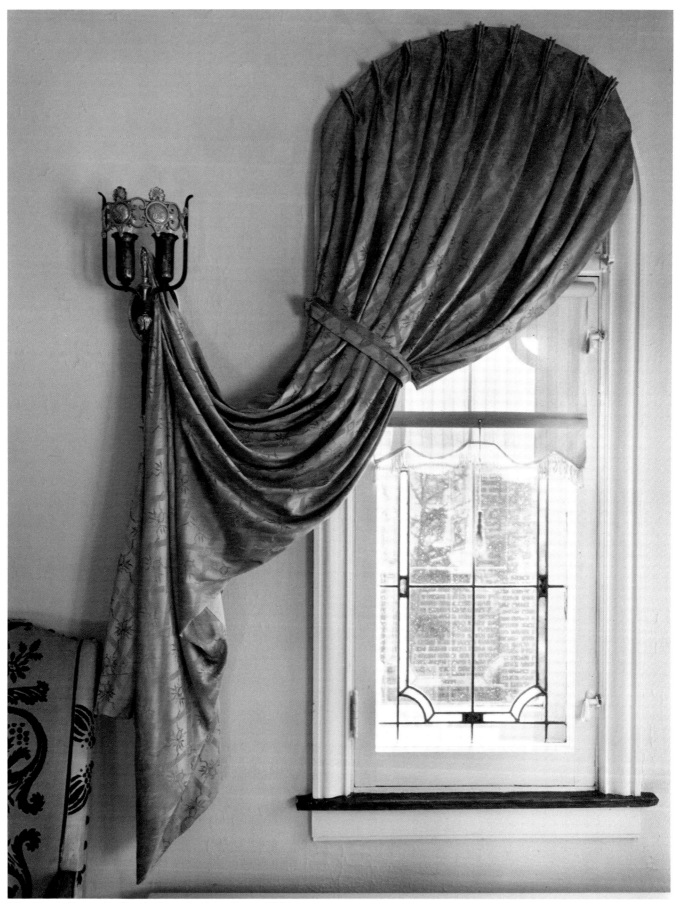

163 Wayne Sorce, *Dr. Soter's Drape in Living Room*, 1976
The Art Institute of Chicago

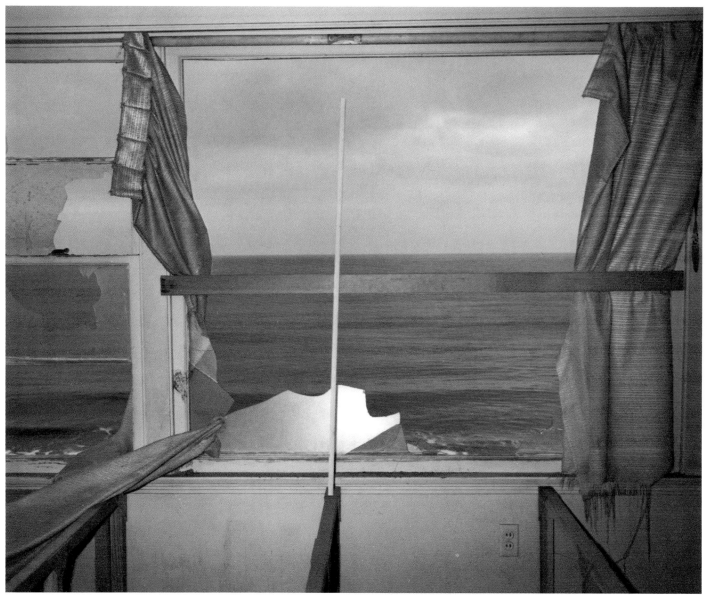

164   John M. Divola, *Zuma Series No. 3*, 1977
San Francisco Museum of Modern Art

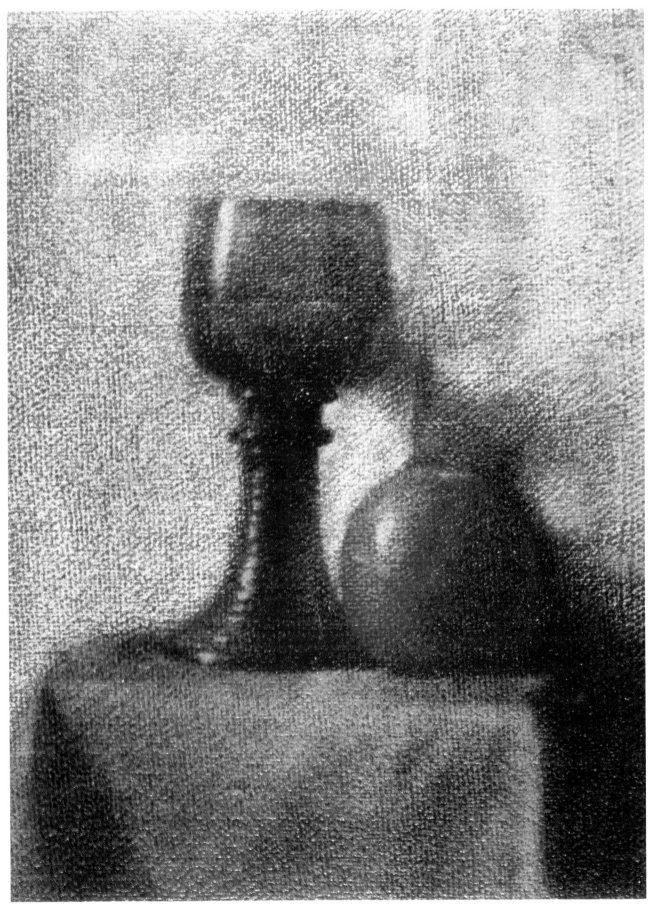

165   Josef Watzek, *Wineglass and Apple*, 1896
Kunstbibliothek Preussischer Kulturbesitz, Berlin

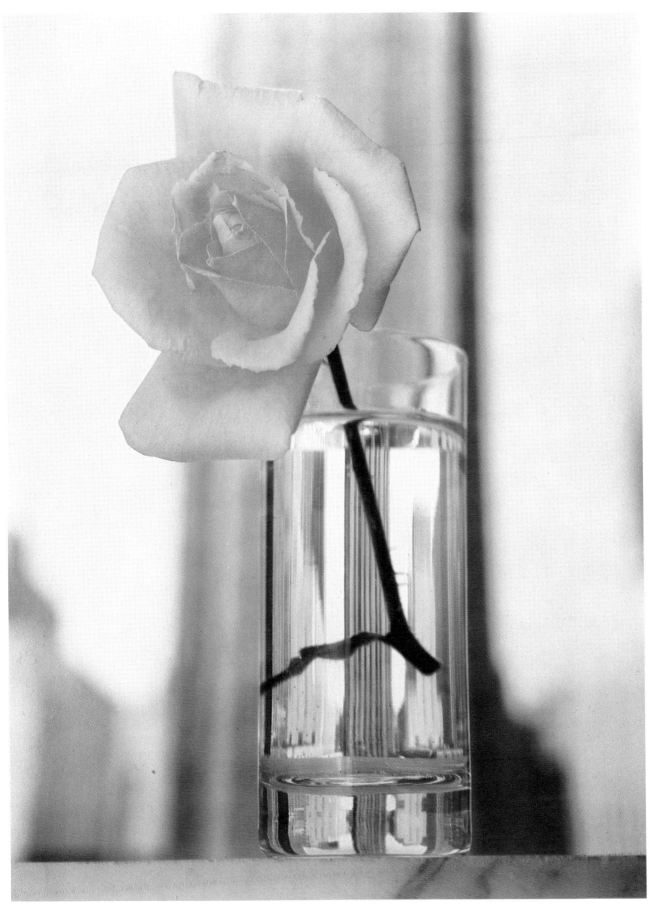

166 Irving Penn, *Yellow Rose and Skyscraper,* 1950
The Museum of Modern Art, New York

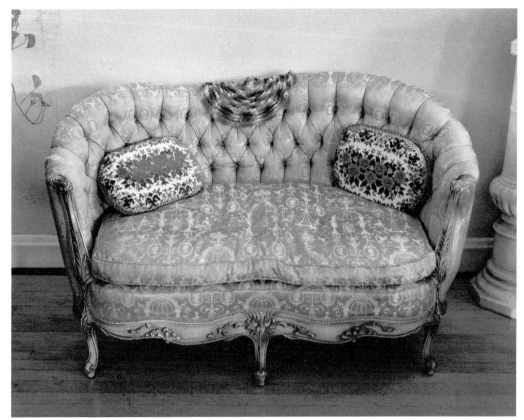

167 Wayne Sorce, *Dr. Soter's Pink Couch,* 1976
The Art Institute of Chicago

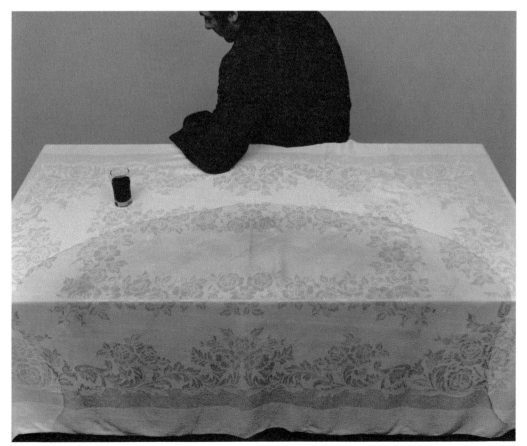

168 Jo Ann Callis, *Man at Table,* 1977
San Francisco Museum of Modern Art

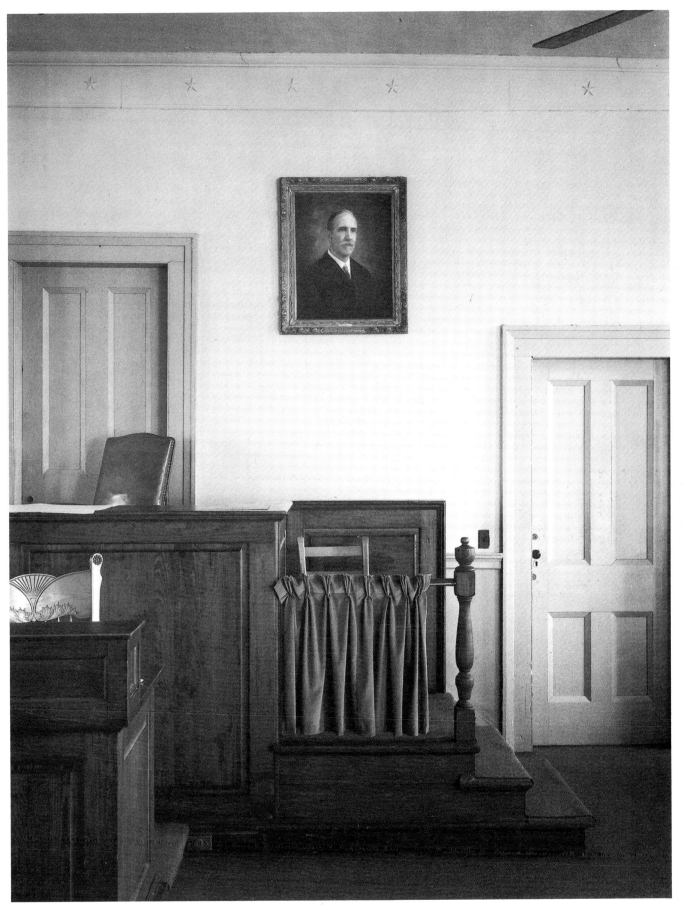

169 Stephen Shore, *Green County Court House*, 1976
The Art Institute of Chicago

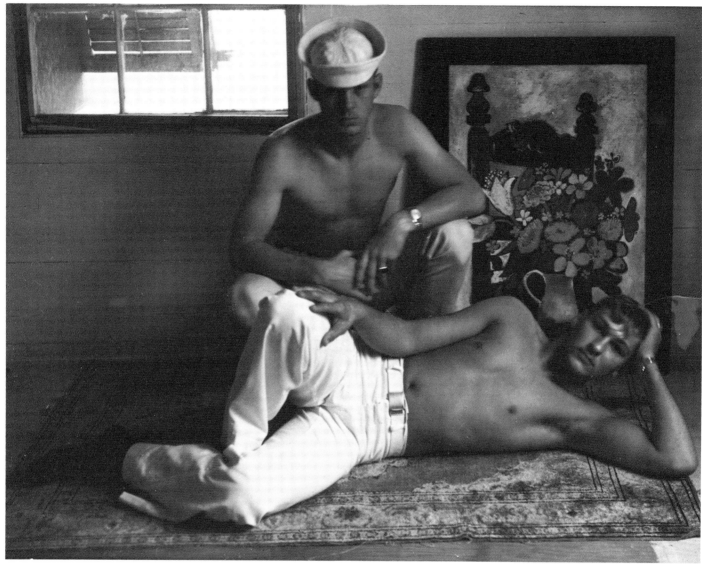

170 Marie Cosindas, *Sailors, Key West*, 1965
     Museum of Fine Arts, Boston

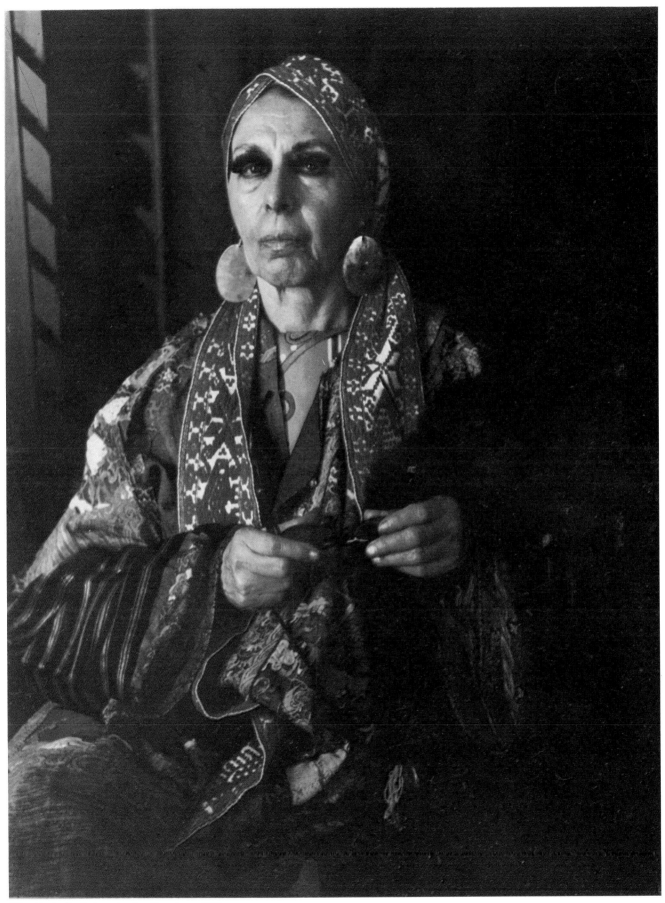

171   Marie Cosindas, *Louise Nevelson*, 1974
Museum of Fine Arts, Boston

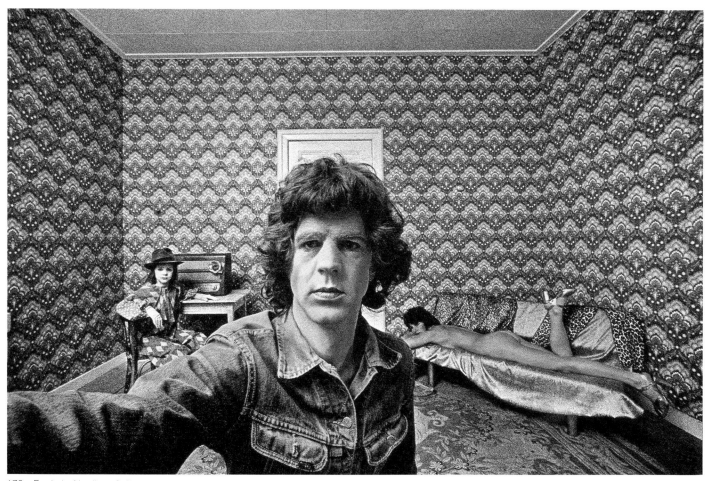

172   Paul de Nooijer, *Self-portrait,* 1976
      Stedelijk Museum, Amsterdam

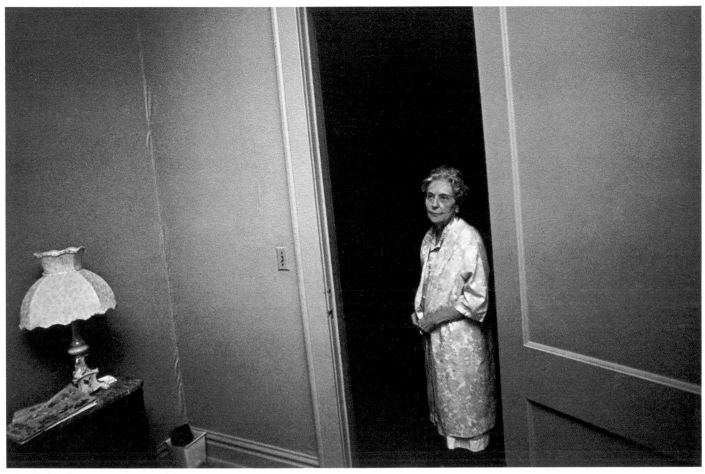

173 William Eggleston, *Sumner, Mississippi*, 1969–1970
The Museum of Modern Art, New York

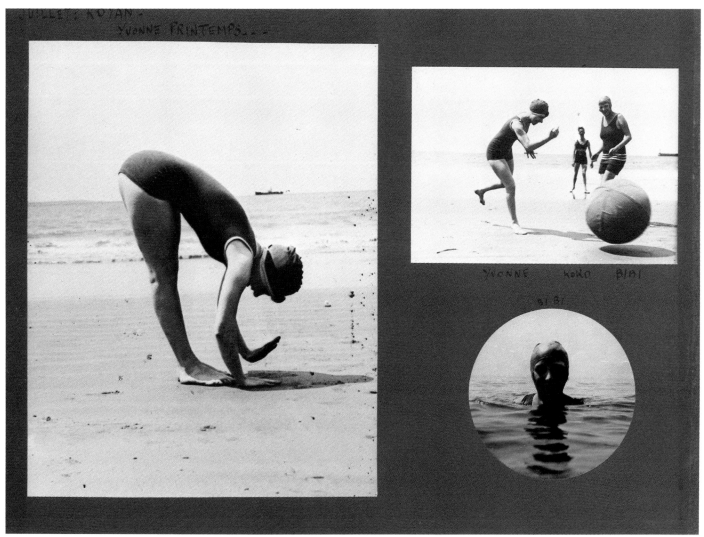

174   Jacques Henri Lartigue, *One Page from the Album,* 1921
Ministère de la Culture, Paris

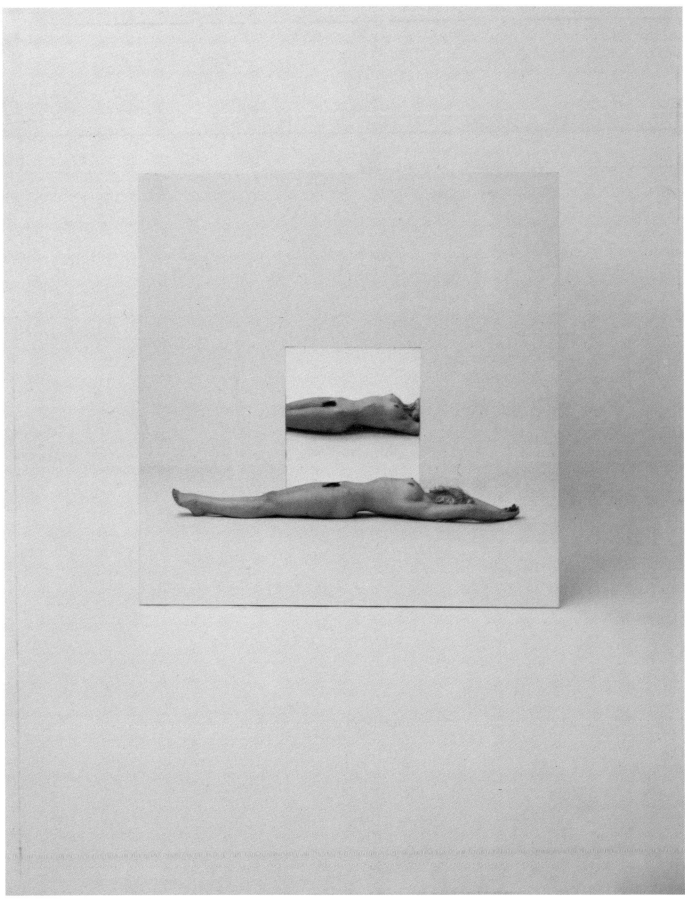

175 Roel Jacobs, *Nude*, 1978
Het Sterckshof Museum, Antwerp

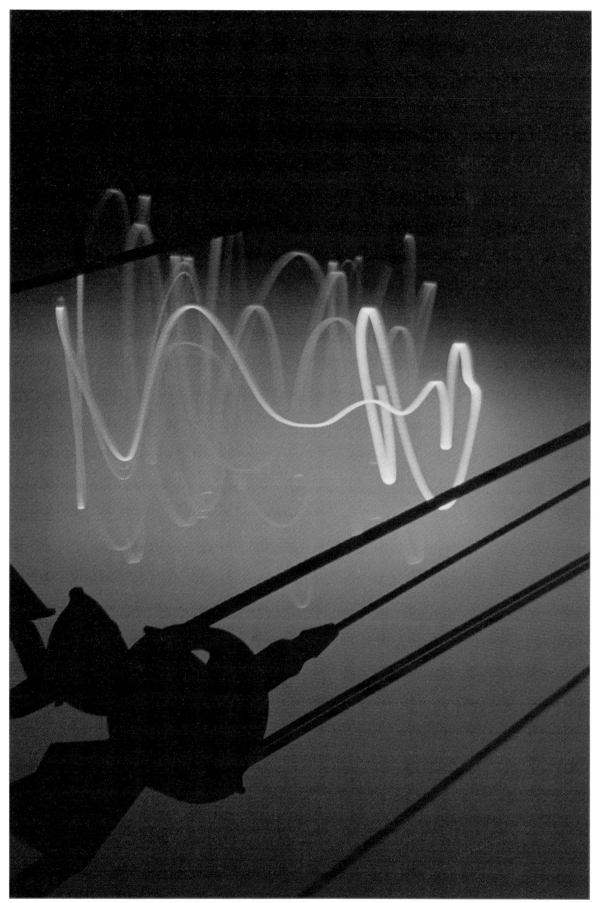

176 Emil Schulthess, *Sunset from the Rolling Icebreaker*, 1958
Stiftung für die Photographie, Kunsthaus, Zürich

ANALOGY

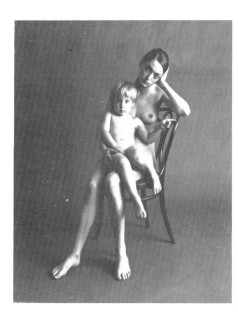
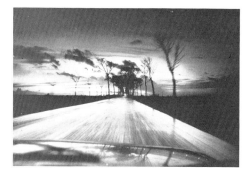
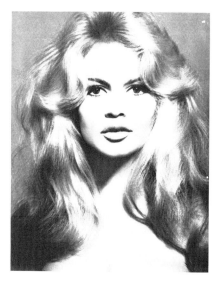
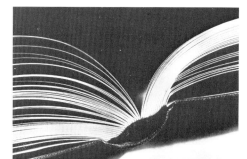
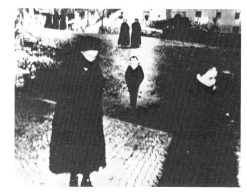
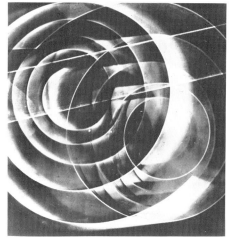
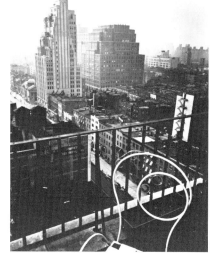

THE OBJECTS

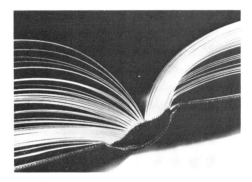

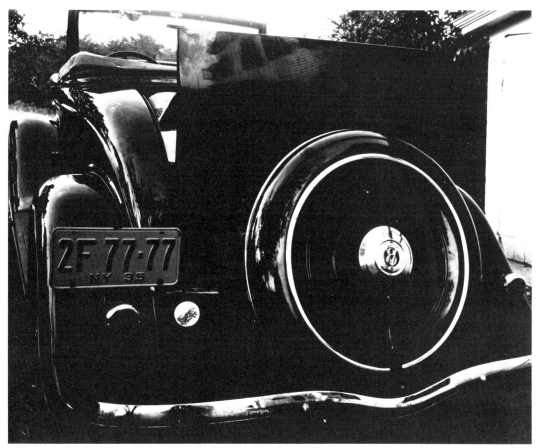

177 Alfred Stieglitz, *Later Lake George*, 1935
The Art Institute of Chicago

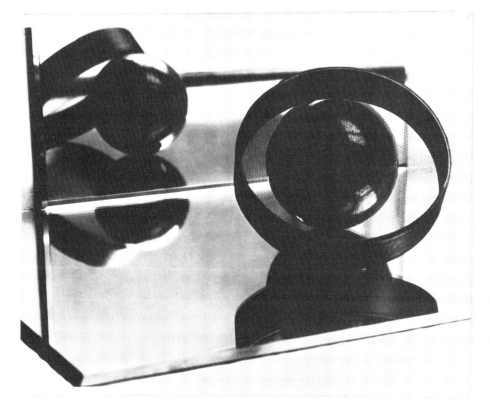

178 Florence Henri, *Reflecting Ball*, 1930
Museum Folkwang, Essen

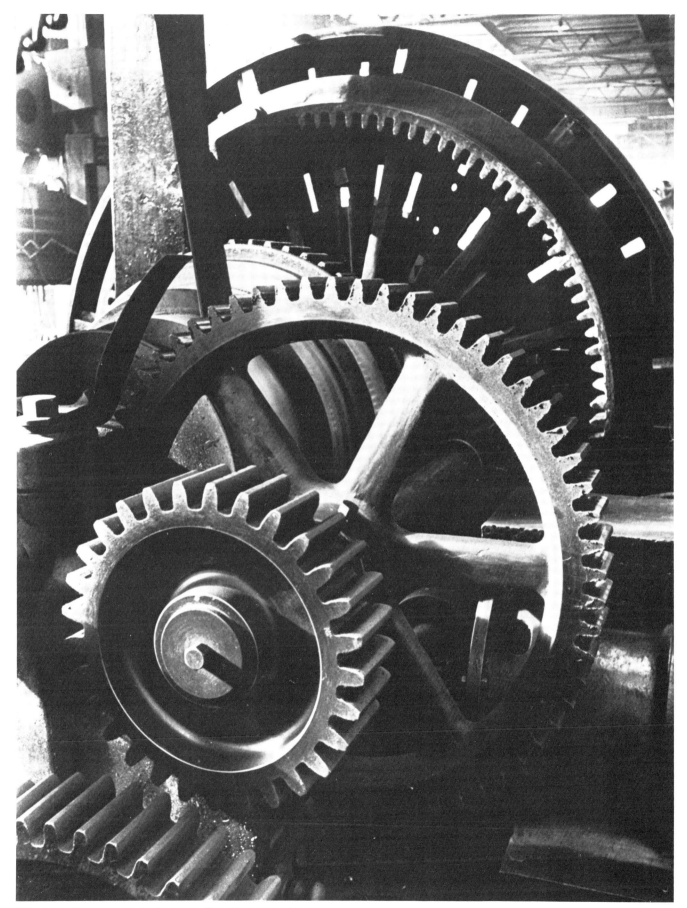

179 Jakob Tuggener, *Lathe in the Oerlikon Engineering Works*, 1935
Stiftung für die Photographie, Kunsthaus Zürich

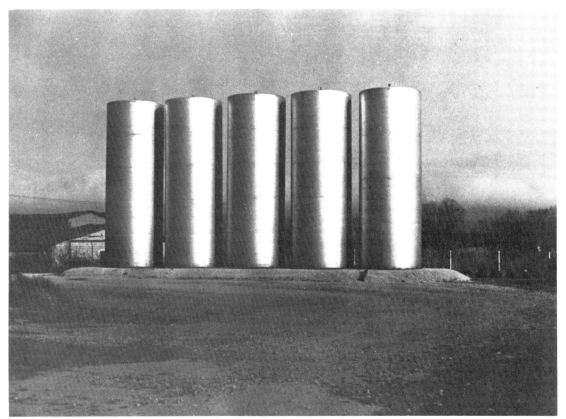

180 Charles Sheeler, *Fuel Tanks, Wisconsin*, no date
The Library of Congress, Washington, D.C.

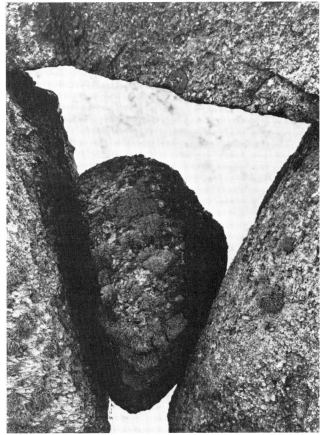

181 Aaron Siskind, *Wedged Rock*, 1954
San Francisco Museum of Modern Art

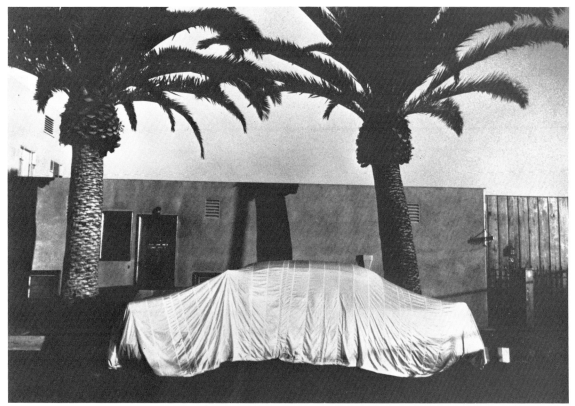

182 Robert Frank, *Long Beach, California*, 1955
Stiftung für die Photographie, Kunsthaus Zürich

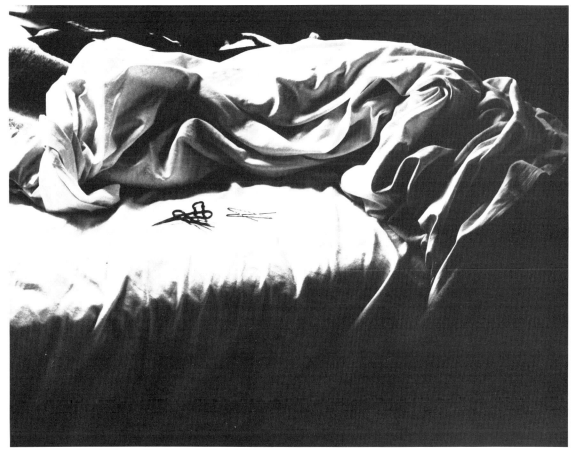

183 Imogen Cunningham, *The Unmade Bed*, 1954
Museum Folkwang, Essen

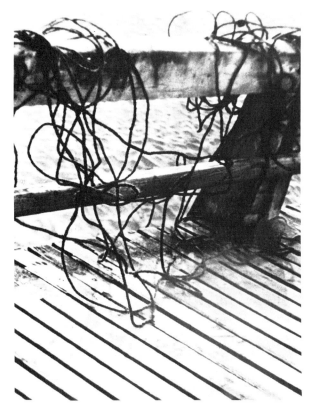

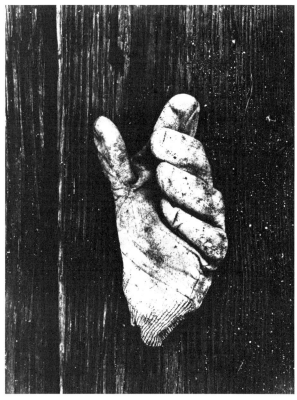

184 André Kertész, *Dew*, no date
Kunstbibliothek Preussischer Kulturbesitz, Berlin

185 Aaron Siskind, *Gloucester I*, 1944
San Francisco Museum of Modern Art

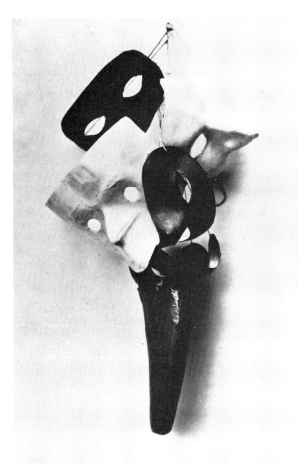

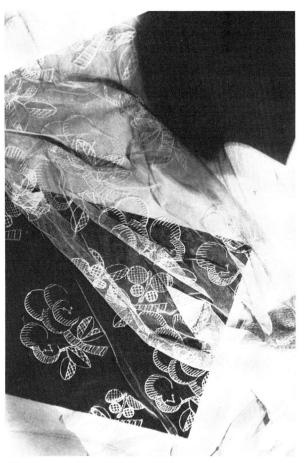

186 Emmanuel Sougez, *Masks*, no date
Museum Folkwang, Essen

187 Hans Finsler, *Fabric*, ca. 1930
Kunstbibliothek Preussischer Kulturbesitz, Berlin

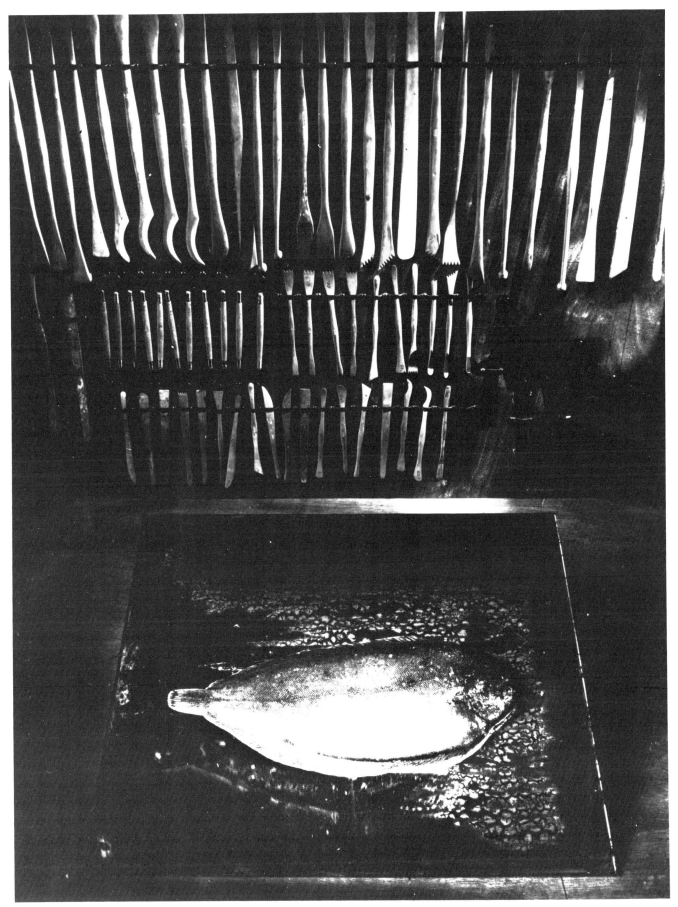

188   Otto Steinert, *Still Life with Fish*, 1958
Deutsche Gesellschaft für Photographie, Cologne

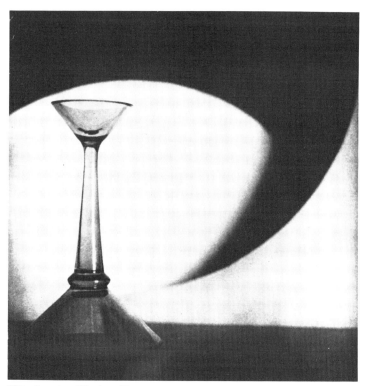

189 Jaroslav Rössler, *Glass*, 1923
    Uměleckoprůmyslové Muzeum v Praze, Prague

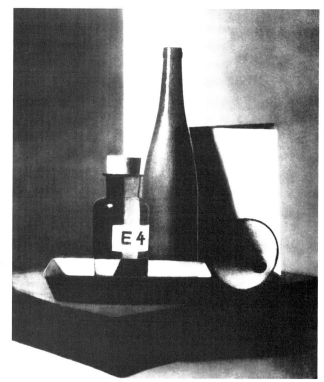

190 Marta Hoepffner, *Still Life with Wine Bottle*, 1945
    Agfa-Gevaert Foto-Historama, Leverkusen

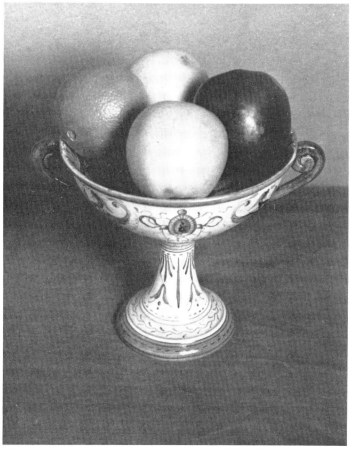

191 Paul Outerbridge, Jr., *Fruit in a Majolica Dish*, 1921
    The Library of Congress, Washington, D.C.

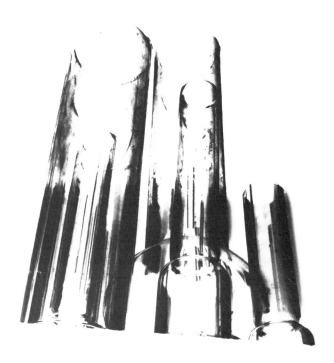

192 Paul Schuitema, *Lampshades*, 1929
    Haags Gemeente Museum, The Hague

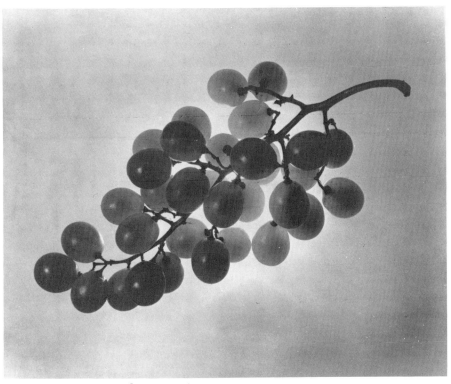

193 Kiyoshi Nishayama, *Grapes*, no date
The Nihon University of Art, Tokyo

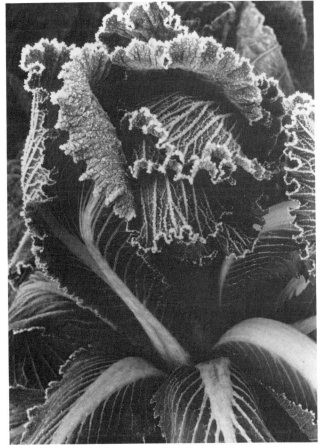

194 Piet Zwart, *Cabbage with Hoarfrost*, 1930
Haags Gemeente Museum, The Hague

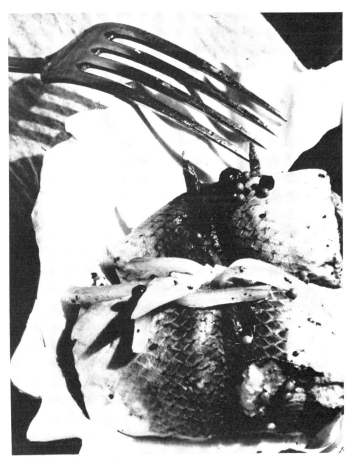

195 Max Burchartz, *Rollmops*, no date
Kunstbibliothek Preussischer Kulturbesitz, Berlin

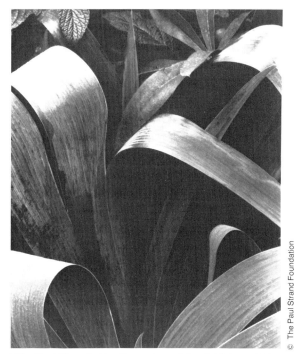

196 Paul Strand, *Iris, Georgetown Island, Maine*, 1928
Museum of Fine Arts, Boston

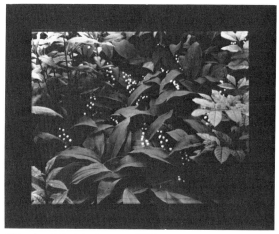

197 Josef Sudek, *Leaves*, 1970
Uměleckoprůmyslové Muzeum v Praze, Prague

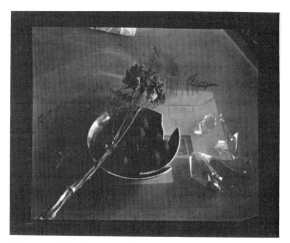

198 Josef Sudek, *Aerial Remembrances, for Dr. Brumlik*,
1971
Uměleckoprůmyslové Muzeum v Praze, Prague

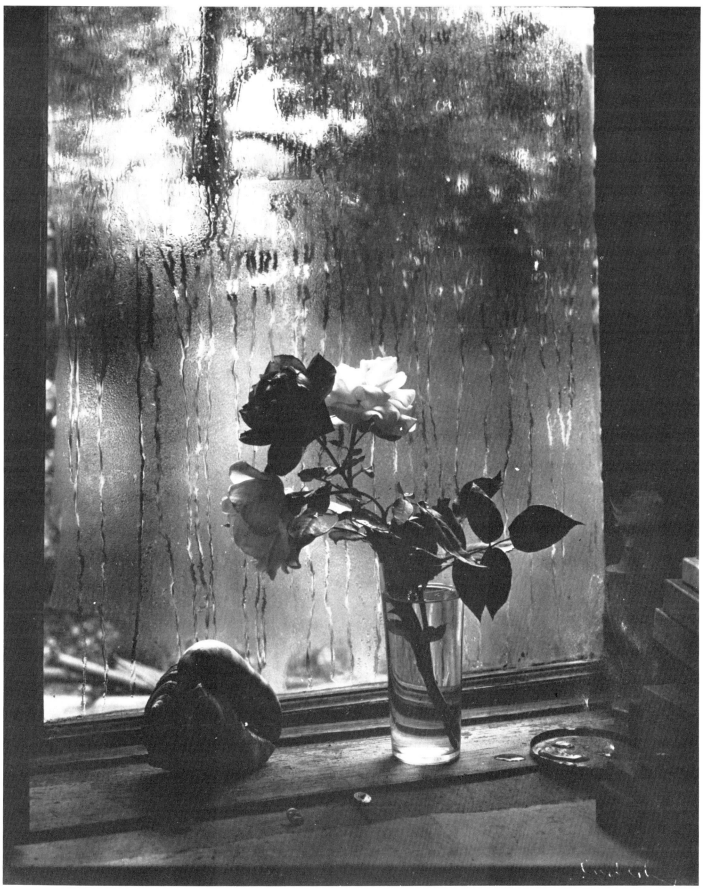

199 Josef Sudek, *Roses*, 1956
Uměleckoprůmyslové Muzeum v Praze, Prague

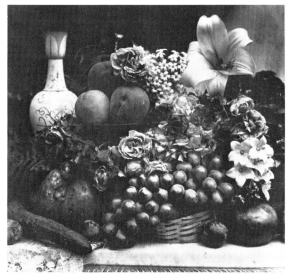

200 Roger Fenton, *Still Life (Fruit and Flowers),* ca. 1860
The Royal Photographic Society of Great Britain, Bath

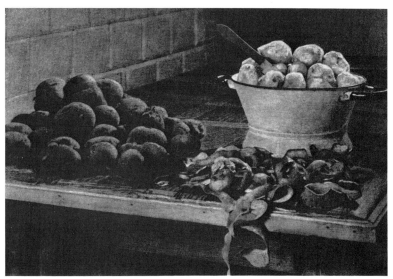

201 Victor Guidalevitch, *Still Life,* no date
Het Sterckshof Museum, Antwerp

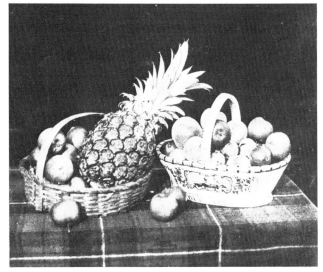

202 William Henry Fox Talbot, *A Fruit Piece,* Plate 24 from *The Pencil of Nature,* ca. 1844
The Fox Talbot Museum, Lacock

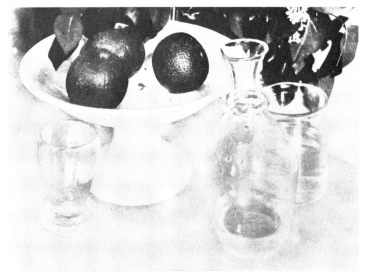

203 Heinrich Kühn, *Still Life with Oranges,* 1903
Museum Folkwang, Essen

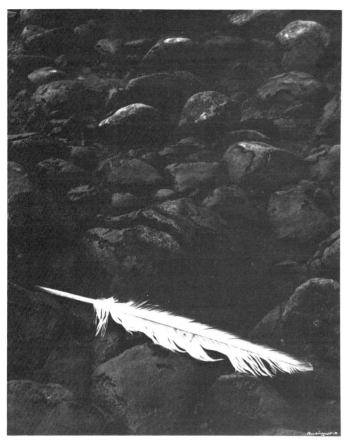

204 Rolf Winquist, *Feather*, 1950
     Fotografiska Museet, Stockholm

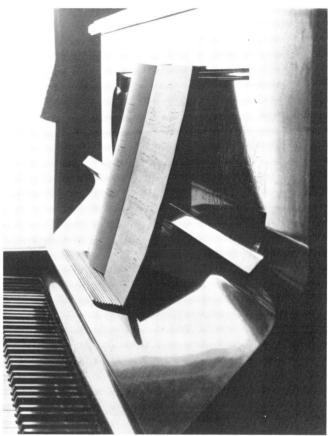

205 Paul Outerbridge, Jr., *Piano*, 1924
     The Library of Congress, Washington, D.C.

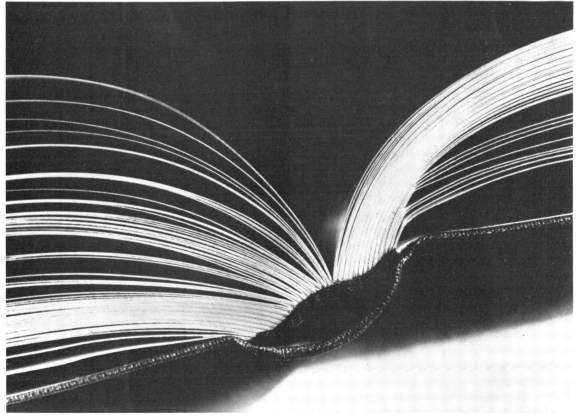

206 Hein Gorny, *Pages of a Book*, no date
     Kunstbibliothek Preussischer Kulturbesitz, Berlin

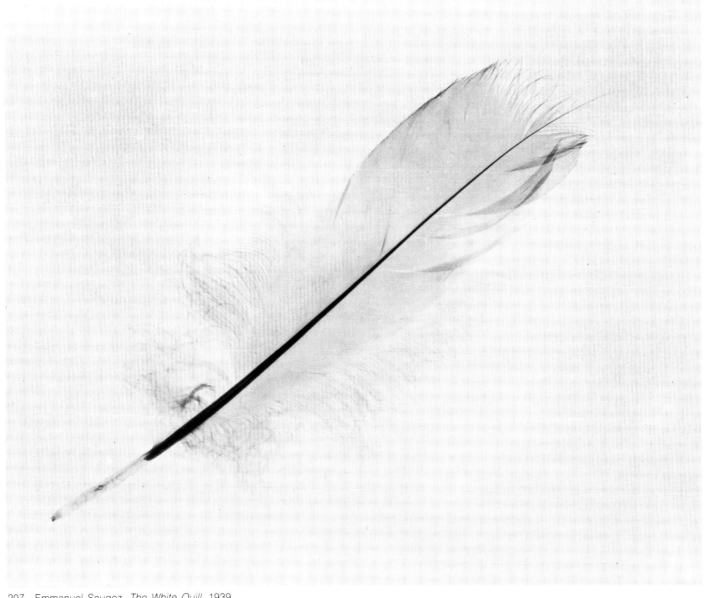

207 Emmanuel Sougez, *The White Quill*, 1939
Bibliothèque Nationale, Paris

THE NUDE

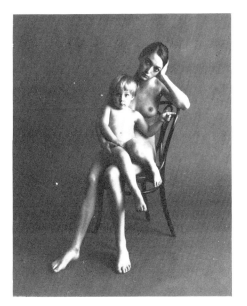

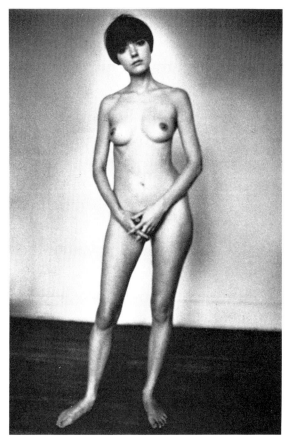

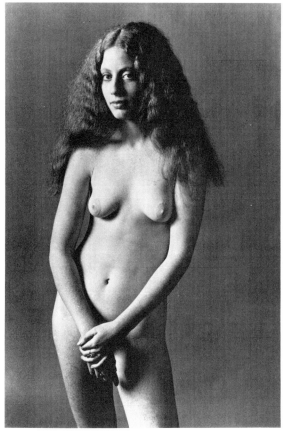

208 Jean-Loup Sieff, *Homage to Seurat*, 1965
Bibliothèque Nationale, Paris

209 Eva Rubinstein, *New York*, 1972
Fotografiska Museet, Stockholm

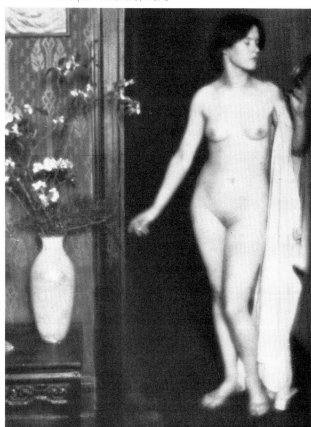

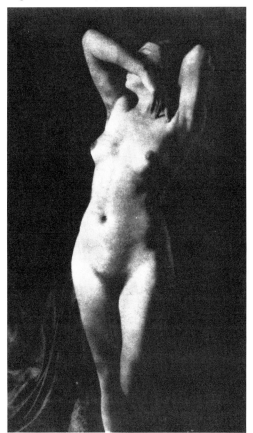

210 Clarence H. White, *Nude*, no date
The Royal Photographic Society of Great Britain, Bath

211 Franz Grainer, *Nude*, no date
Münchner Stadtmuseum, Munich

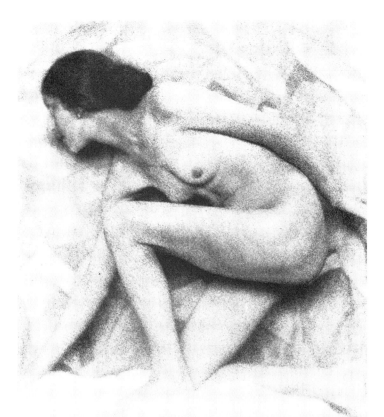

212 Erna Lendvai-Dircksen, *Nude*, 1921
Kunstbibliothek Preussischer Kulturbesitz, Berlin

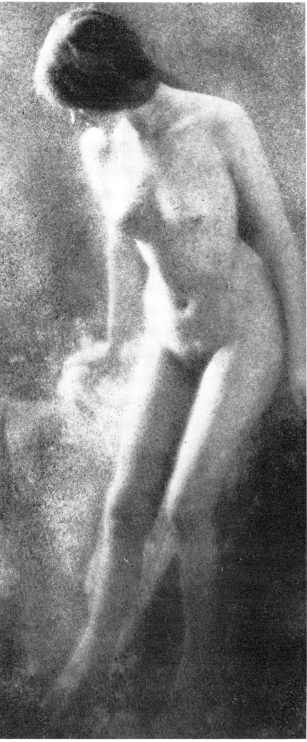

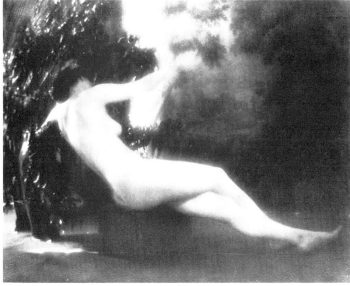

213 Francis Bruguière, *Daphne*, 1915
The Library of Congress, Washington, D.C.

214 Robert Demachy, *Untitled*, ca. 1900
Société Française de Photographie, Paris

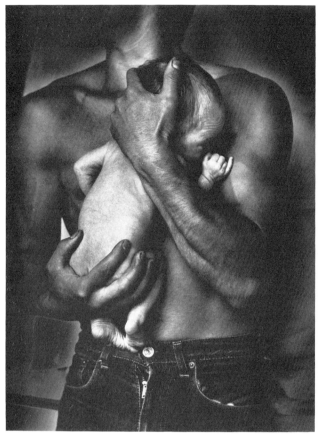

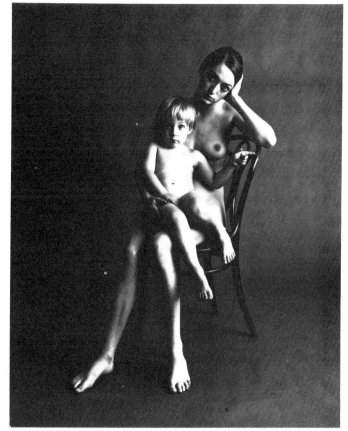

215 Jan Saudek, *Man and Baby,* no date
      Stedelijk Museum, Amsterdam

216 Jean-François Bauret, *Woman and Child (Nudes),* 1971
      Bibliothèque Nationale, Paris

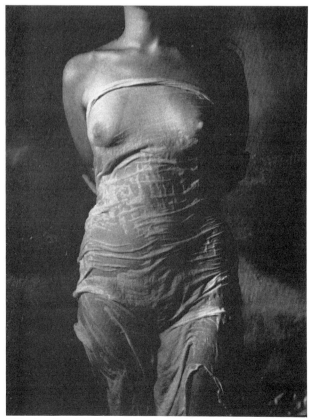

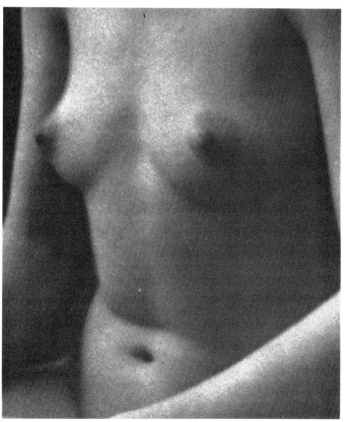

217 Jan Saudek, *Female Torso,* no date
      Stedelijk Museum, Amsterdam

218 Paul Outerbridge, Jr., *Torso,* 1923
      Museum of Fine Arts, Boston

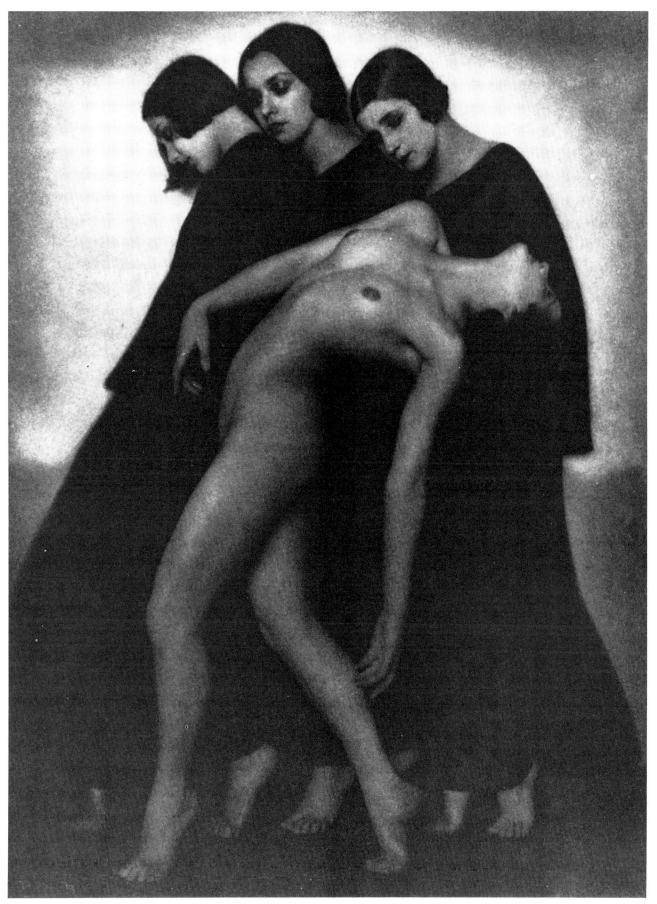

219   Rudolf Koppitz, *Motion Study*, 1926
      The Royal Photographic Society of Great Britain, Bath

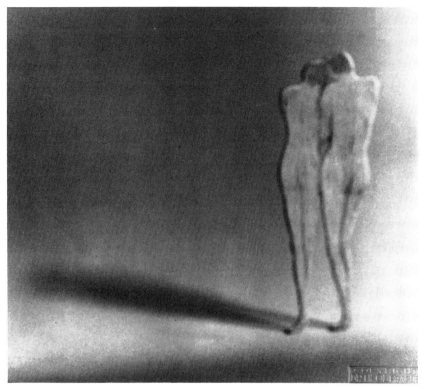

220 Frantisek Drtikol, *The Imaginary Photograph*, 1930
Uměleckoprůmyslové Muzeum v Praze, Prague

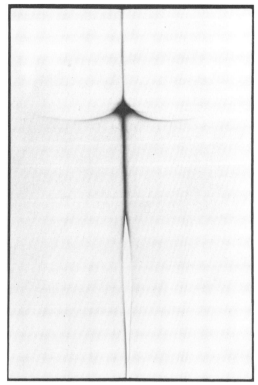

221 Eikoh Hosoe, *Nude*, no date
The Nihon University of Art, Tokyo

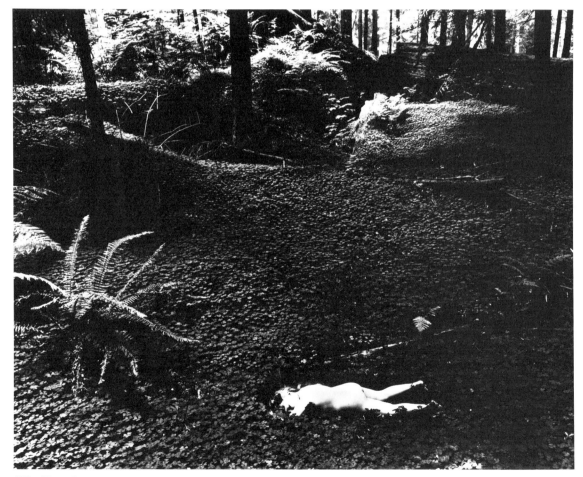

222 Wynn Bullock, *Child in Forest*, 1954
San Francisco Museum of Modern Art

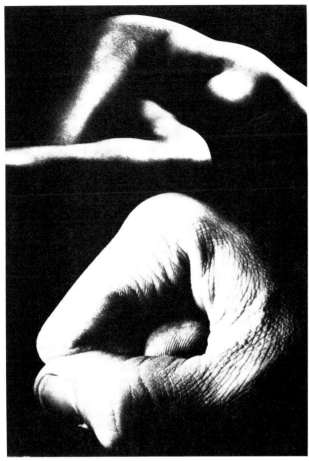

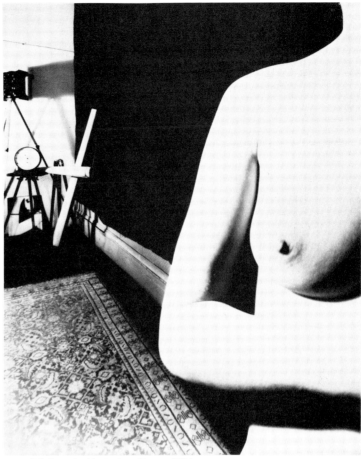

223 Jerry Uelsmann, *Equivalent,* 1964
     The Royal Photographic Society of Great Britain, Bath

224 Bill Brandt, *Nude in a Room,* 1961
     Museum Ludwig, Cologne

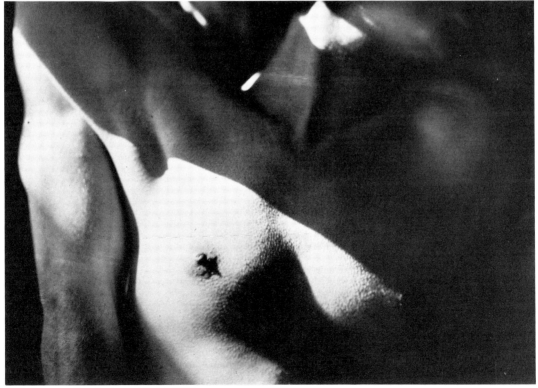

225 Imogen Cunningham, *Nude,* 1928
     Museum Folkwang, Essen

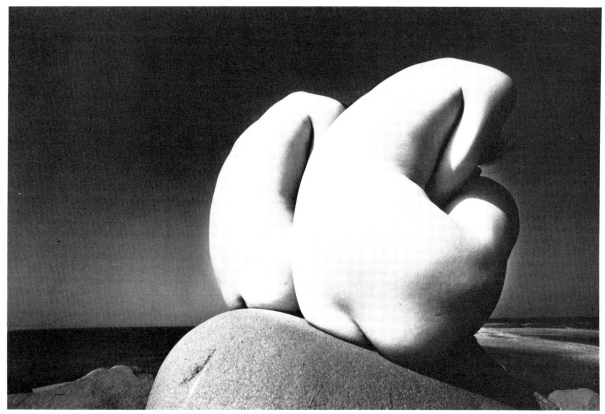

226 Kishin Shinoyama, *Nude*, no date
The Nihon University of Art, Tokyo

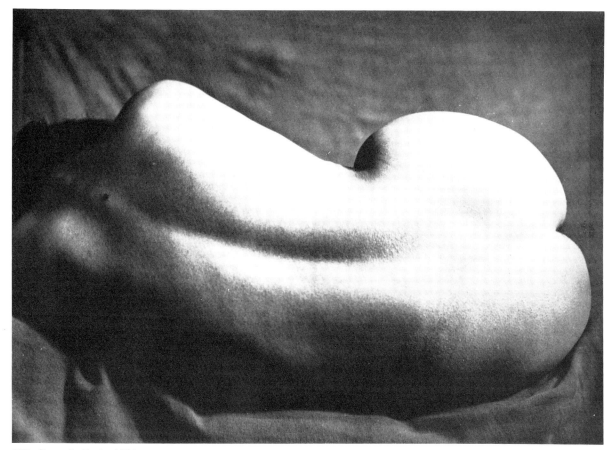

227 Brassaï, *Nude*, 1934
Bibliothèque Nationale, Paris

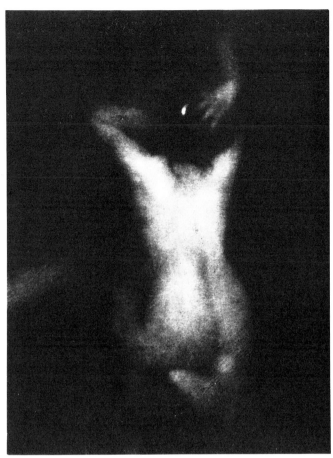

228 Edward Steichen, *Dolor*, ca. 1922
Kunstbibliothek Preussischer Kulturbesitz, Berlin

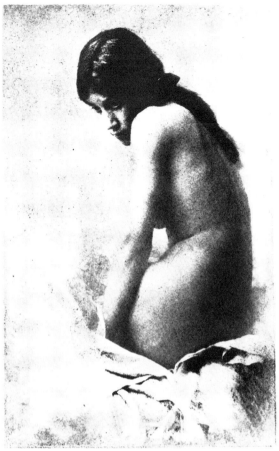

229 Robert Demachy, *Perplexity*, 1906
The Royal Photographic Society of Great Britain,
Bath

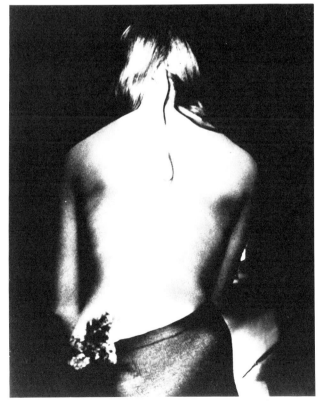

230 Sanne Sannes, *Nude Back*, no date
Stedelijk Museum, Amsterdam

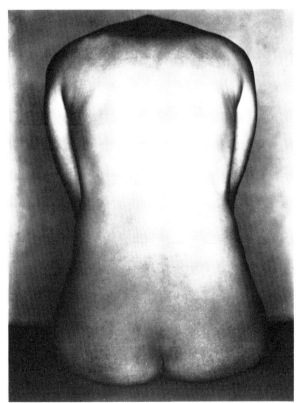

231 Edward Weston, *Nude*, 1927
San Francisco Museum of Modern Art

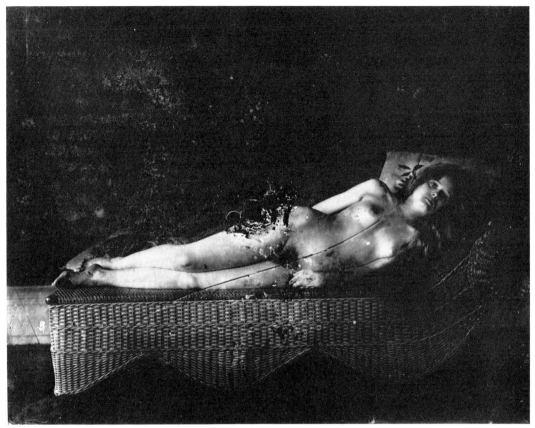

232 E.J. Bellocq, *Nude*, ca. 1912
Het Sterckshof Museum, Antwerp

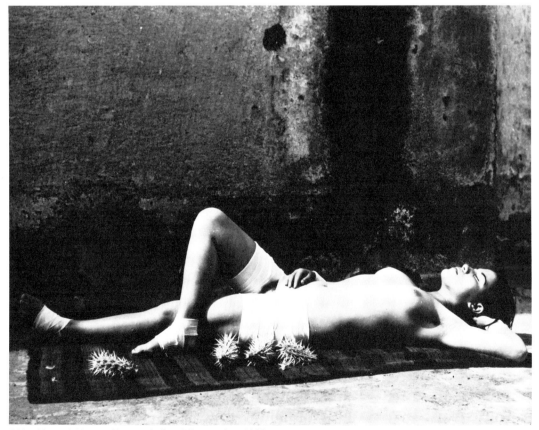

233 Manuel Alvarez Bravo, *A Good Reputation*, 1938
Bibliothèque Nationale, Paris

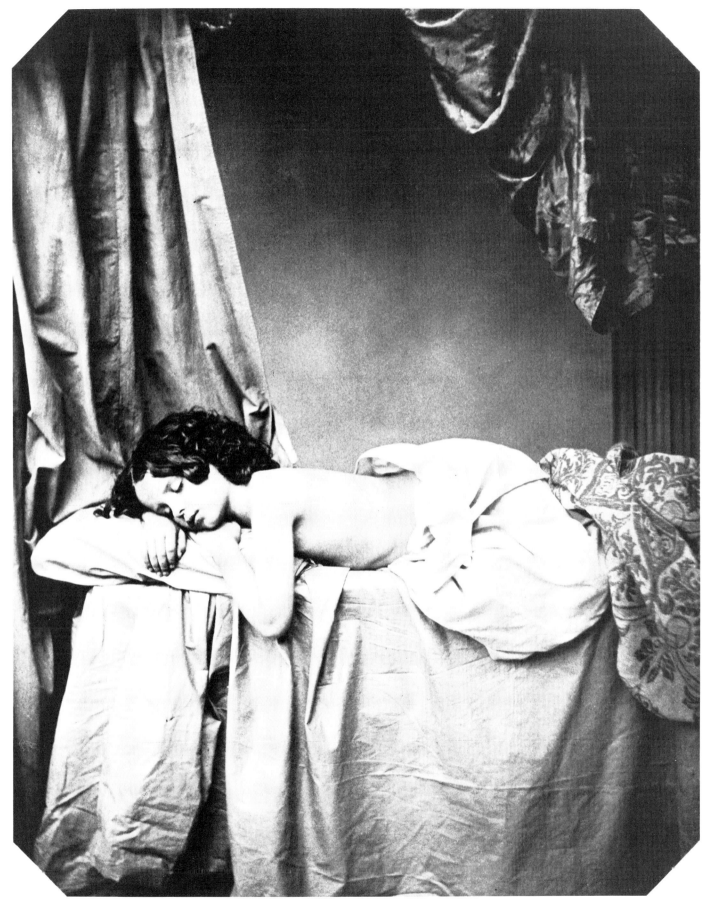

234 Franz Hanfstaengl, *Untitled*, 1855
Münchner Stadtmuseum, Munich

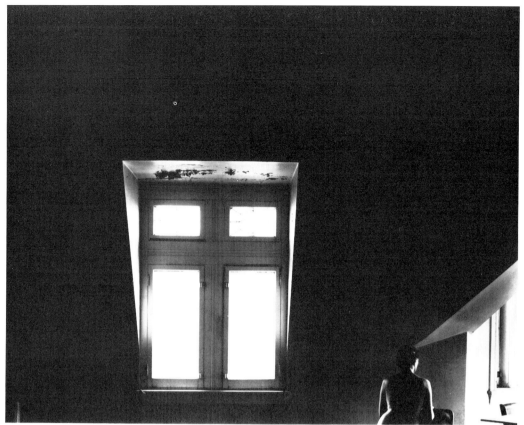

235 Harry Callahan, *Eleanor*, 1948
Museum of Fine Arts, Boston

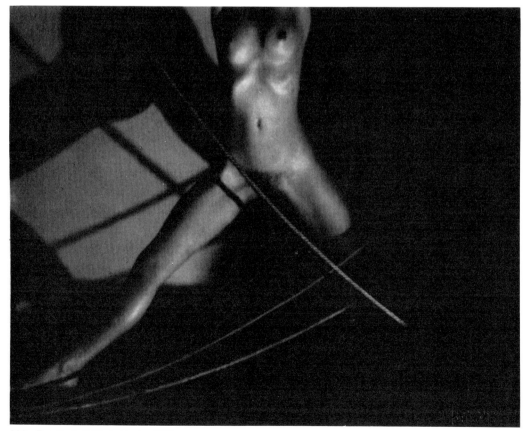

236 Frantisek Drtikol, *Nude*, 1929
Uměleckoprůmyslové Muzeum v Praze, Prague

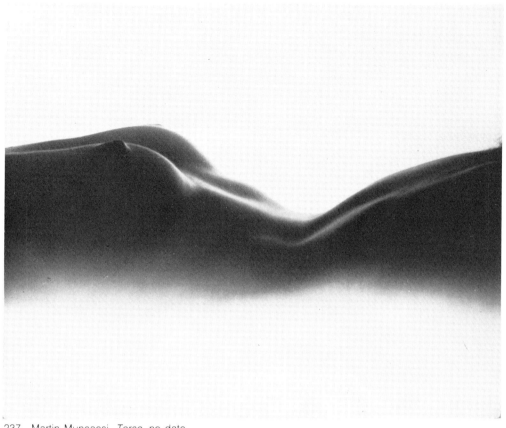

237   Martin Muncacsi, *Torso*, no date
      Museum Ludwig, Cologne

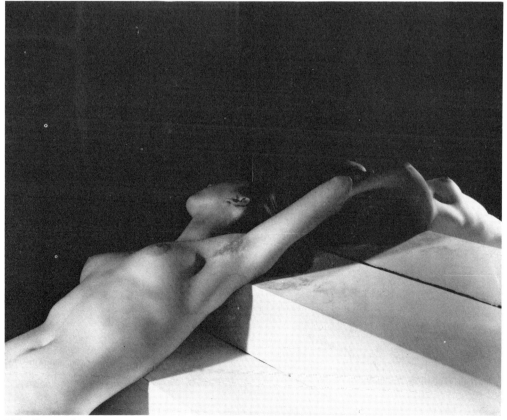

238   George Platt Lynes, *Nude in a Room*, no date
      Museum Ludwig, Cologne

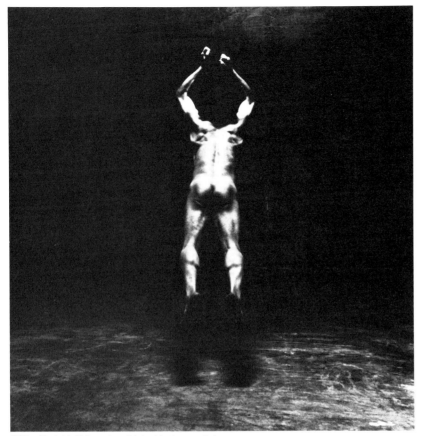

239 Noriaki Yokosuka, *Male Nude*, no date
The Nihon University of Art, Tokyo

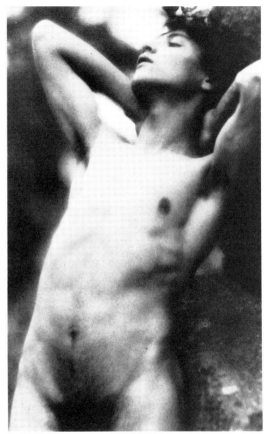

240 F. Holland Day, *Nude Youth*, no date
The Library of Congress, Washington, D.C.

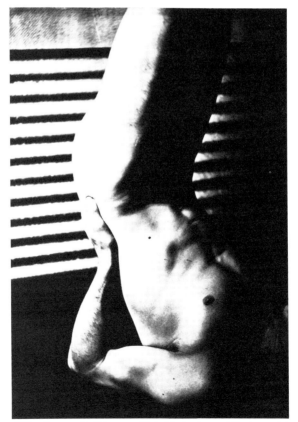

241 George Platt Lynes, *Male Nude, Legs Lifted*, no date
The Art Institute of Chicago

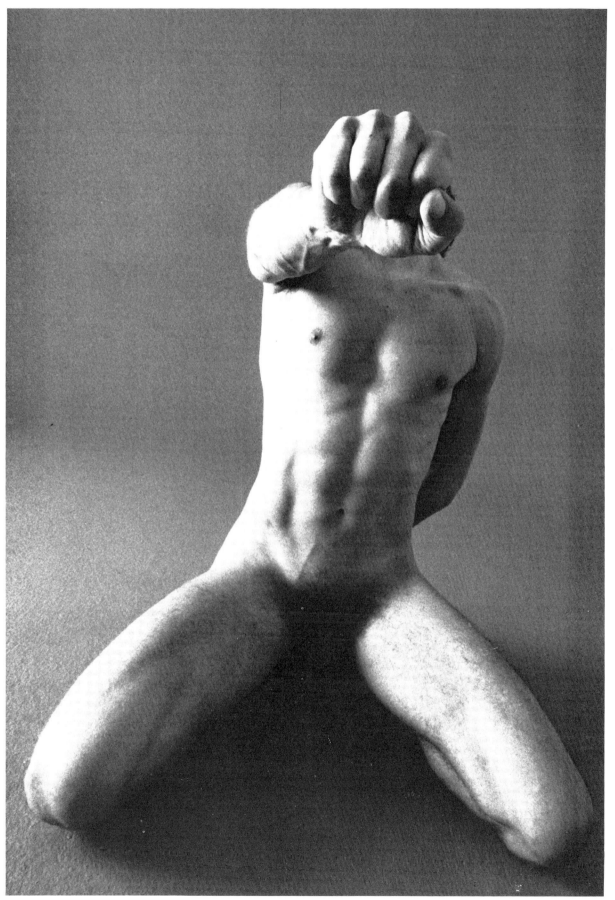

242   Christian Vogt, *Male Nude,* 1969
Stiftung für die Photographie, Kunsthaus Zürich

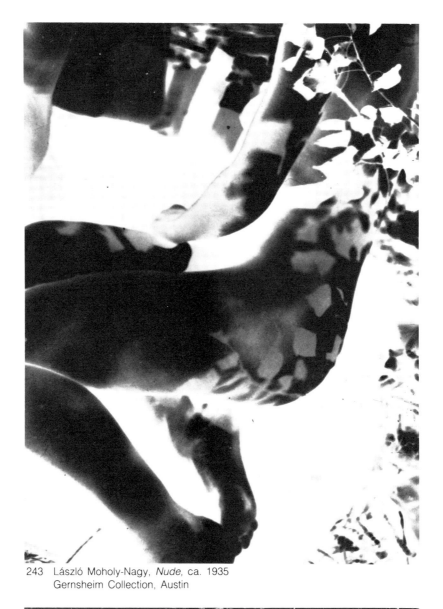

243 László Moholy-Nagy, *Nude,* ca. 1935
Gernsheim Collection, Austin

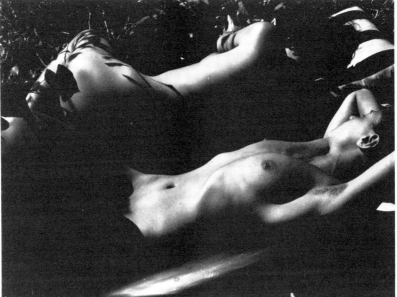

244 László Moholy-Nagy, *Two Nudes,* 1927–1929
Museum Folkwang, Essen

THE LANDSCAPE

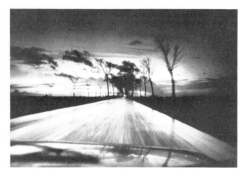

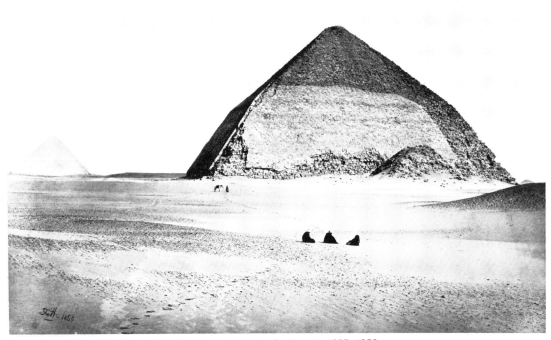

245 Francis Frith, *The Pyramids of Dahshoor from the Southwest,* 1857–1858
Fotografiska Museet, Stockholm

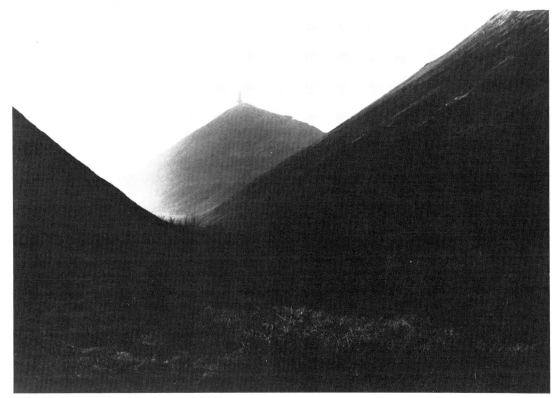

246 Otto Steinert, *Saar Landscape 2,* 1953
Deutsche Gesellschaft für Photographie, Cologne

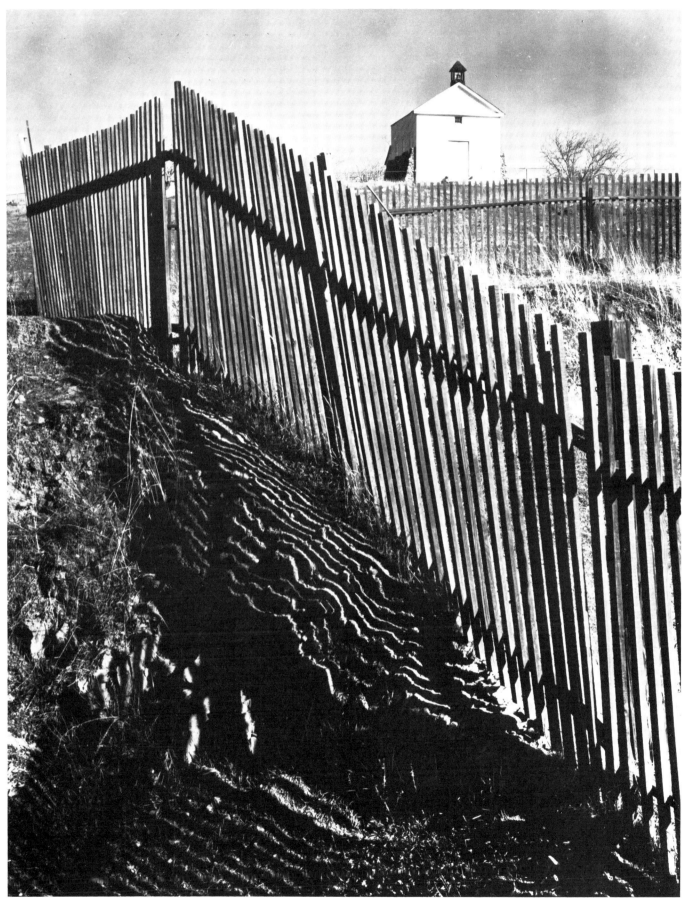

247   Ansel Adams, *House with Fence*, 1948
San Francisco Museum of Modern Art

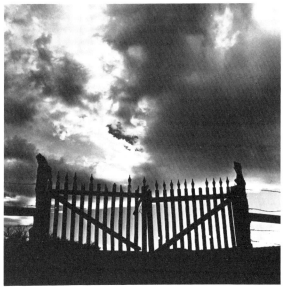

248 George A. Tice, *Cemetery Gates*, 1965
The Art Institute of Chicago

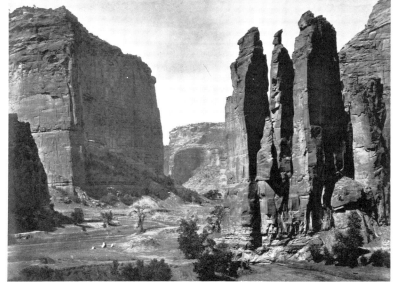

249 Timothy O'Sullivan, *Canyon de Chelle, New Mexico*, 1873
Museum für Kunst und Gewerbe, Hamburg

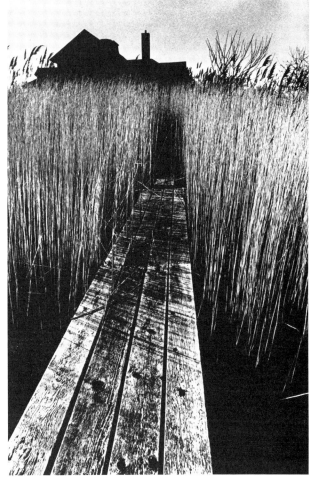

250 Jeanloup Sieff, *Jetty in the Reeds*, no date
Het Sterckshof Museum, Antwerp

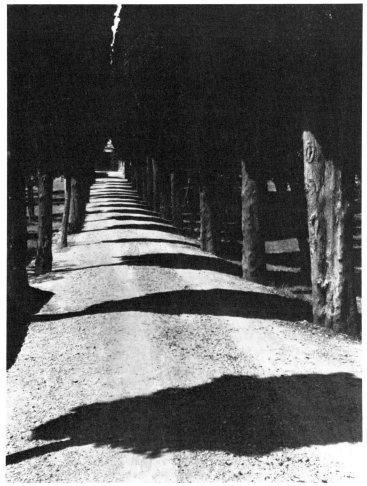

251 Theodor and Oskar Hofmeister, *Cypress Alley*, 1903
Museum für Kunst und Gewerbe, Hamburg

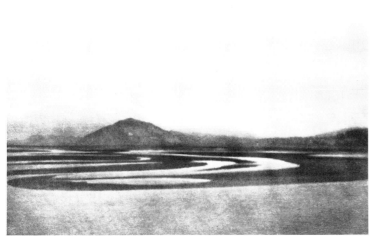

252 George Davison, *Near Portmadoc*, 1920
Kodak Museum, Harrow

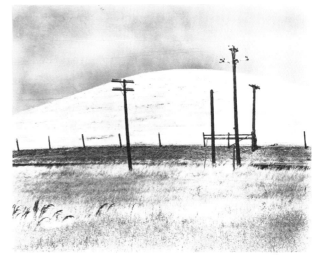

253 Edward Weston, *Powerlines and Telephone Poles*, 1939
San Francisco Museum of Art

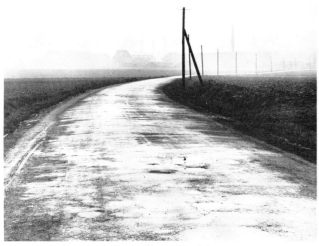

254 Albert Renger-Patzsch, *Street*, no date
Kunstbibliothek Preussischer Kulturbesitz, Berlin

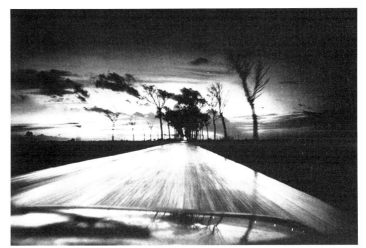

255 Filip Tas, *Long Avenue without Leentjie (Little Helen)*, 1979
Het Sterckshof Museum, Antwerp

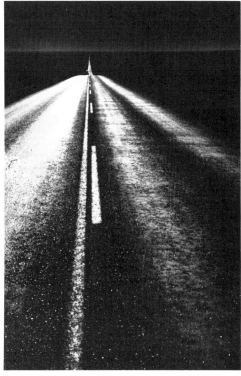

256 Robert Frank, *U.S. 285, New Mexico*, 1958
The Art Institute of Chicago

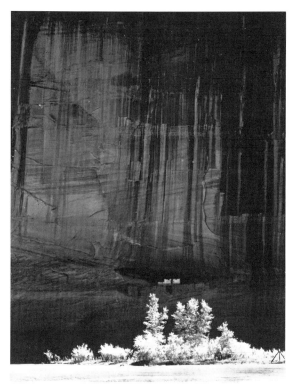

257 Ansel Adams, *Small House in Mountain*, 1950
San Francisco Museum of Modern Art

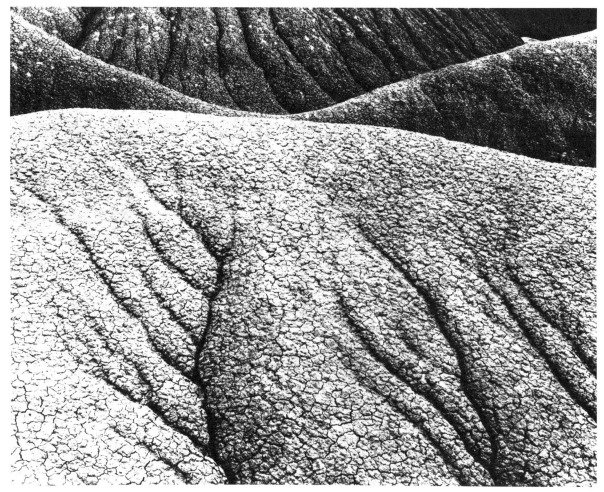

258 Minor White, *Three Tides*, 1959
San Francisco Museum of Modern Art

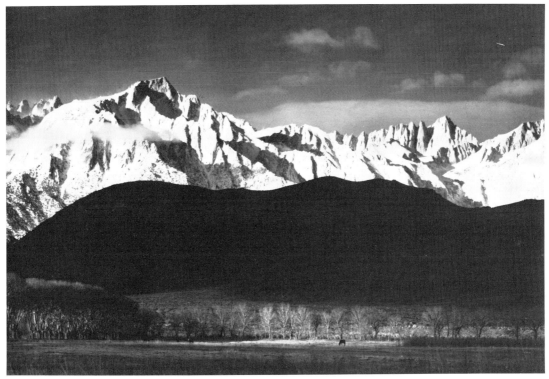

259   Ansel Adams, *Lone Pine Peak, Mount Whitney, Sierra Nevada, California,* 1944
      The Royal Photographic Society of Great Britain, Bath

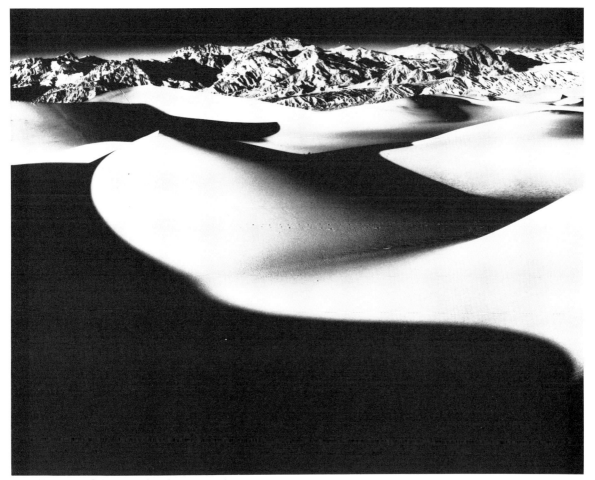

260   Yoshikazu Shirakawa, *Landscape,* no date
      The Nihon University of Art, Tokyo

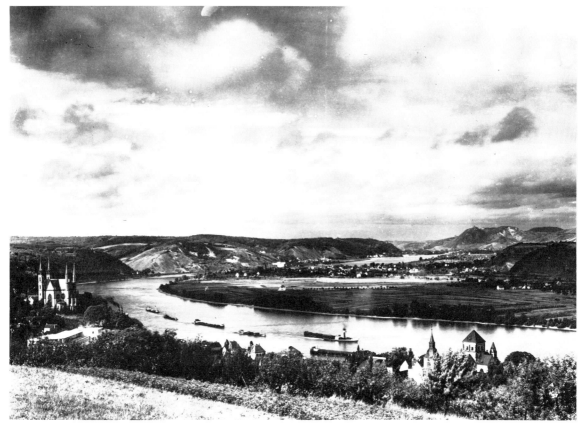

261 August Sander, *Siebengebirge,* ca. 1936
       Museum Ludwig, Cologne

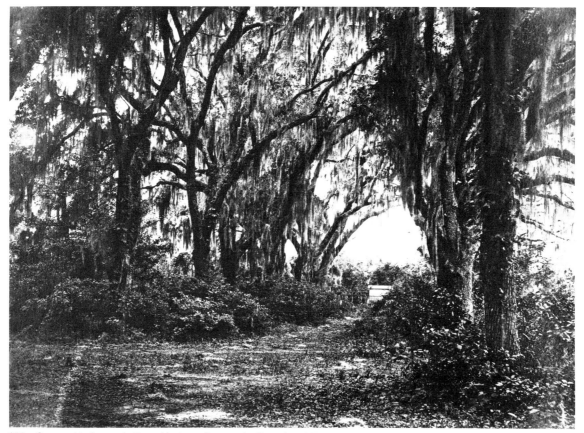

262 George N. Barnard, *Buen-Ventura, Savannah, Georgia,* 1865
       The Library of Congress, Washington, D.C.

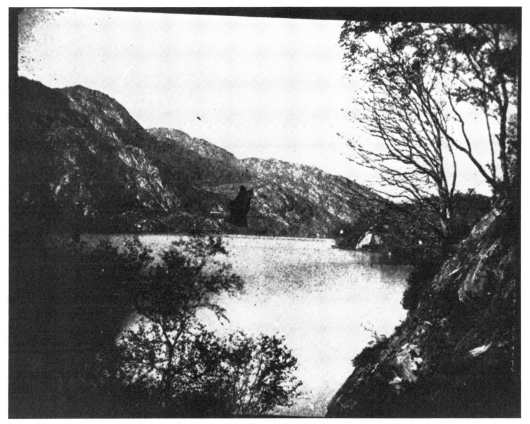

263   William Henry Fox Talbot, *Loch Katrine* from *Sun Pictures in Scotland*, ca. 1845
       The Fox Talbot Museum, Lacock

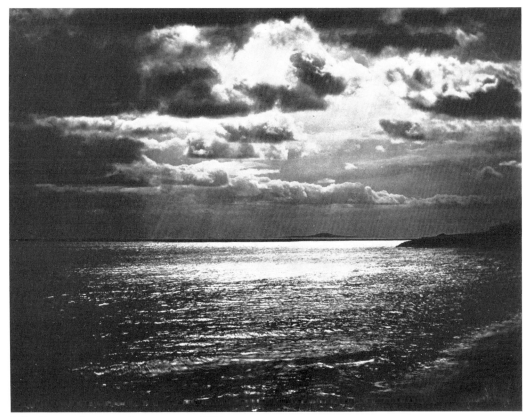

264   Gustave Le Gray, *Seascape*, ca. 1857
       Victoria and Albert Museum, London

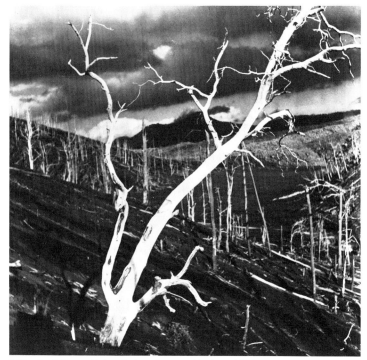

265   Paul Senn, *Volcanic Landscape*, Mexico, 1951
Stiftung für die Photographie, Kunsthaus Zürich

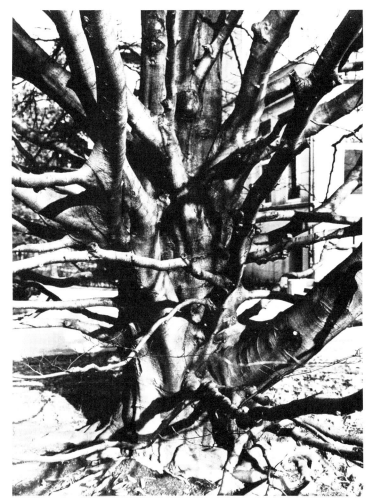

266   Albert Renger-Patzsch, *The Copper Beech*, 1925
Kunstbibliothek Preussischer Kulturbesitz, Berlin

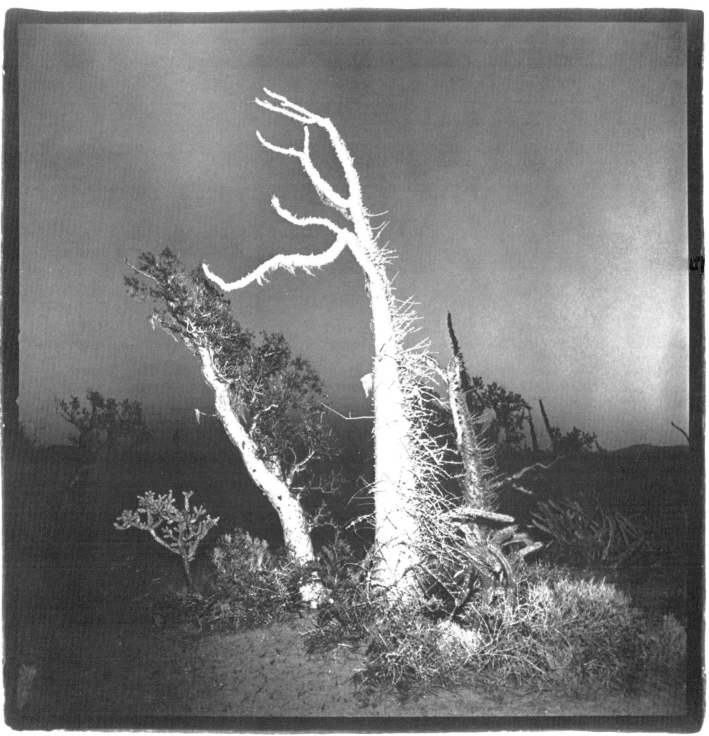

267 Richard Misrach, *Boojum II,* 1977
San Francisco Museum of Modern Art

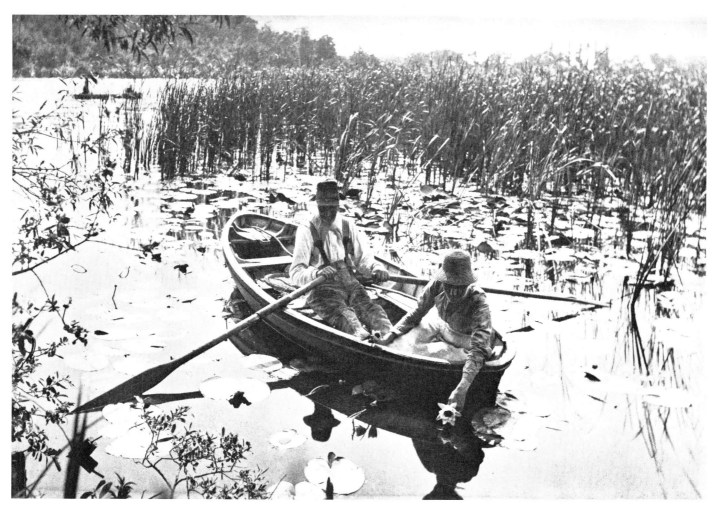

273 Peter Henry Emerson, *Gathering Waterlilies*, 1885
George Eastman House, Rochester

THE PORTRAIT

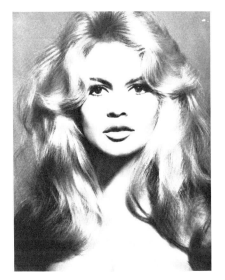

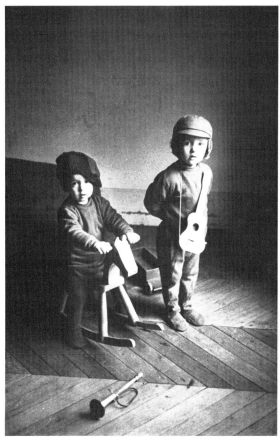

274 Frank Horvat, *Two Little Boys*, 1961
Bibliothèque Nationale, Paris

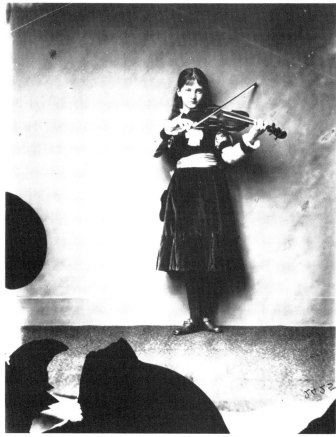

275 Lewis Carroll, *Alexandra (Xie) Kitchin*, 1876
Gernsheim Collection, Austin

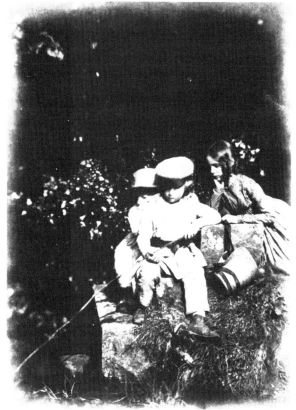

276 David Octavius Hill and Robert Adamson, *A Minnow
Pool, the Finlay Children*, 1843–1848
Museum Ludwig, Cologne

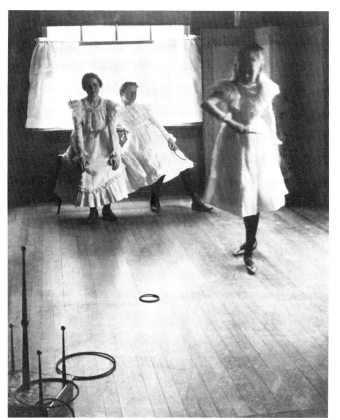

277 Clarence H. White, *Ring Toss*, 1899
The Library of Congress, Washington, D.C.

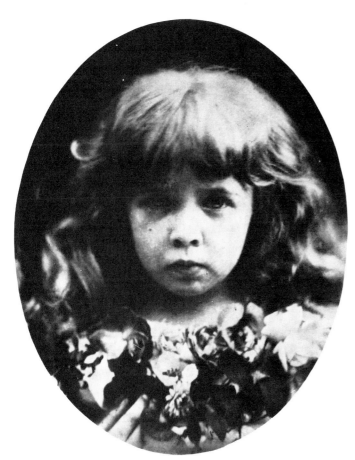

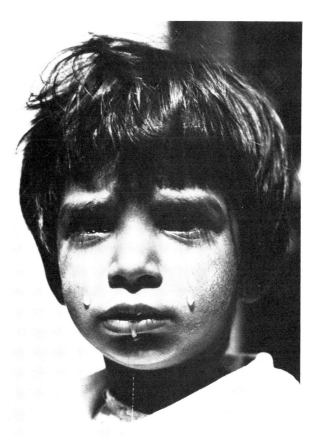

278 Julia Margaret Cameron, *Untitled (Girl)*, no date
The Royal Photographic Society of Great Britain, Bath

279 Werner Bischof, *Hungary*, 1947
Museum Ludwig, Cologne

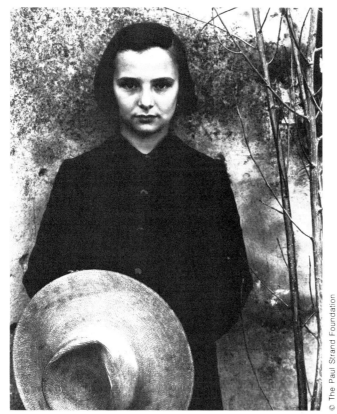

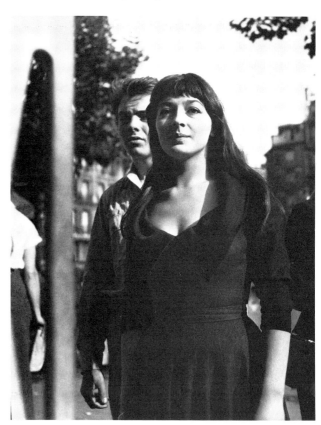

280 Paul Strand, *Tailor's Apprentice, Luzzara, Italy*, 1953
Museum of Fine Arts, Boston

281 Emmy Andriesse, *Juliet Greco*, 1950
Stedelijk Museum, Amsterdam

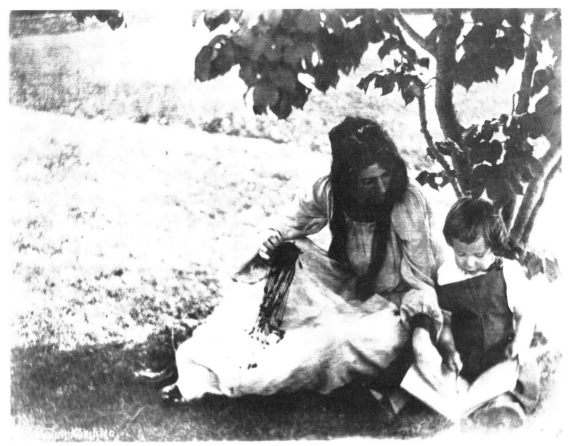

282 Gertrude Käsebier, *The Picture Book*, 1905
     The Library of Congress, Washington, D.C.

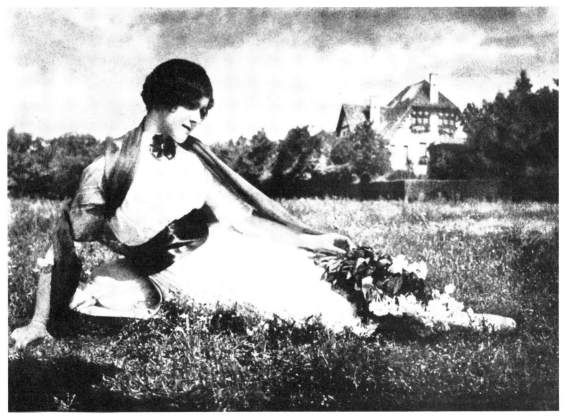

283 Nicola Perscheid, *Young Girl*, no date
     Kunstbibliothek Preussischer Kulturbesitz, Berlin

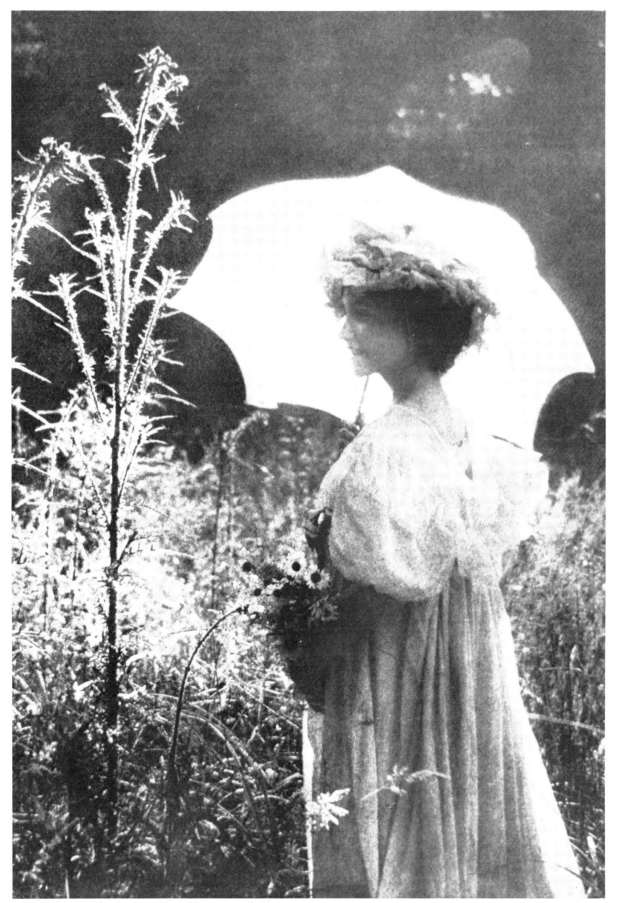

284 Emile Joachim Constant Puyo, *Woman,* ca. 1896
Société Française de Photographie, Paris

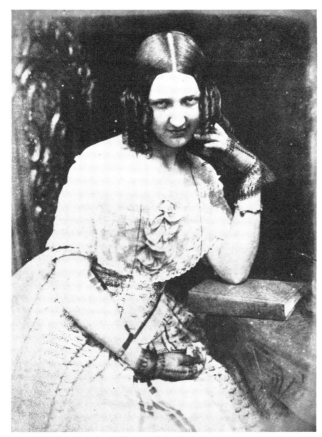

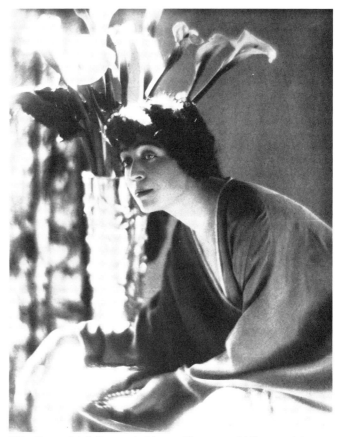

285 David Octavius Hill and Robert Adamson,
     Portrait of a Lady, no date
     Museum Folkwang, Essen

286 Baron Adolf Gayne de Meyer, *Woman and Lilies*, no date
     The Library of Congress, Washington, D.C.

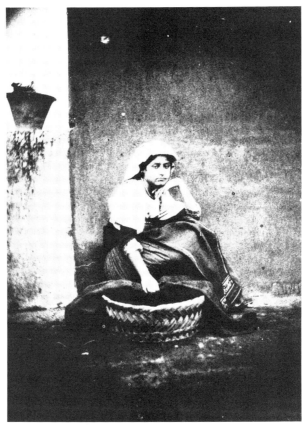

287 Charles Nègre, *Woman of Arles*, 1852
     Het Sterckshof Museum, Antwerp

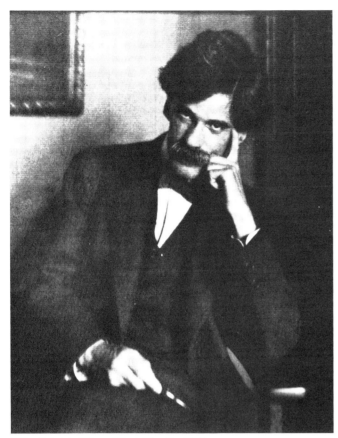

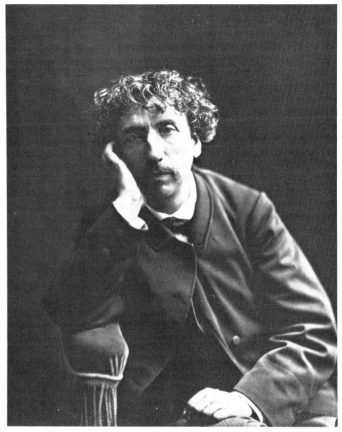

288 Heinrich Kühn, *Alfred Stieglitz*, 1904
Museum Folkwang, Essen

289 Antoine Samuel Adam-Salomon, *Charles Garnier*, 1865
Bibliothèque Nationale, Paris

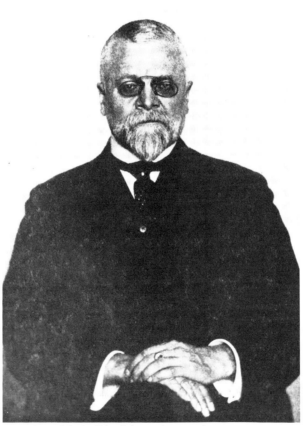

290 Hugo Erfurth, *Fritz Schumacher,* no date
Agfa-Gevaert Foto-Historama, Leverkusen

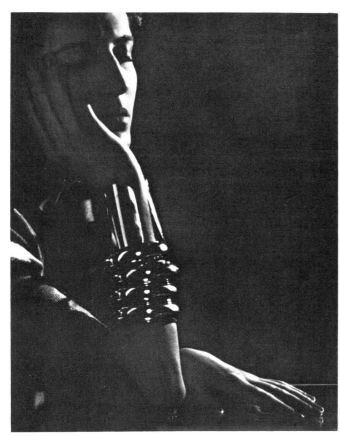

291 Man Ray, *Woman*, 1930
Bibliothèque Nationale, Paris

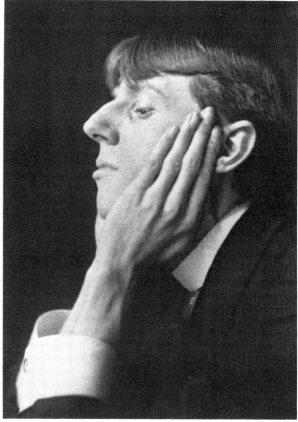

292 Frederick H. Evans, *Aubrey Beardsley*, ca. 1895
National Portrait Gallery, London

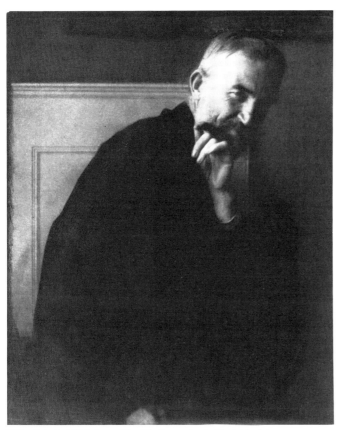

293 Edward Steichen, *The Photographer's Best Model:
George Bernard Shaw*, 1907
The Museum of Modern Art, New York

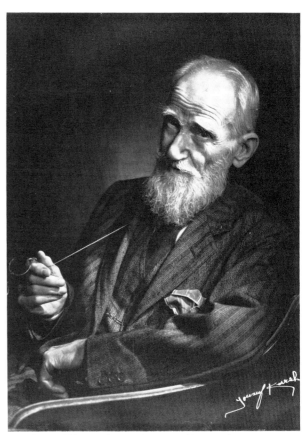

294 Yousuf Karsh, *George Bernard Shaw*, 1934
Museum Ludwig, Cologne

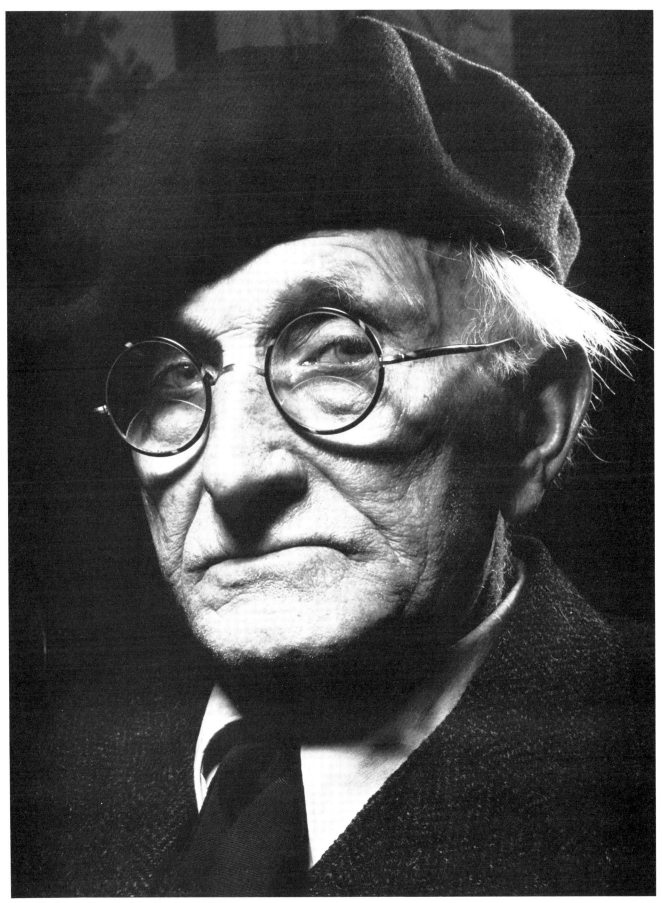

295 Chargesheimer, *August Sander*, 1956
The Museum of Modern Art, New York

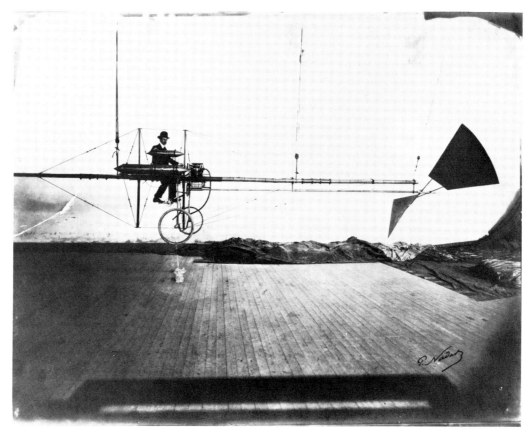

296　Nadar, *Santos Dumont,* ca. 1906
　　 Bibliothèque Nationale, Paris

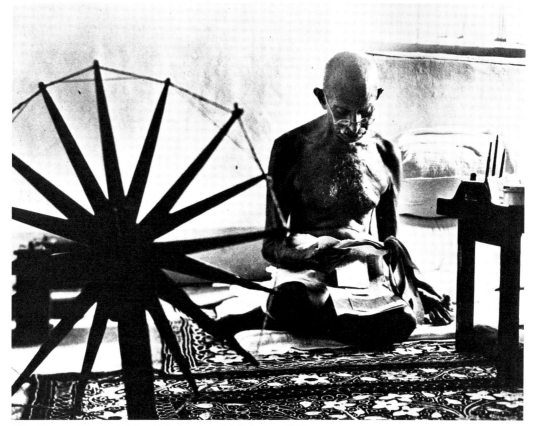

297　Margaret Bourke-White, *Mahatma Gandhi, Spinning,* 1946
　　 The Art Institute of Chicago

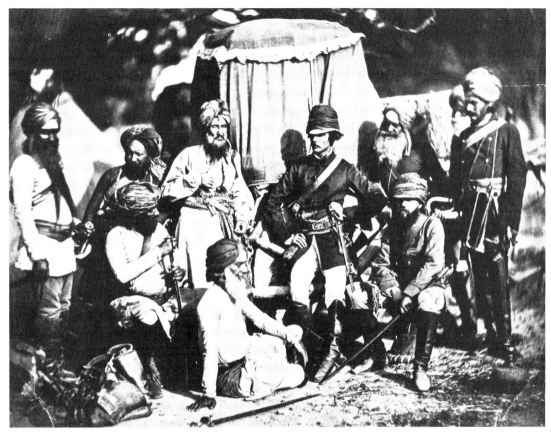

298 Felice A. Beato, *Bragière Sikhs*, 1857
Det kongelige Bibliotek, Copenhagen

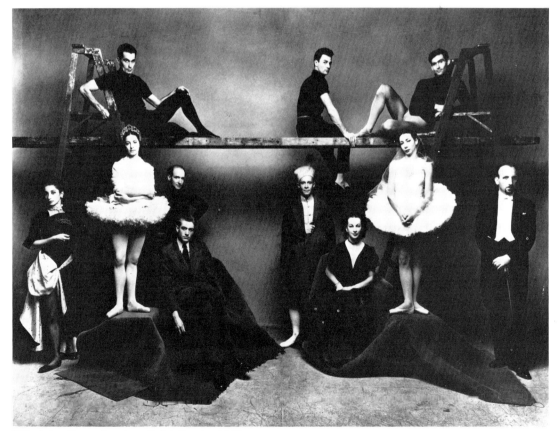

299 Irving Penn, *American Ballet Theatre*, 1947
Museum für Kunst und Gewerbe, Hamburg

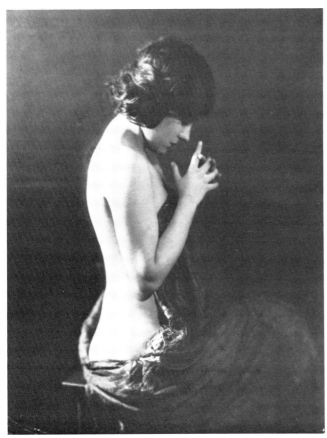

300 Alfred Cheney Johnston, *Gloria Swanson*, 1920
Museum Ludwig, Cologne

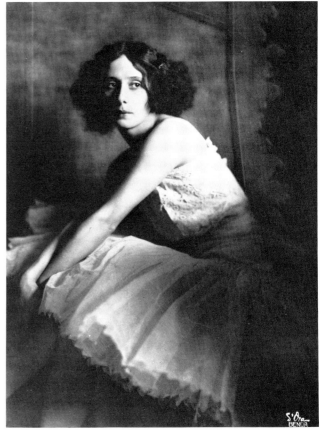

301 Madame d'Ora, *Anna Pavlova*, 1913
Museum für Kunst und Gewerbe, Hamburg

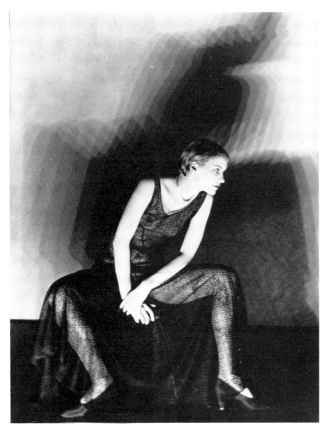

302 Man Ray, *Lee Miller*, 1930
Museum Ludwig, Cologne

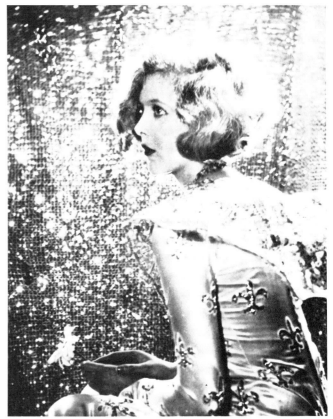

303 Sir Cecil Beaton, *Nana Beaton*, ca. 1925
Museum Ludwig, Cologne

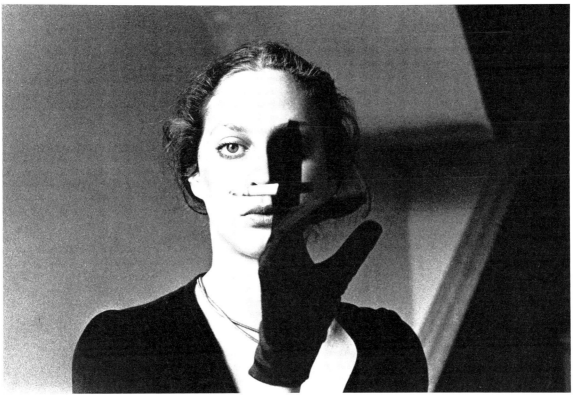

304 Ralph Gibson, *Untitled*, 1974
Fotografiska Museet, Stockholm

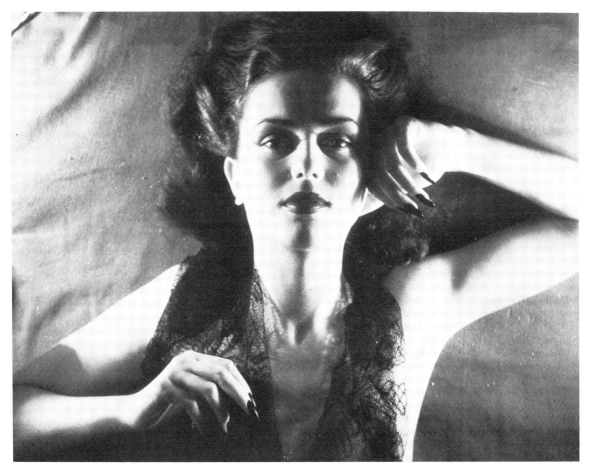

305 Jacques Henry Lartigue, *Paris, Florette*, 1944
Bibliothèque Nationale, Paris

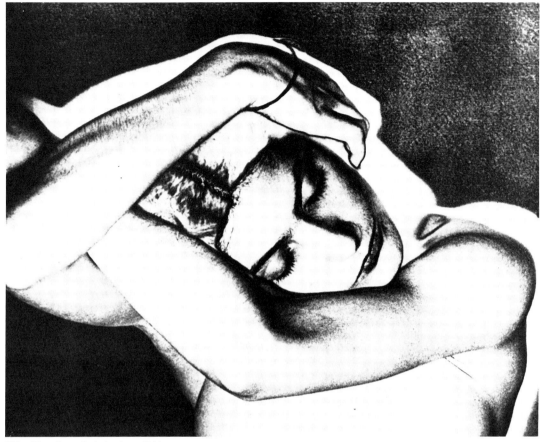

306 Man Ray, *Solarization*, 1931
Museum Ludwig, Cologne

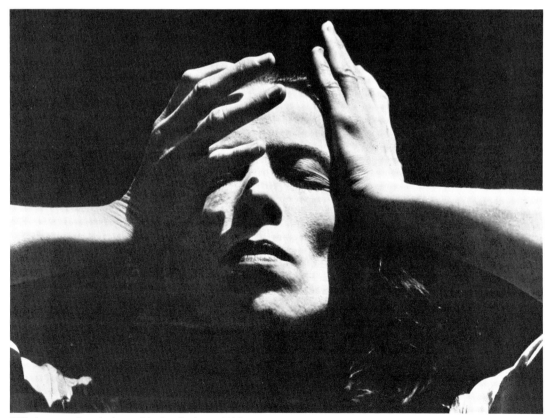

307 Imogen Cunningham, *Martha Graham*, 1931
San Francisco Museum of Modern Art

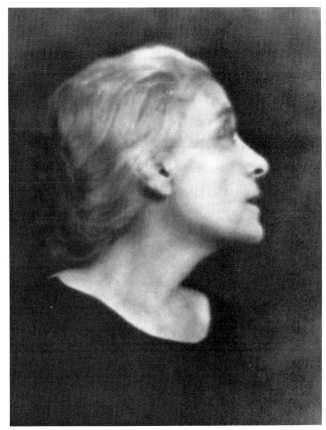

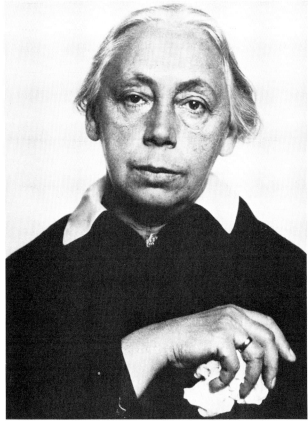

308　Arnold Genthe, *Last Portrait of Eleonora Duse*, no date
　　　Museum of Fine Arts, Boston

309　Hugo Erfurth, *Käthe Kollwitz*, 1935
　　　Deutsche Gesellschaft für Photographie, Cologne

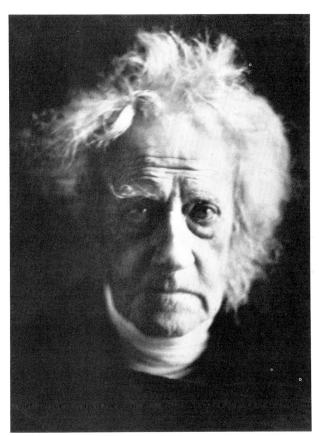

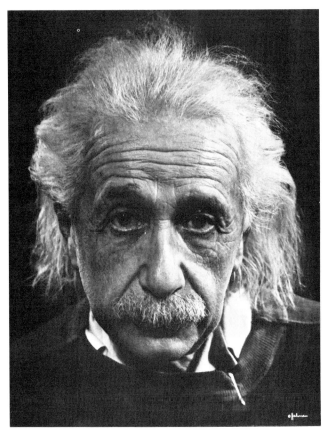

310　Julia Margaret Cameron, *Sir John Herschel*, 1867
　　　Kunstbibliothek Preussischer Kulturbesitz, Berlin

311　Philippe Halsman, *Albert Einstein*, 1947
　　　The Royal Photographic Society of Great Britain, Bath

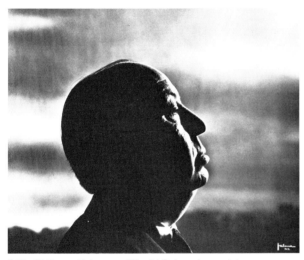

312   Philippe Halsman, *Alfred Hitchcock,* no date
       The Royal Photographic Society of Great Britain, Bath

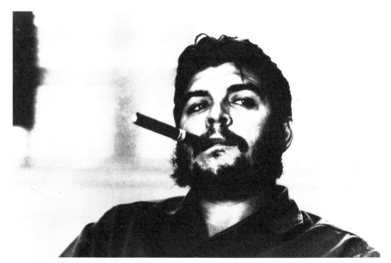

313   René Burri, *Che Guevara,* 1963
       Stiftung für die Photographie, Kunsthaus Zurich

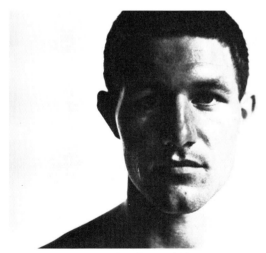

314   Duane Michals, *Ray Barry,* 1963
       The Art Institute of Chicago

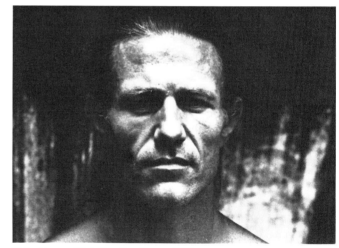

315   Duane Michals, *Ray Barry,* 1977
       The Art Institute of Chicago

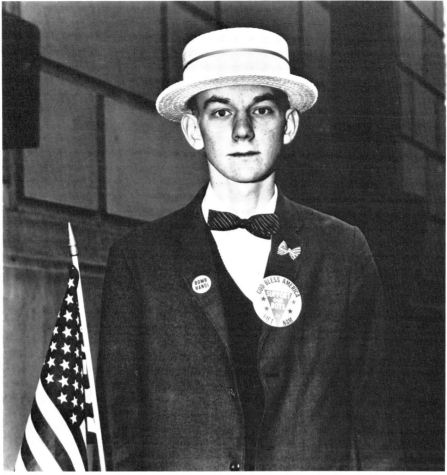

316   Diane Arbus, *Patriotic Boy with Straw Hat, Button and Flag, Waiting to March in a Pro-War-Parade, New York City*, 1967
San Francisco Museum of Modern Art

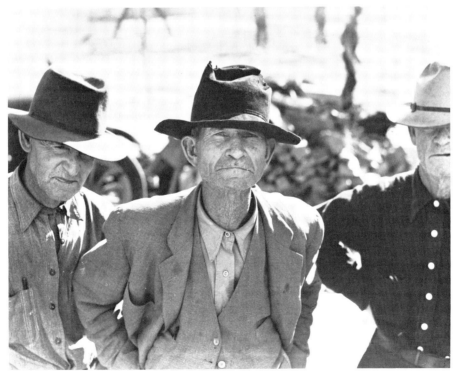

317   Dorothea Lange, *Once a Missouri Farmer, now a Migratory Farm Worker in California*, 1936
The Library of Congress, Washington, D.C.

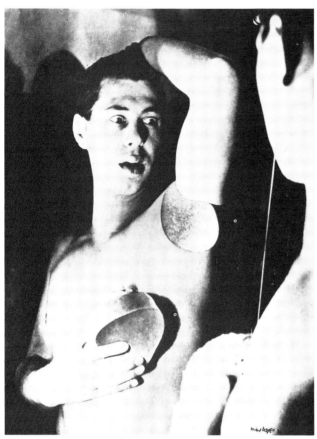

318 Herbert Bayer, *Self-portrait,* 1932
Museum Folkwang, Essen

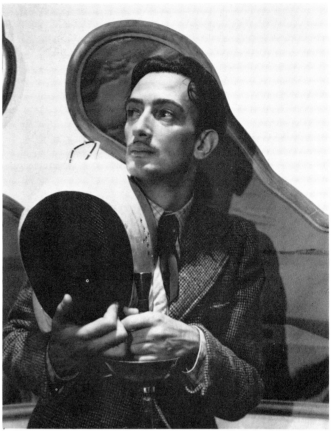

319 Sir Cecil Beaton, *Salvador Dali,* 1935
Museum Ludwig, Cologne

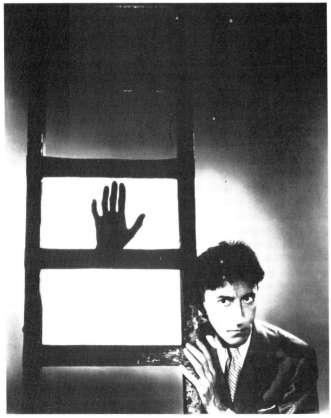

320 George Platt Lynes, *Jean Cocteau,* 1930
Museum Ludwig, Cologne

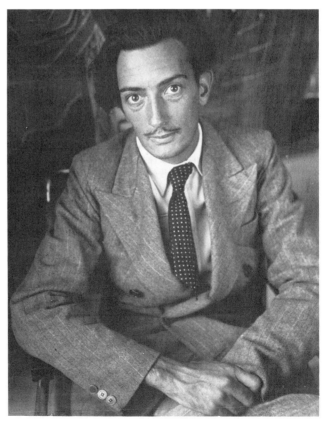

321 Brassaï, *Salvador Dali,* 1932
Bibliothèque Nationale, Paris

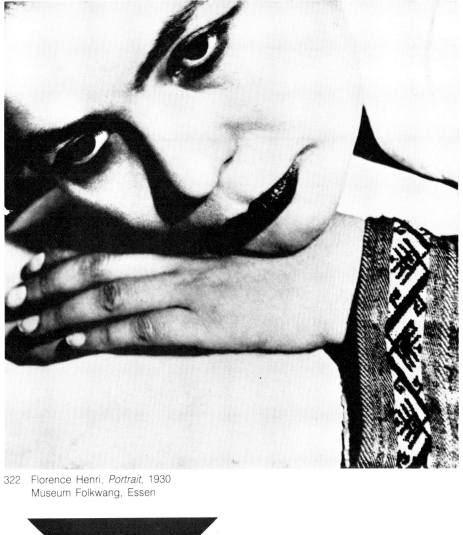

322 Florence Henri, *Portrait*, 1930
Museum Folkwang, Essen

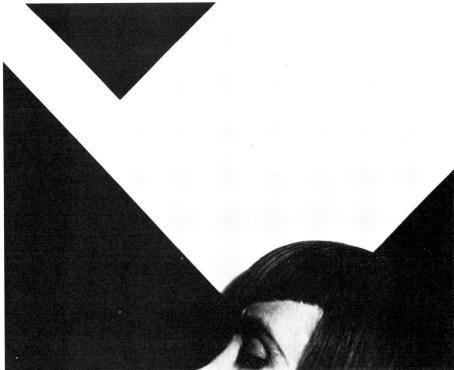

323 Edward Weston, *Ruth Shaw*, 1922
The Art Institute of Chicago

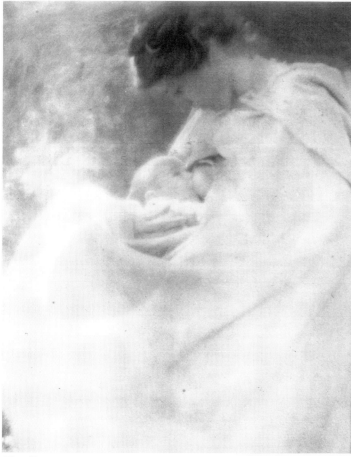

324 F. Holland Day, *Mother and Child*, ca. 1905
     The Library of Congress, Washington, D.C.

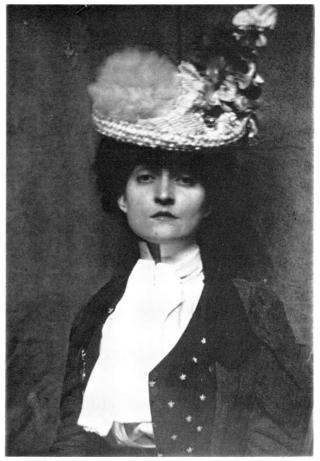

325 Frank Eugene, *Portrait of Woman*, no date
     The Art Institute of Chicago

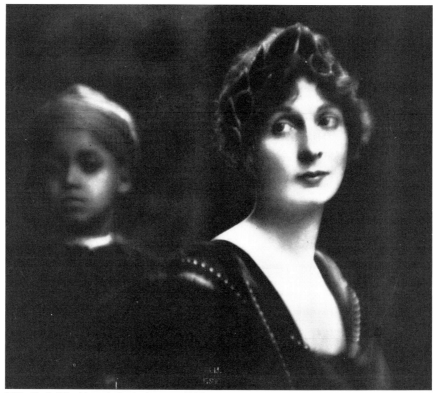

326 Emil Otto Hoppé, *Lady Lavery*, 1914
     Bibliothèque Nationale, Paris

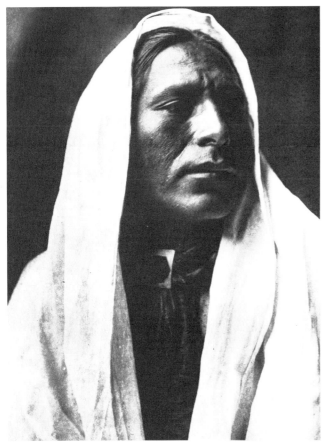

327 Edward Sheriff Curtis, *Lahla (Willow) Taos*, 1905
Art Museum, University of New Mexico, Albuquerque

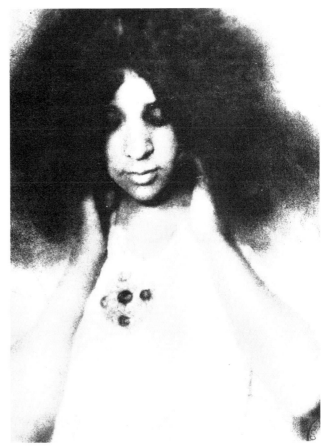

328 Robert Demachy, *Untitled*, ca. 1900
Société Française de Photographie, Paris

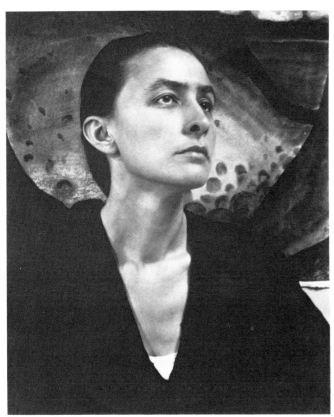

329 Alfred Stieglitz, *Georgia O'Keeffe*, 1918
The Art Institute of Chicago

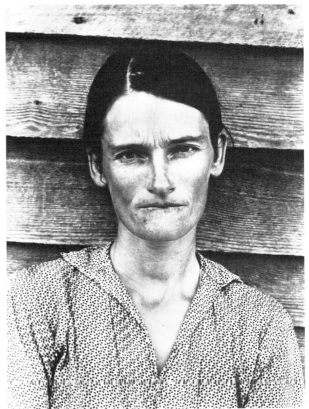

330 Walker Evans, *Tenant Farmer's Wife*, 1936
San Francisco Museum of Modern Art

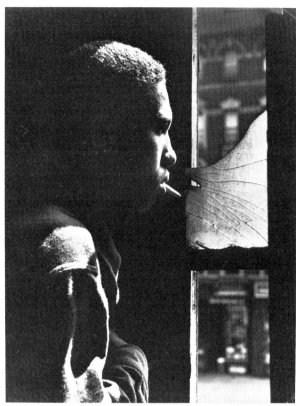

331 Gordon Parks, *Red Jackson*, 1948
     Museum Ludwig, Cologne

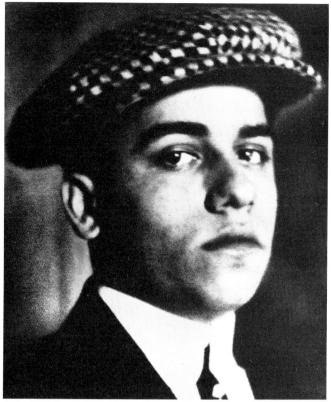

332 F. Holland Day, *Young Man in Checkered Cap*, no date
     The Library of Congress, Washington, D.C.

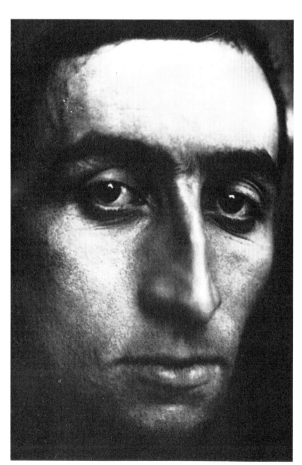

333 Erna Lendvai-Dircksen, *Miner from Upper Silesia*,
     no date
     Agfa-Gevaert Foto-Historama, Leverkusen

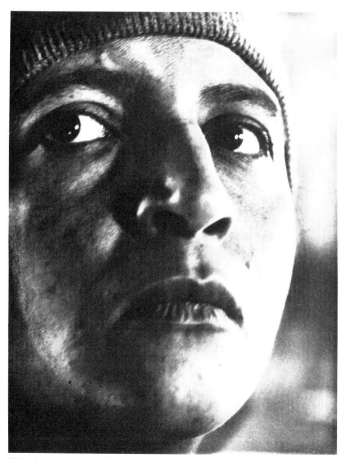

334 Helmar Lerski, *Typist*, before 1931
     Museum für Kunst und Gewerbe, Hamburg

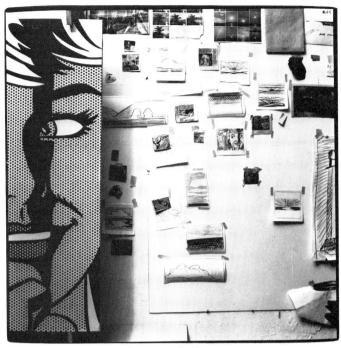

335 Ugo Mulas, *Roy Lichtenstein*, 1964
Università di Parma

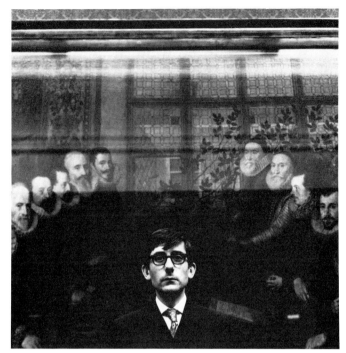

336 Sir Cecil Beaton, *Dr. Roy Strong*, no date
National Portrait Gallery, London

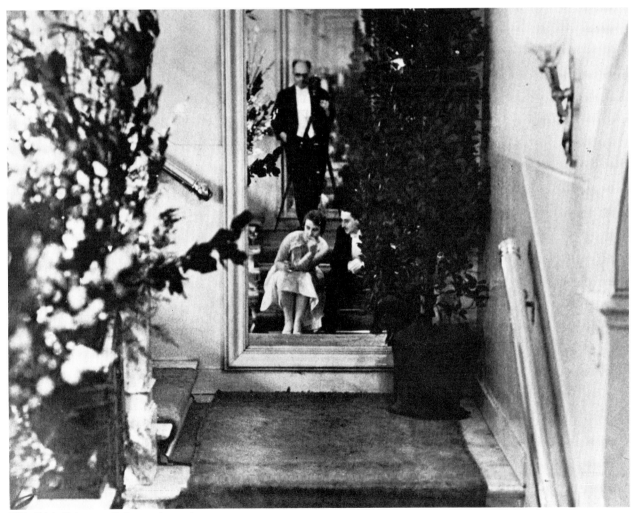

337 Erich Salomon, *Self-portrait*, no date
Museum Folkwang, Essen

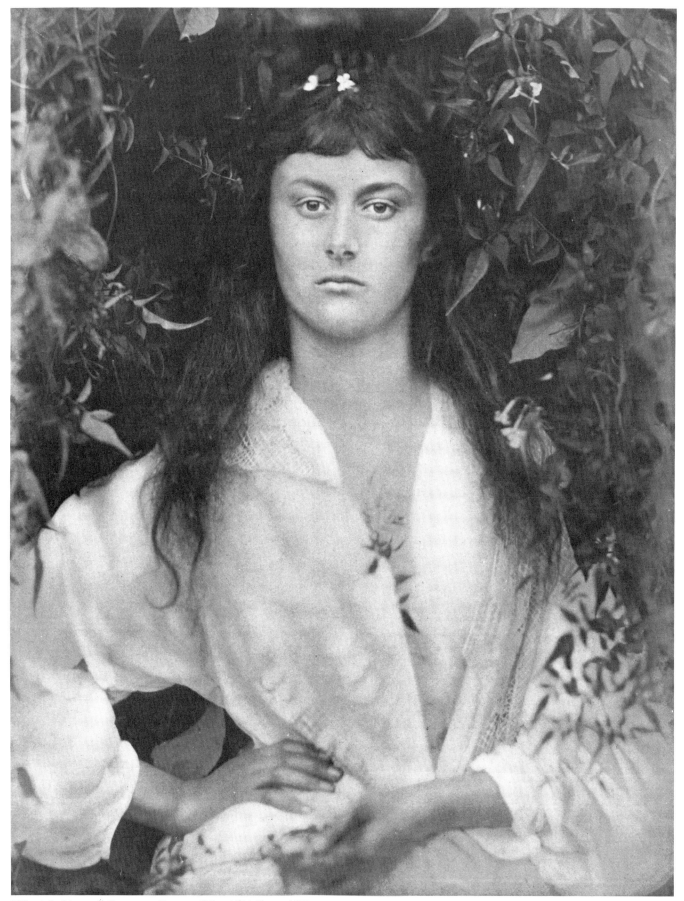

338 Julia Margaret Cameron, *Pomona (Alice Liddell)*, ca. 1872
The Royal Photographic Society of Great Britain, Bath

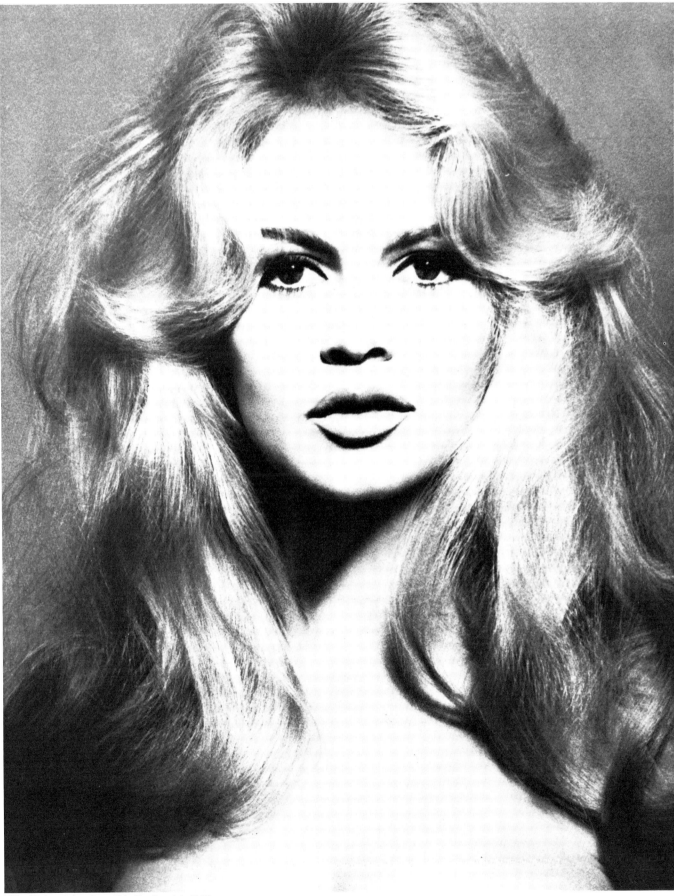

339 Richard Avedon, *Brigitte Bardot*, 1959
Museum Ludwig, Cologne

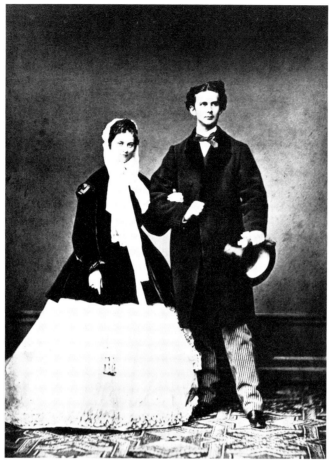

340   Josef Albert, *Ludwig II of Bavaria and his Bride*, 1867
       Münchner Stadtmuseum, Munich

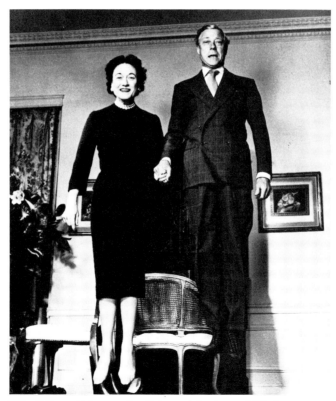

341   Philippe Halsman, *The Duke and Duchess of Windsor*,
       before 1958
       The Royal Photographic Society of Great Britain, Bath

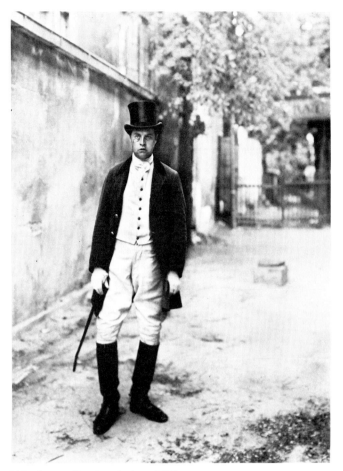

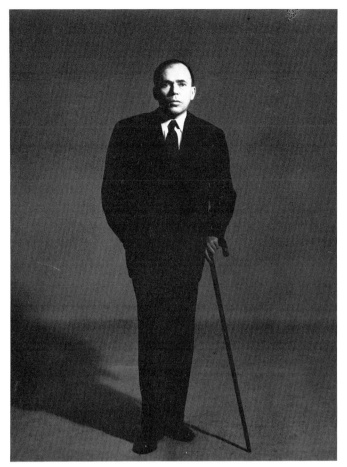

342 August Sander, *Jockey*, 1932
Museum Ludwig, Cologne

343 Liselotte Strelow, *Oscar Fritz Schuh*, 1955
Deutsche Gesellschaft für Photographie, Cologne

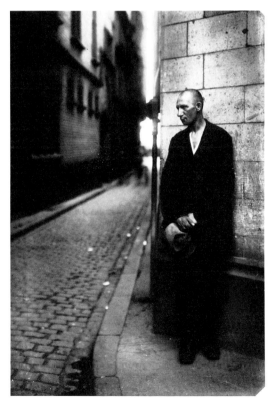

344 August Sander, *Unemployed*, 1932
Museum Ludwig, Cologne

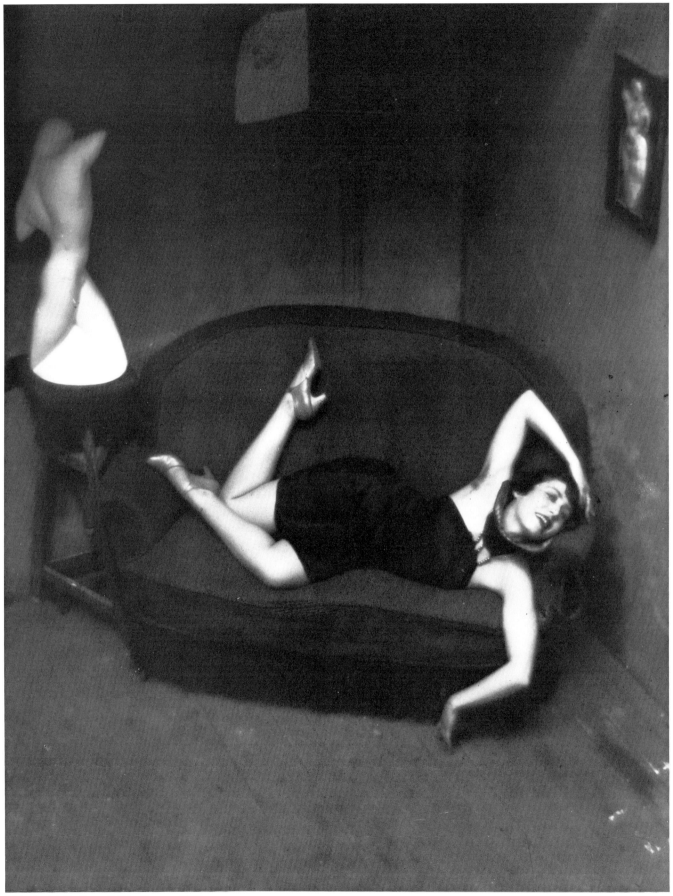

345 André Kertész, *Satiric Dancer*, 1926
Fotografiska Museet, Stockholm

THE CITY

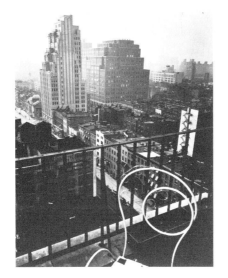

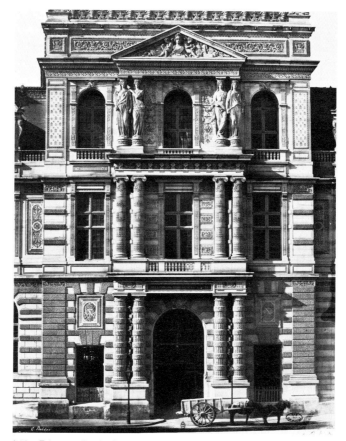

346 Edouard-Denis Baldus, *Paris, Le Louvre*, 1860
Bibliothèque Nationale, Paris

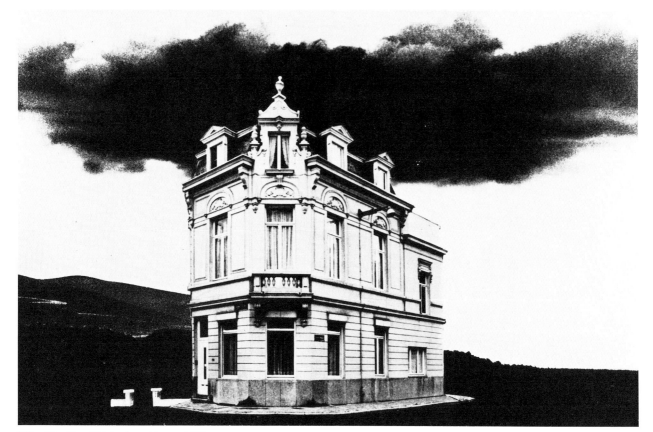

347 Filip Tas, *Think-alone House*, 1979
Het Sterckshof Museum, Antwerp

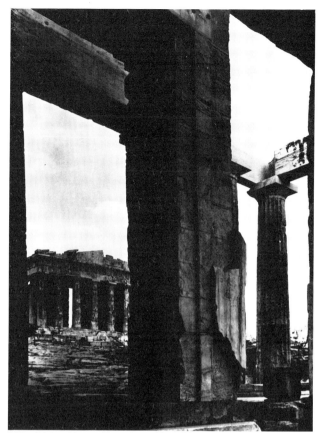

348 Walter Hege, *Propyläen, East Wing*, 1928–1929
Museum Folkwang, Essen

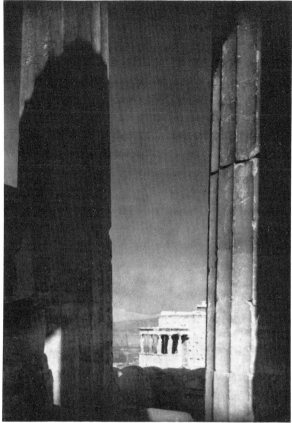

349 Edward Steichen, *Athens*, 1921
George Eastman House, Rochester

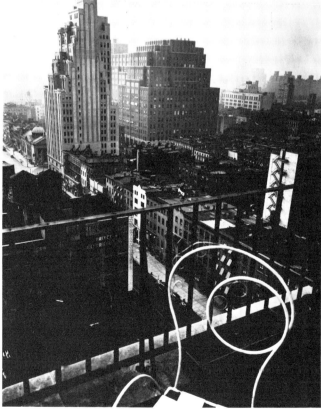

350 Berenice Abbott, *N.Y.C., Changing New York*, 1937
The Art Institute of Chicago

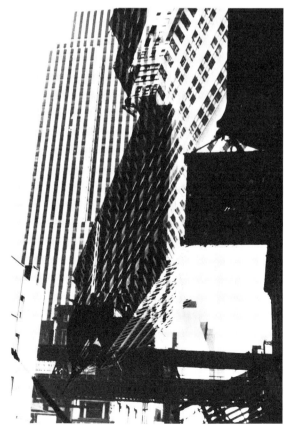

351 Francis Bruguière, *Skyscrapers*, 1920
Het Sterckshof Museum, Antwerp

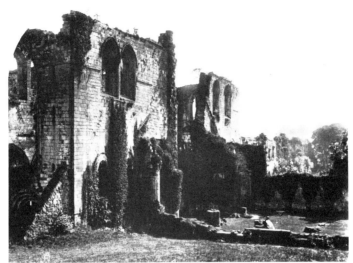

352 Roger Fenton, *Furness Abbey, The Transepts from the Northwest*,
     ca. 1856
     The Royal Photographic Society of Great Britain, Bath

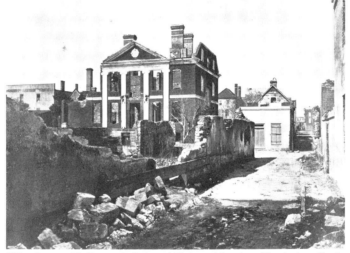

353 George N. Barnard, *Ruins of Pickney Mansion, Charleston, South
     Carolina*, 1865
     The Library of Congress, Washington, D.C.

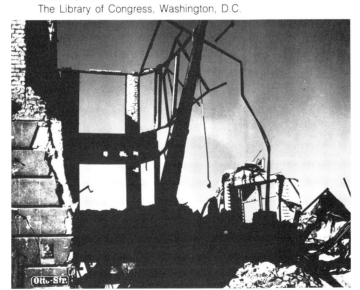

354 Herbert List, *Munich*, 1945
     Museum Folkwang, Essen

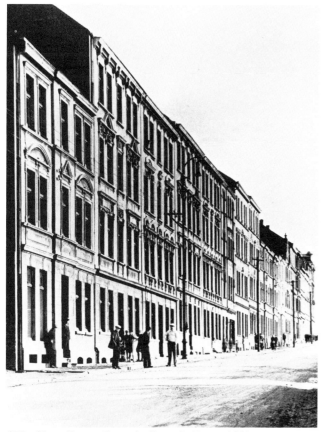

355 Albert Renger-Patzsch, *Street in Essen*, 1932
Kunstbibliothek Preussischer Kulturbesitz, Berlin

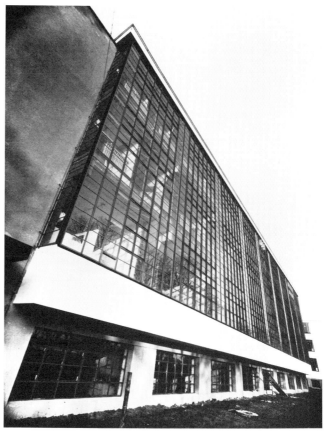

356 Lucia Moholy, *Bauhaus*, 1925–1926
Museum Ludwig, Cologne

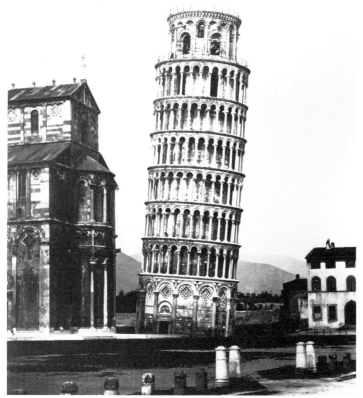

357 Louis-Auguste and Auguste-Rosalie Bisson, *Belltower, Pisa*,
ca. 1860
Gernsheim Collection, Austin

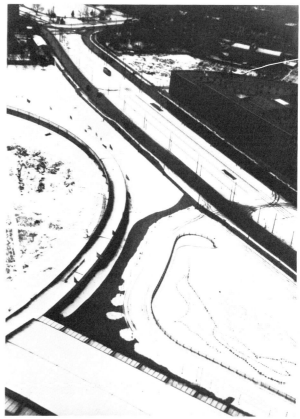

358 László Moholy-Nagy, *Untitled*, no date
The Art Institute of Chicago

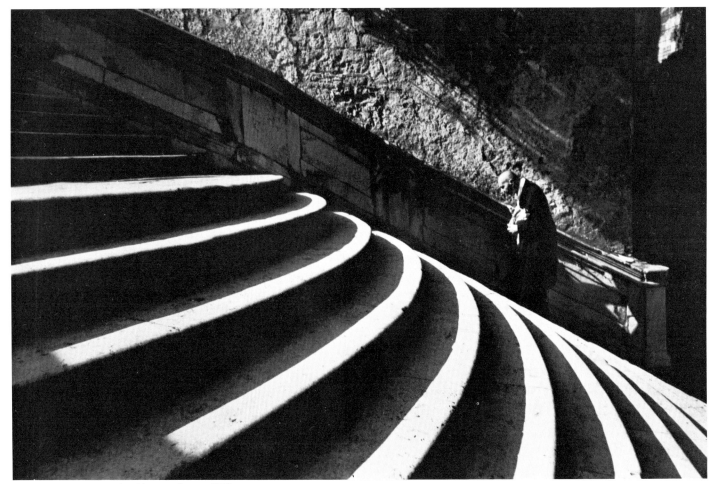

359   Eva Rubinstein, *Old Man on Steps*, 1973
      Bibliothèque Nationale, Paris

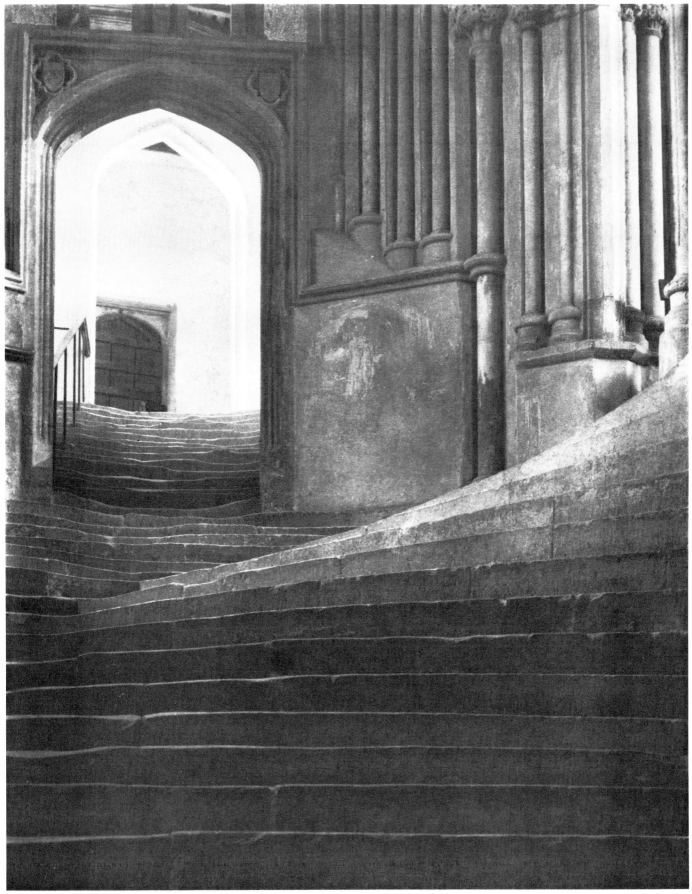

360 Frederick H. Evans, *A Sea of Steps*, 1903
Museum für Kunst und Gewerbe, Hamburg

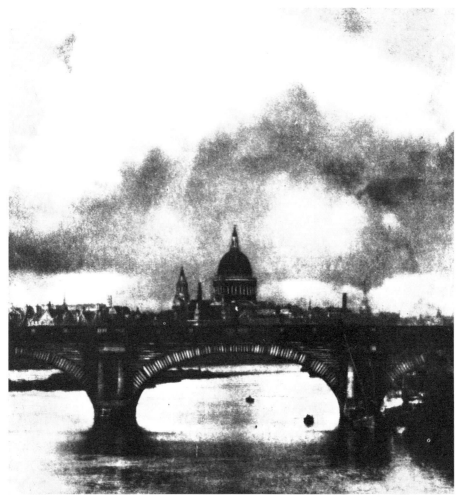

361   Alvin Langdon Coburn, *St. Paul's from the River,* before 1910
      The Royal Photographic Society of Great Britain, Bath

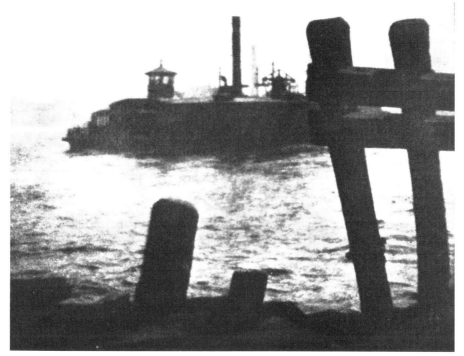

362   Alvin Langdon Coburn, *New York Ferry,* 1910
      The Royal Photographic Society of Great Britain, Bath

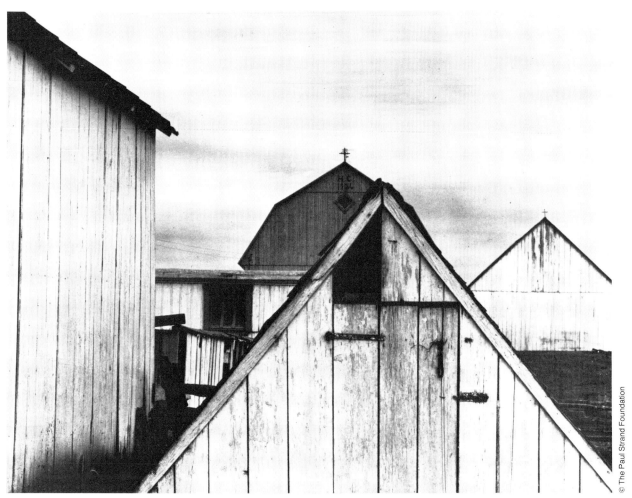

363 Paul Strand, *Barns and Sheds,* 1936
San Francisco Museum of Modern Art

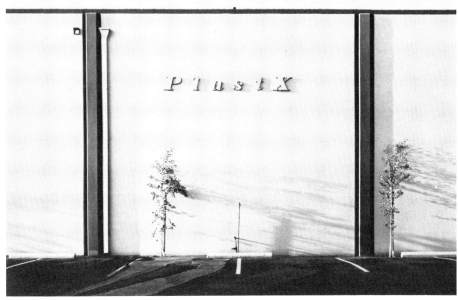

364 Lewis Baltz, *South Wall PlastX, 350 Lear, Costa Mesa,* 1974
Art Museum, University of New Mexico, Albuquerque

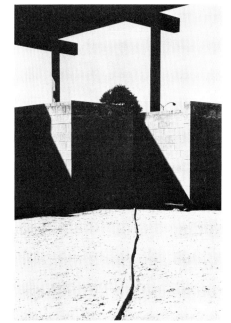

365 Ray K Metzker *Untitled,* 1972
Art Museum, University of
New Mexico, Albuquerque

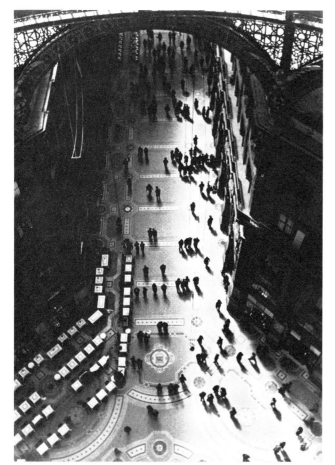

366 Bruno Stefani, *The Galeria, Milan*, 1930
Università di Parma

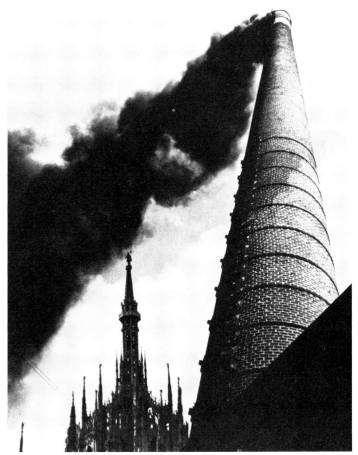

367 Bruno Stefani, *Milan*, 1938
Università di Parma

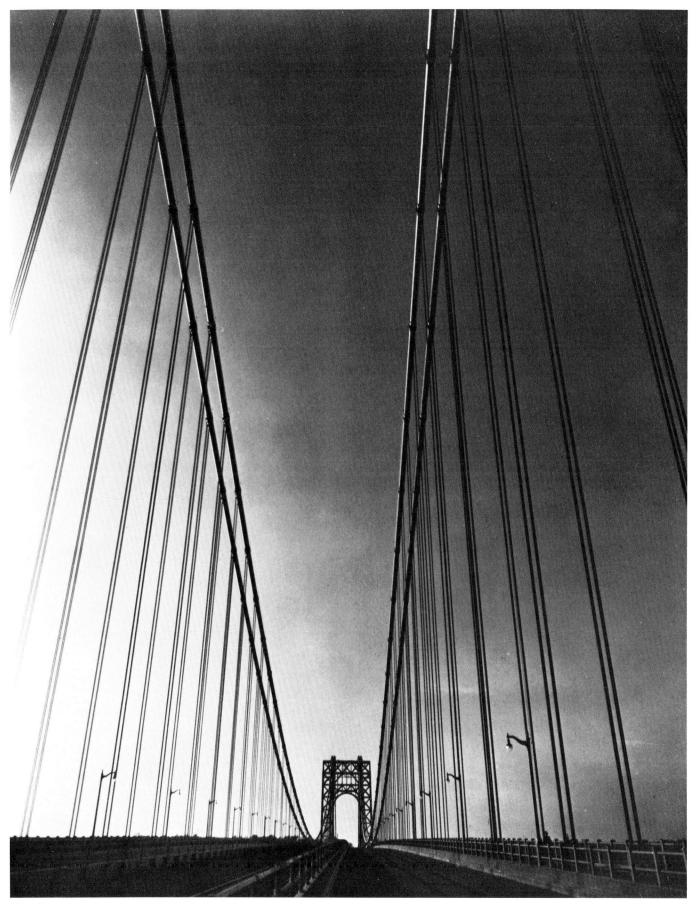

368   Edward Steichen, *George Washington Bridge, New York*, 1931
George Eastman House, Rochester

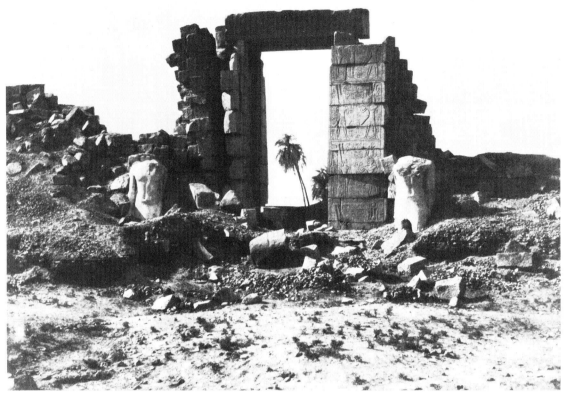

369 Félix Teynard, *Karnak,* ca. 1850
Det kongelige Bibliotek, Copenhagen

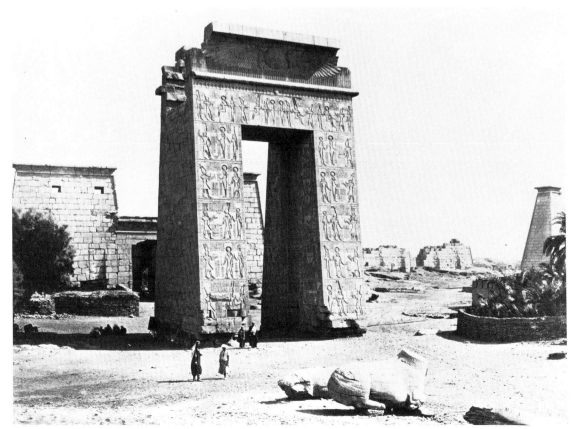

370 Francis Frith, *Egypt,* 1858
Det kongelige Bibliotek, Copenhagen

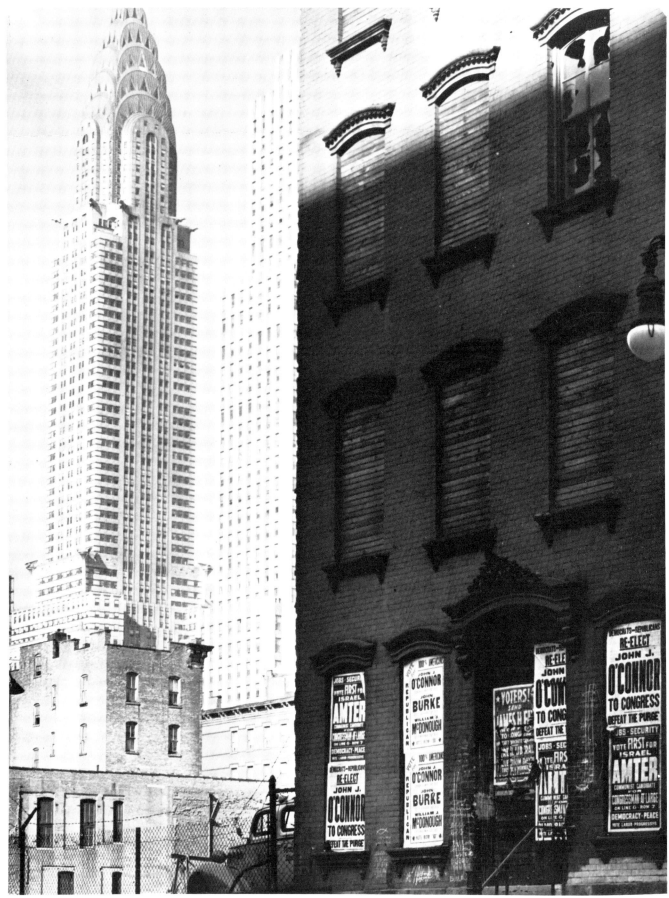

371   Berenice Abbott, *News Building,* 1938
The Art Institute of Chicago

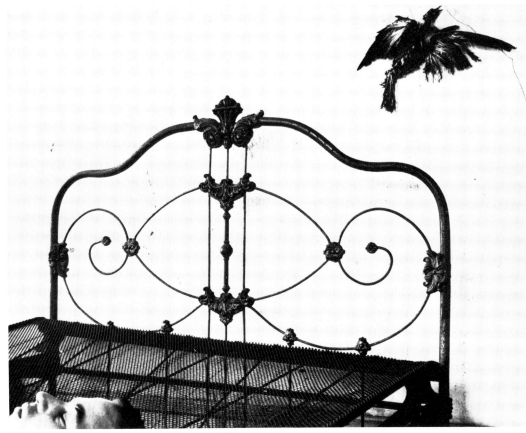

372 Ralph Eugene Meatyard, *Untitled,* ca. 1960
     Art Museum, University of New Mexico, Albuquerque

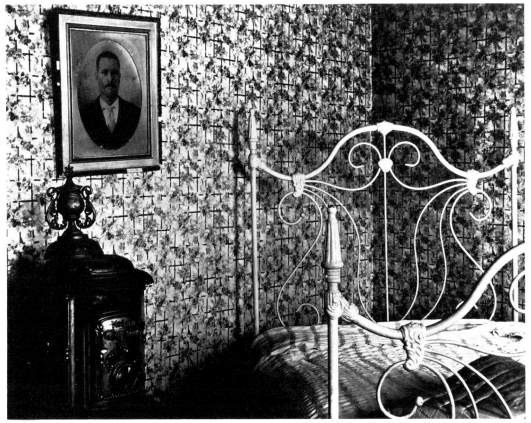

373 Walker Evans, *Bed and Stove,* 1931
     San Francisco Museum of Modern Art

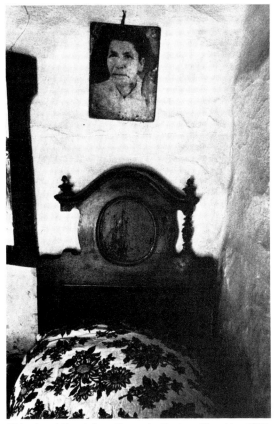

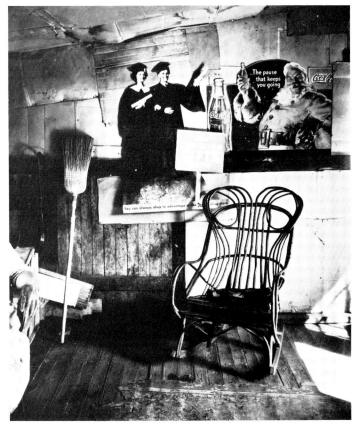

374 Josef Koudelka, *Gypsy in Eastern Slovakia*, 1965
Stiftung für die Photographie, Kunsthaus Zürich

375 Walker Evans, *West Virginia Coal Miner's House*, 1936
The Art Institute of Chicago

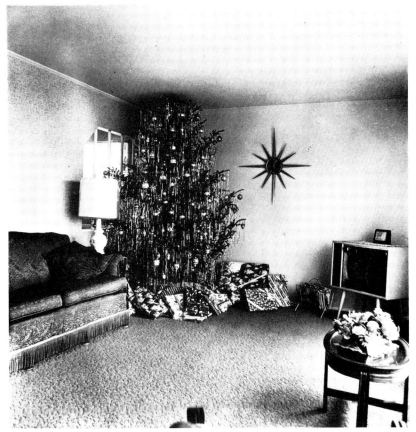

376 Diane Arbus, *Christmas Tree*, 1962
San Francisco Museum of Modern Art

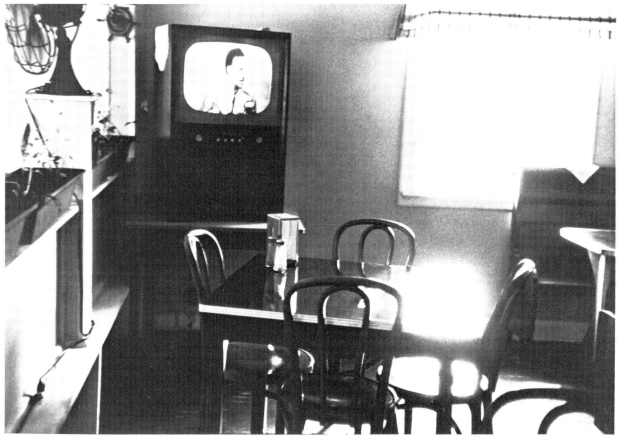

377 Robert Frank, *U.S. 1, South Carolina*, 1955
Stiftung für die Photographie, Kunsthaus, Zürich

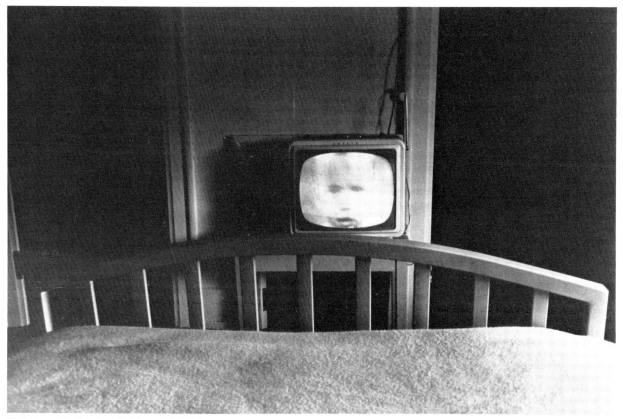

378 Lee Friedlander, *Child on TV*, 1962
San Francisco Museum of Modern Art

THE EVENT

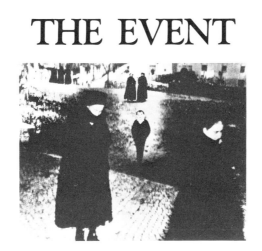

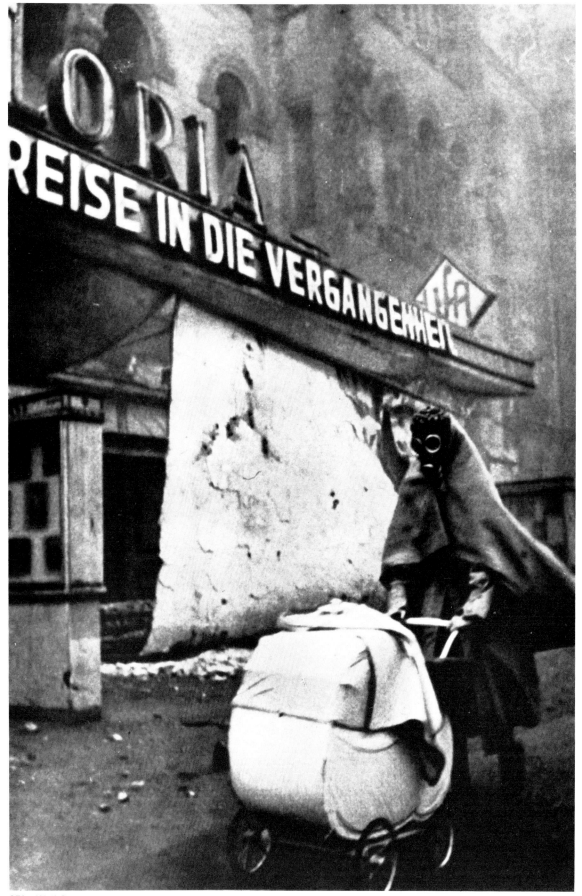

379 Wolf Strache, *Journey into the Past,* ca. 1945
Museum Folkwang, Essen

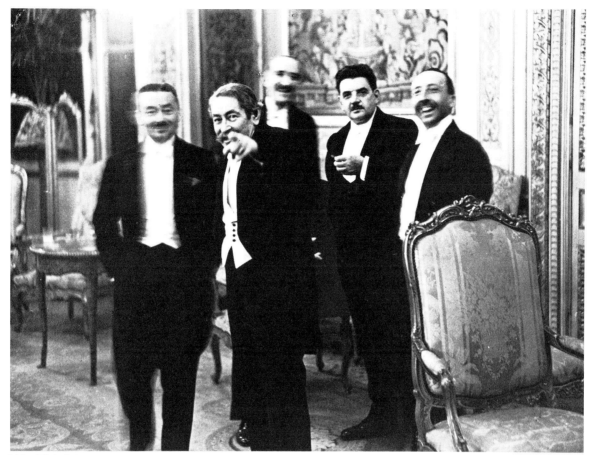

380 Erich Salomon, *The King of Indiscretion—There He Is!*, 1931
Museum Folkwang, Essen

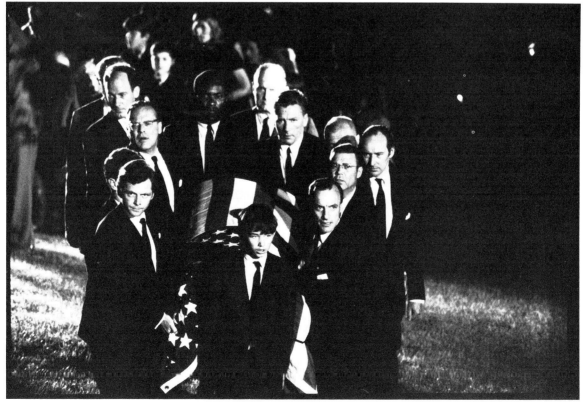

381 Robert Lebeck, *Kennedy's Burial*, 1968
Museum Folkwang, Essen

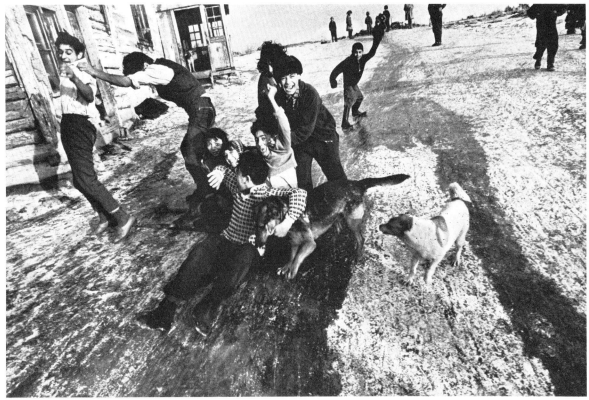

382   Josef Koudelka, *Gypsy Children*, 1964
      Stiftung für die Photographie, Kunsthaus Zürich

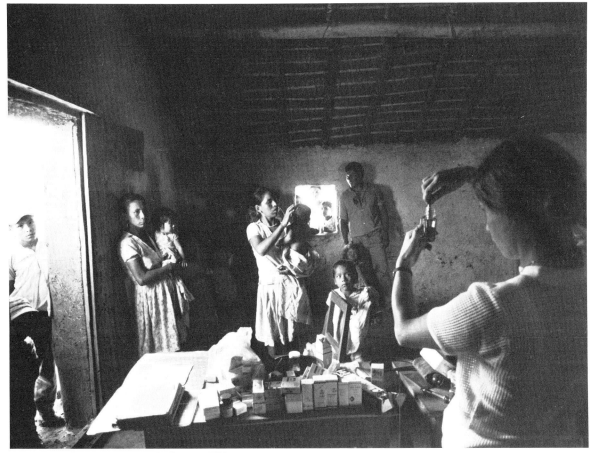

383   Hilmar Pabel, *Volunteers in Bolivia*, 1975
      Museum Folkwang, Essen

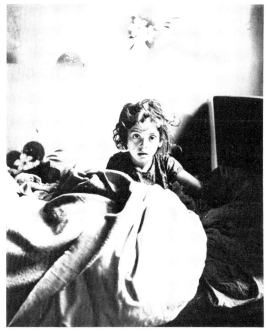

384 Roman Vishniac, *Jewish Child*, 1938
Münchner Stadtmuseum, Munich

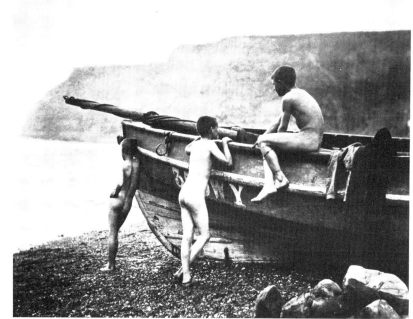

385 Frank Meadow Sutcliffe, *Natives of these Isles*, 1885
The Royal Photographic Society of Great Britain, Bath

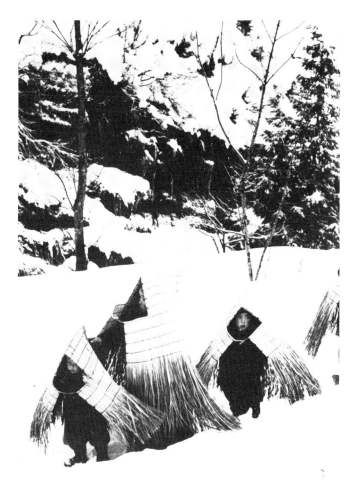

386 Hiroshi Hamaya, *Snowcountries Children*, 1956
Museum Ludwig, Cologne

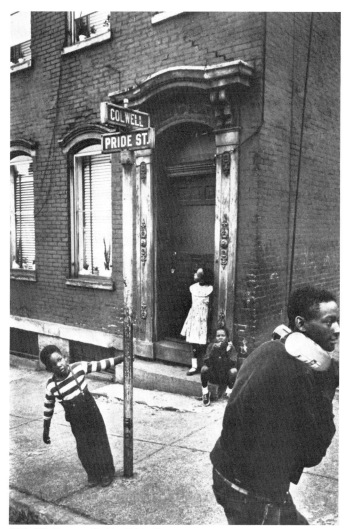

387 W. Eugene Smith, *Pride Street*, no date
Museum Ludwig, Cologne

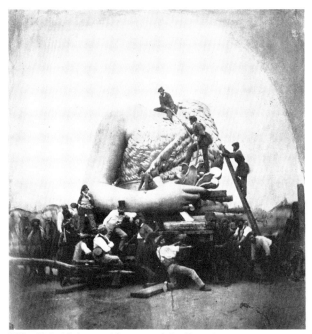

388   Alois Löcherer, *Montage of the Bavaria,* 1850
      Münchner Stadtmuseum, Munich

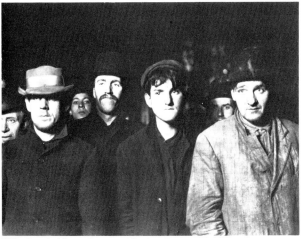

389   Lewis Hine, *Bowery Mission Bread Line, 2 A.M.,*
      New York, 1907
      The Library of Congress, Washington, D.C.

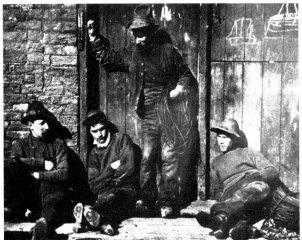

390   Frank Meadow Sutcliffe, *Hawksfield,* no date
      The Royal Photographic Society of Great Britain, Bath

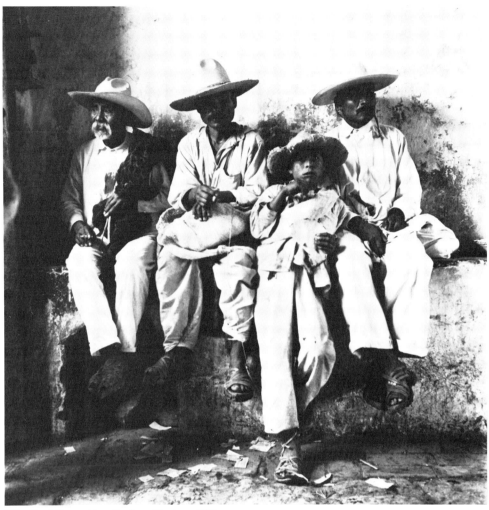

391 Paul Senn, *Hog Traders,* Mexico, 1951
Stiftung für die Photographie, Kunsthaus Zürich

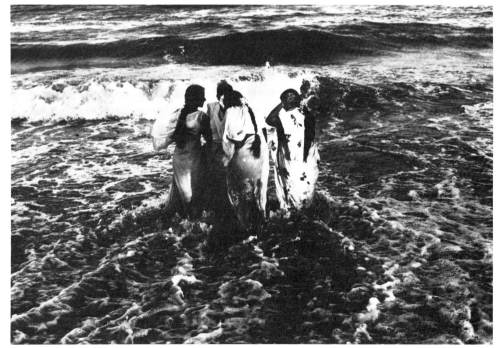

392 Edouard Boubat, *Madras,* 1971
Museum Folkwang, Essen

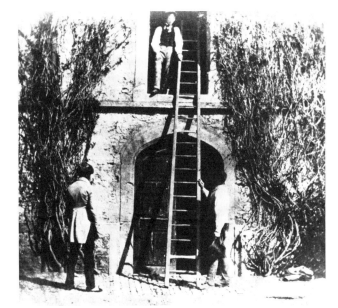

393 William Henry Fox Talbot, *The Ladder*, Plate 14 from *The Pencil of Nature*, ca. 1844
The Fox Talbot Museum, Lacock

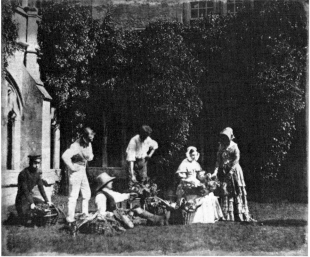

394 William Henry Fox Talbot, *The Fruit Sellers, Group Portrait Taken in Cloister Courtyard of Lacock Abbey*, ca. 1842
The Fox Talbot Museum, Lacock

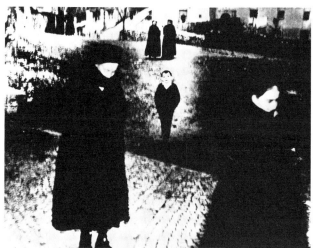

395 Mario Giacomelli, *Scanno*, 1963
Università di Parma

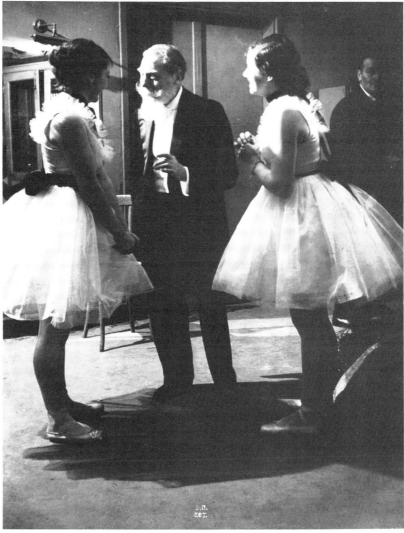

396 Brassaï, *Backstage at the Opera*, 1938
Bibliothèque Nationale, Paris

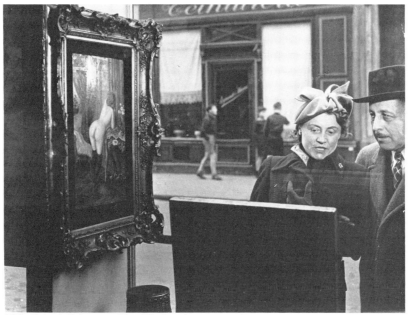

397 Robert Doisneau, *The Windowshopper*, no date
Het Sterckshof Museum, Antwerp

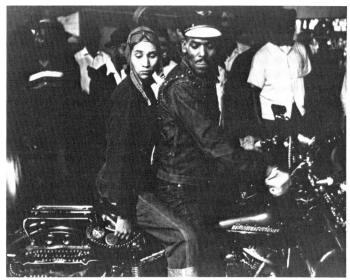

398 Robert Frank, *Indianapolis*, 1955
Stiftung für die Photographie, Kunsthaus Zürich

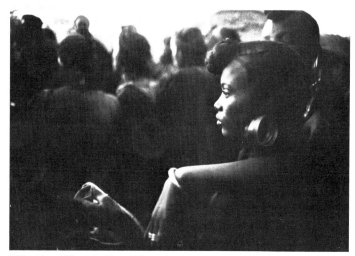

399 Marc Riboud, *Neger Barroros*, 1963
Bibliothèque Nationale, Paris

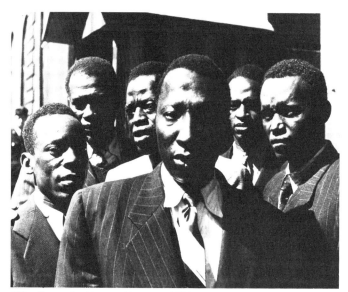

400 Emmy Andriesse, *Negroes*, 1950
Stedelijk Museum, Amsterdam

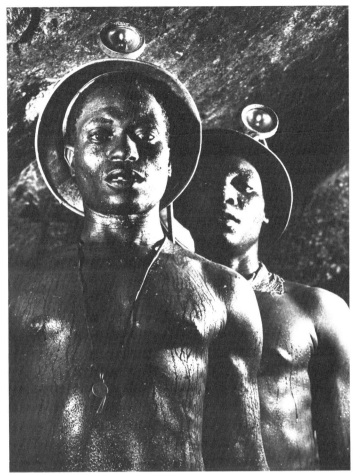

401 Margaret Bourke-White, *A Mile Underground*, 1950
The Art Institute of Chicago

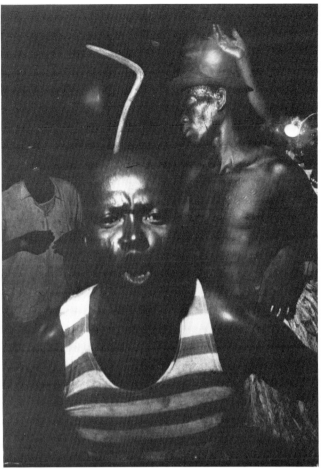

402 Ed van der Elsken, *Africa*, 1957
Stedelijk Museum, Amsterdam

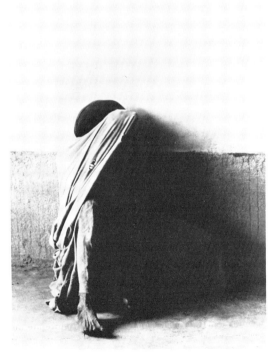

403 Thomas Höpker, *Leprosy in Ethiopia*, 1964
Museum für Kunst und Gewerbe, Hamburg

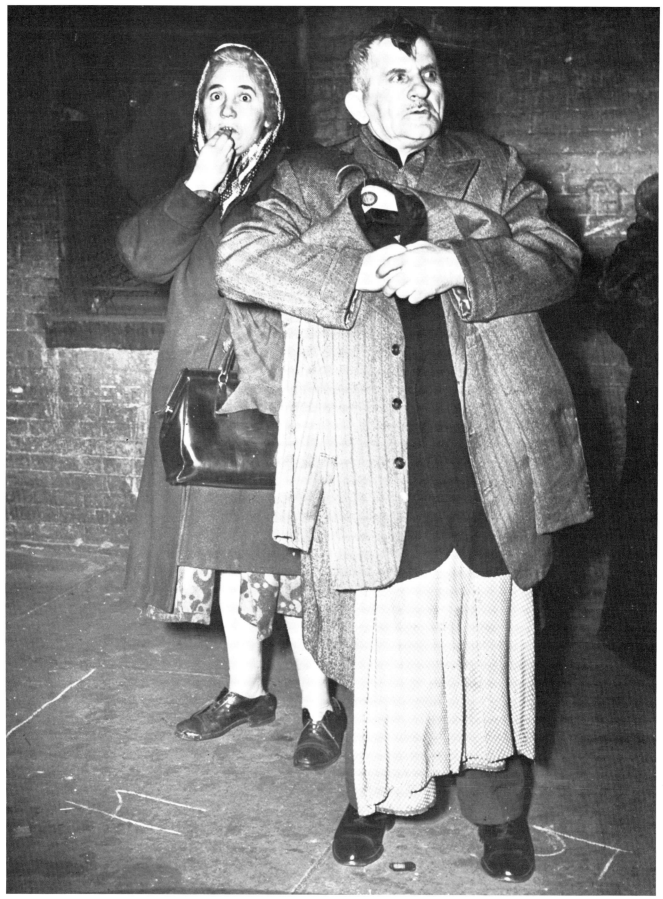

404 Weegee, *A Couple Driven Out*, 1945
Bibliothèque Nationale, Paris

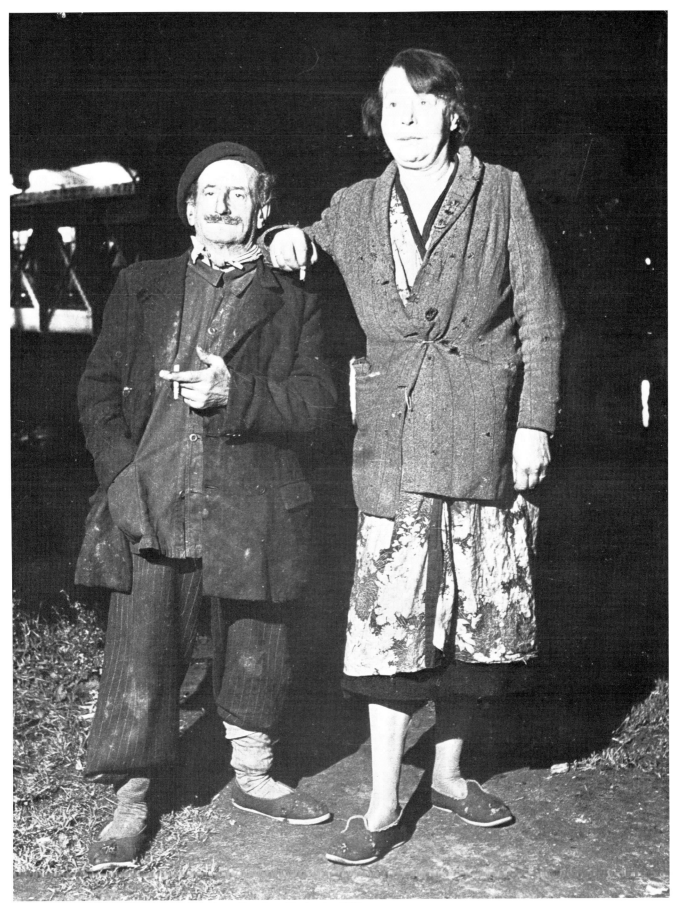

405 Robert Doisneau, *Monsieur and Madame Garafino, Clochards,* 1952
Bibliothèque Nationale, Paris

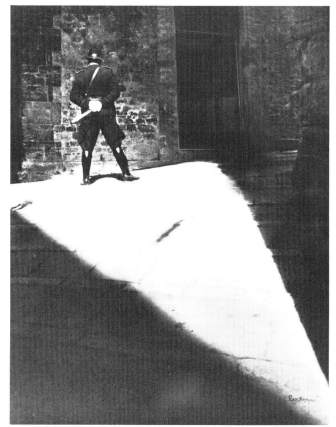

406 Emil Otto Hoppé, *Triangles, Magic*, 1926
Bibliothèque Nationale, Paris

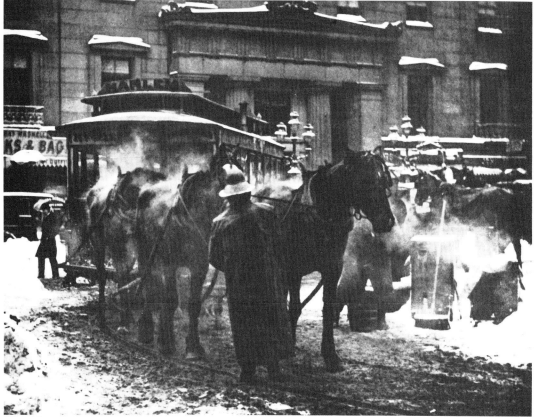

407 Alfred Stieglitz, *The Terminal*, 1893
The Art Institute of Chicago

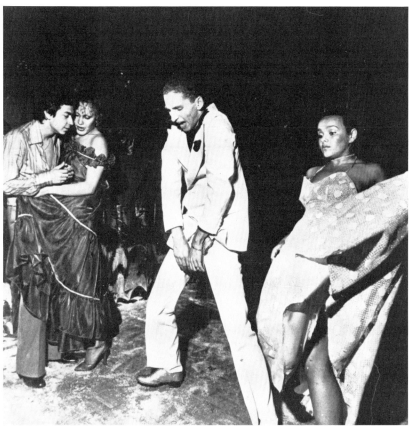

408   Larry Fink, *Studio 54*, 1977
      Museum of Fine Arts, Boston

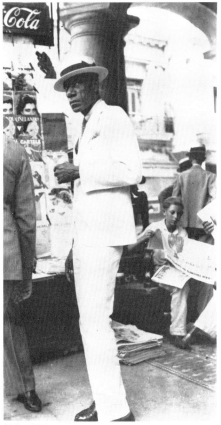

409   Walker Evans, *Citizen in
      Downtown Havana*, 1932
      The Art Institute of Chicago

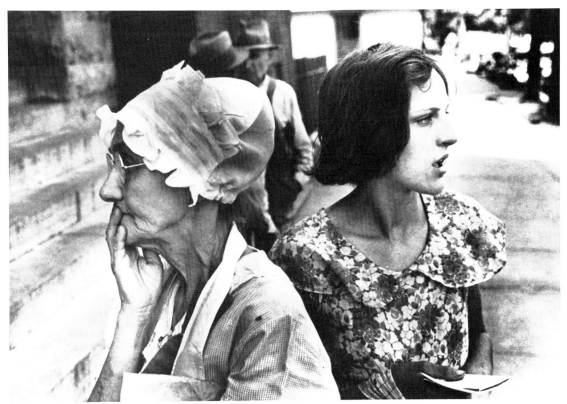

410 Ben Shahn, *Urbana*, 1938
San Francisco Museum of Modern Art

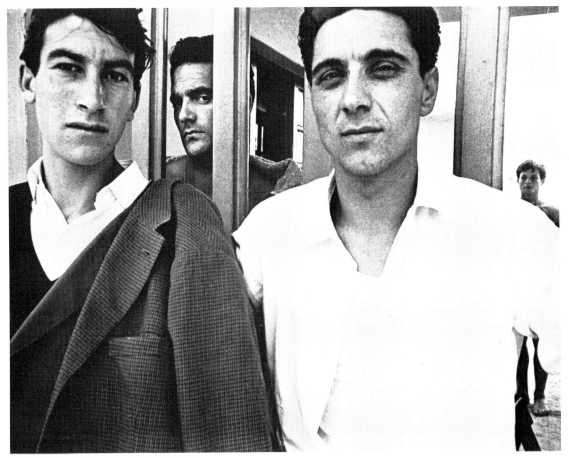

411 William Klein, *Rome (Looks)*, 1956
Bibliothèque Nationale, Paris

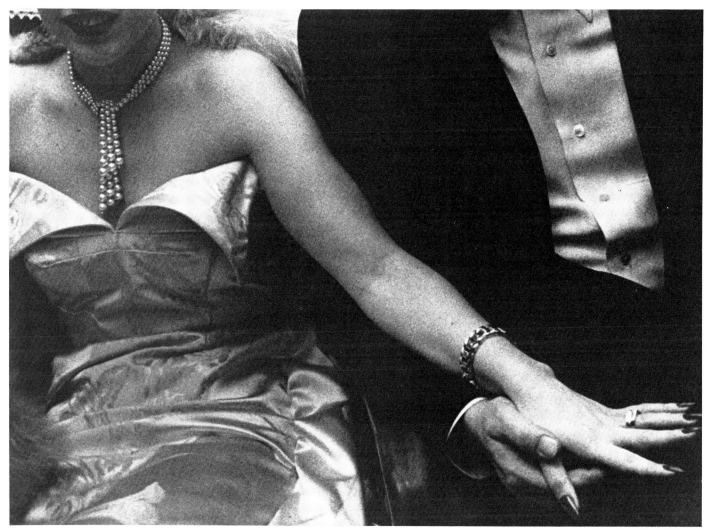

412 Jakob Tuggener, *Ticinesi Ball, Grand Hotel Dolder, Zürich*, 1948
Stiftung für die Photographie, Kunsthaus Zürich

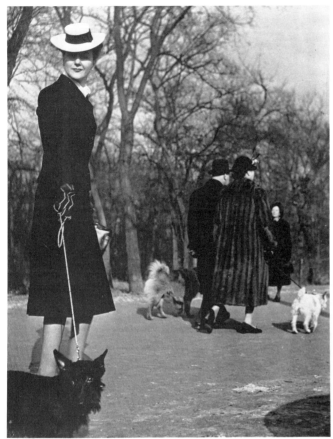

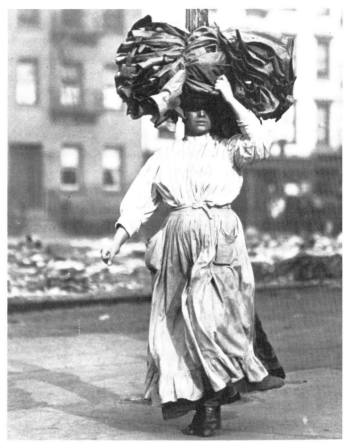

413 Brassaï, *Woman with Dog*, no date
Het Sterckshof Museum, Antwerp

414 Lewis Hine, *First Work in America*, 1910
The Art Institute of Chicago

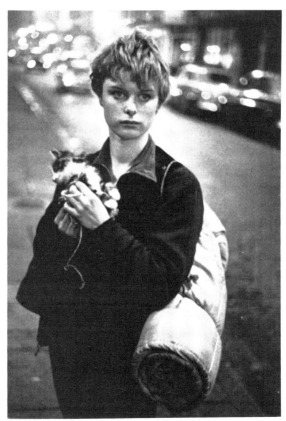

415 Bruce Davidson, *London Life*, 1964
The Art Institute of Chicago

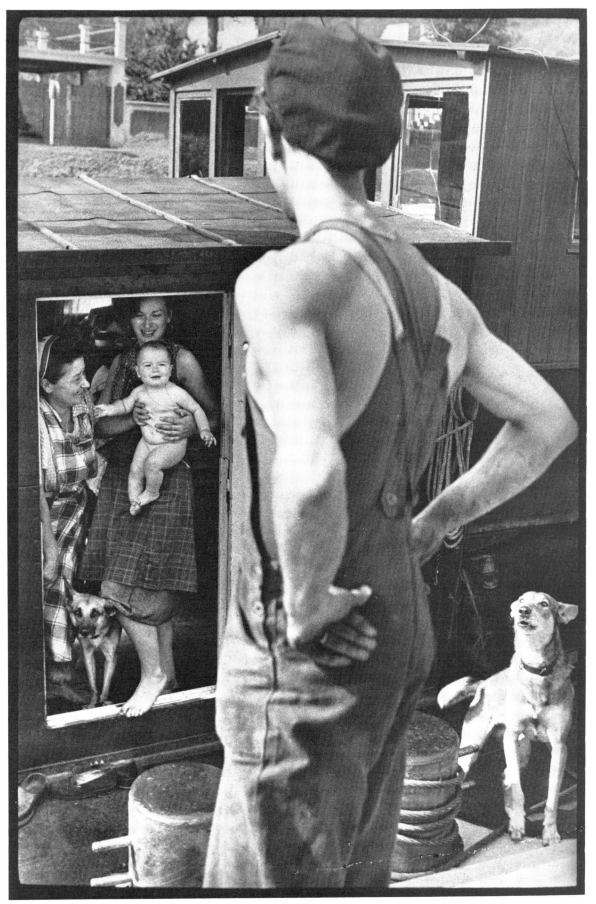

416   Henry Cartier-Bresson, *Seine Bargeman*, 1957
      Museum Ludwig, Cologne

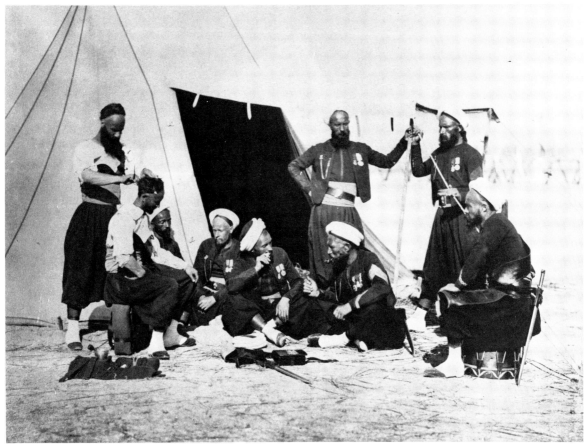

417 Gustave Le Gray, *A Picture Taken at Camp de Chalon*, 1857
Société Française de Photographie, Paris

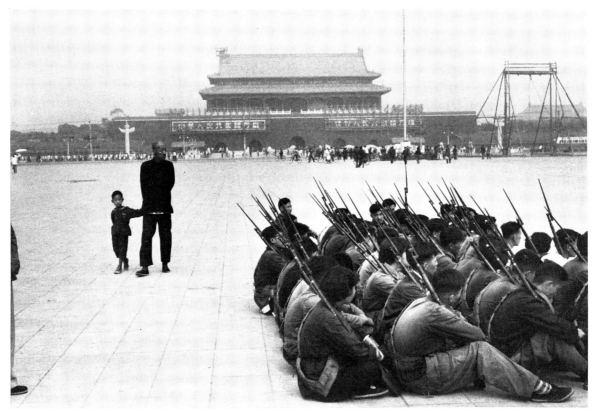

418 Henri Cartier-Bresson, *China*, 1958
Bibliothèque Nationale, Paris

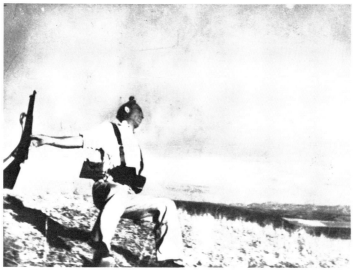

419 Robert Capa, *Falling Spanish Soldier*, 1936
Stedelijk Museum, Amsterdam

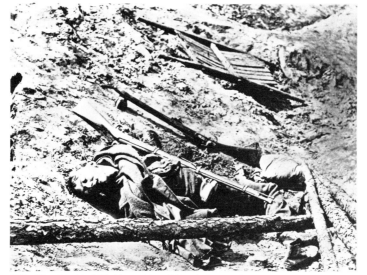

420 Timothy H. O'Sullivan, *Dead Confederate Soldier in Trenches of
Fort Mahone at Petersburg, Virginia,* April 3, 1865
The Library of Congress, Washington, D.C.

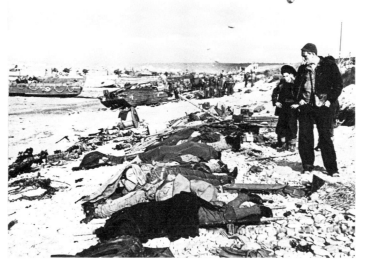

421 Robert Capa, *D-Day Plus One: The Dead on Normandy Beach,*
1944
Stedelijk Museum, Amsterdam

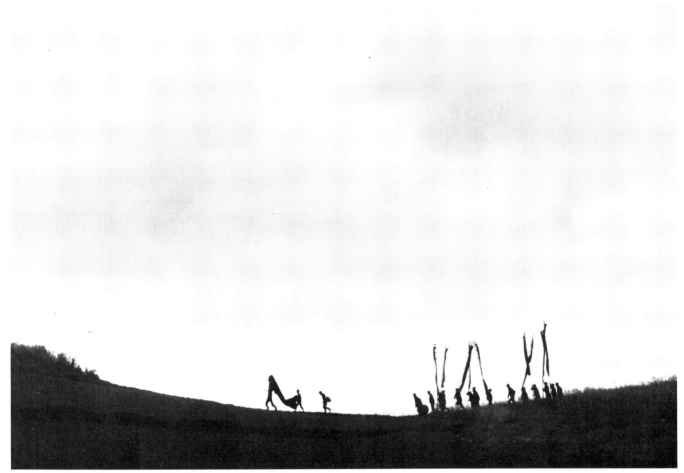

422 Shoji Ueda, *Procession*, no date
The Nihon University of Art, Tokyo

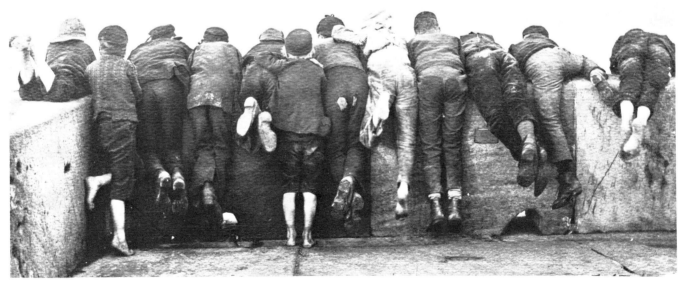

423 Frank Meadow Sutcliffe, *Stern Realities*, 1900
The Royal Photographic Society of Great Britain, Bath

THE VISIONS

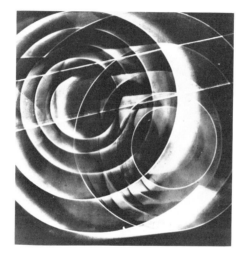

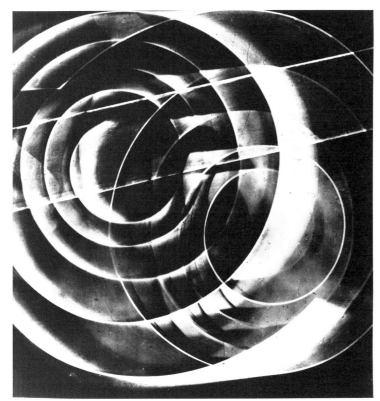

424 Luigi Veronesi, *Photogram on Motion Picture Film*, 1936
Università di Parma

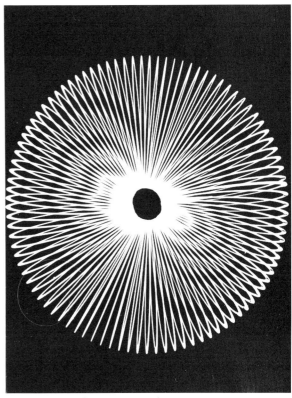

425 Man Ray, *Rayograph*, no date
Het Sterckshof Museum, Antwerp

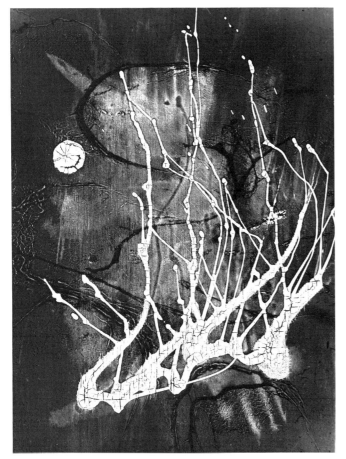

426 Heinz Hajek-Halke, *Light Graphic*, no date
Deutsche Gesellschaft für Photographie, Cologne

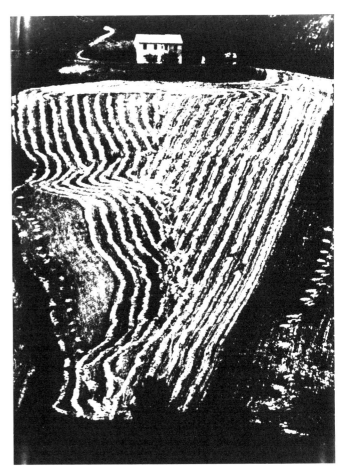

427 Mario Giacomelli, From *The Earth*, 1955–1968
Università di Parma

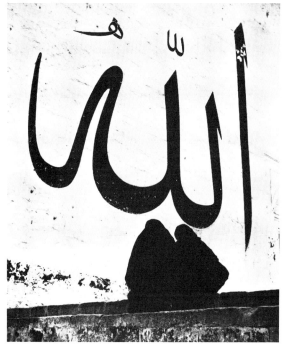

428   Ara Güler, *Turkey, Edirne,* 1956
Bibliothèque Nationale, Paris

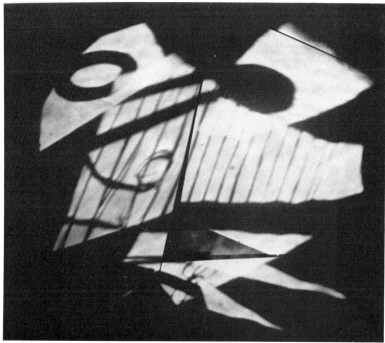

429   Jaromir Funke, *Shadows,* 1927
Uměleckoprůmyslové Muzeum v Praze, Prague

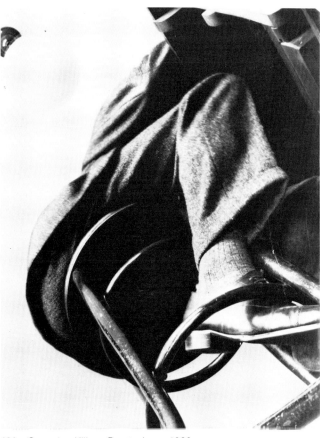

430   Gerardus Kiljan, *Barstool,* ca. 1930
Haags Gemeente Museum, The Hague

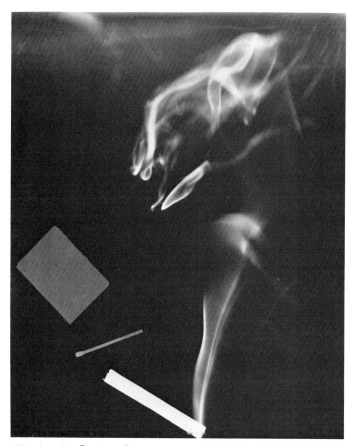

431   Jaroslav Rössler, *Cigarette,* 1929
Uměleckoprůmyslové Muzeum v Praze, Prague

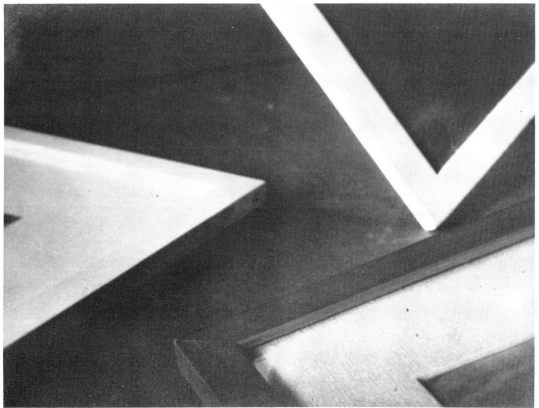

432   Jaromir Funke. *Corners*, no date
Uměleckoprümyslové Muzeum v Praze. Prague

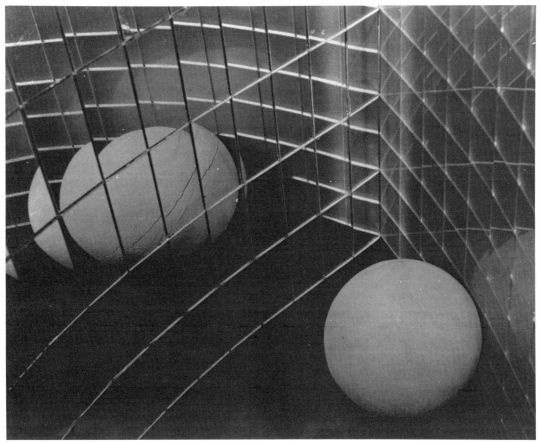

433   Luigi Veronesi. *Photography*. 1938
Università di Parma

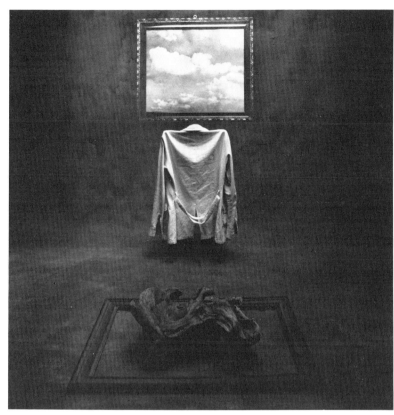

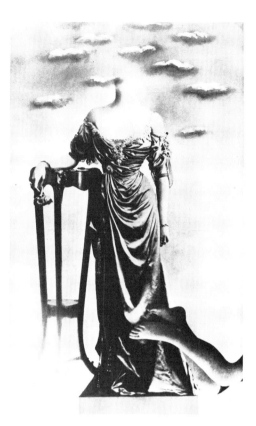

434 Rudolf Lichtsteiner. *Moment. Self-portrait.* 1972
Stiftung für die Photographie. Kunsthaus Zürich

435 Herbert Bayer. *Monument.* 1932
Museum Folkwang. Essen

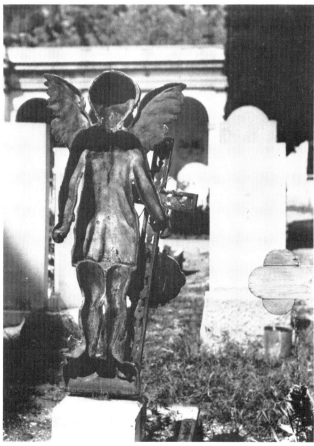

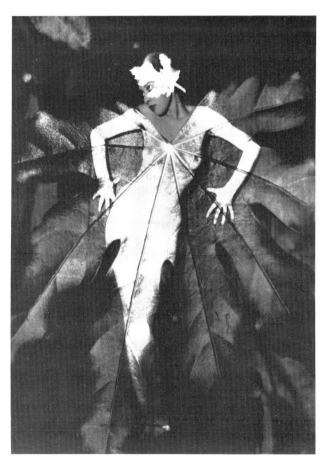

436 Antonio Migliori. From *The Cemeteries.* 1952
Università di Parma

437 Heinz Hajek-Halke. *Nude,* no date
Museum Folkwang, Essen

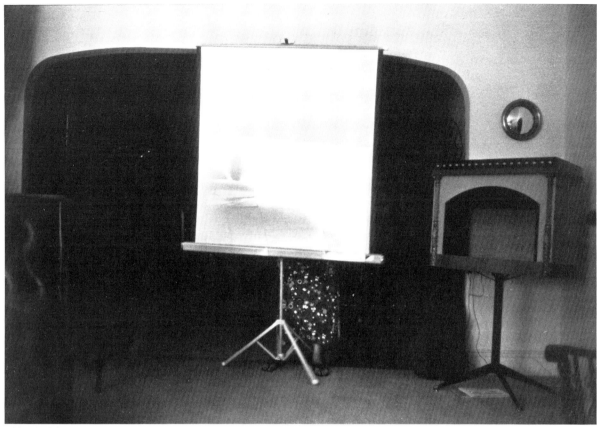

438   Joel Meyerowitz, *New Jersey Home*, 1966
      Museum of Fine Arts, Boston

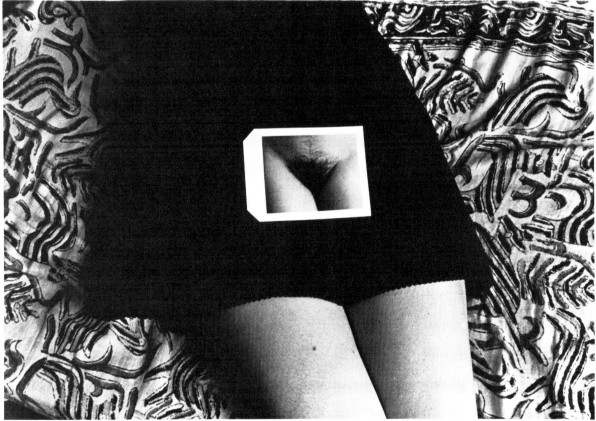

439   Kenneth Josephson, *Polapan*, 1973
      The Art Institute of Chicago

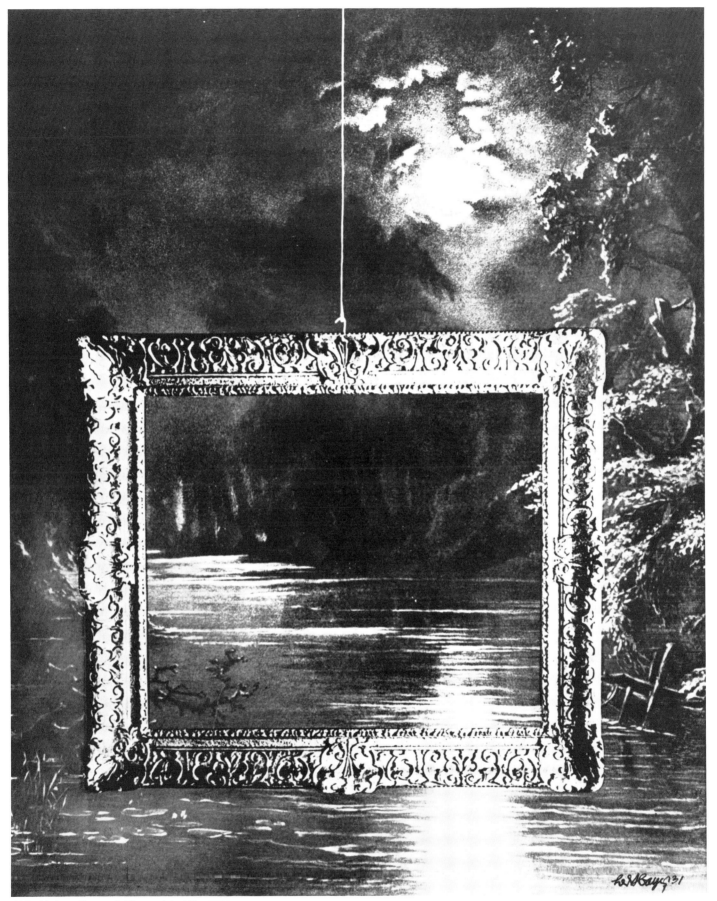

440   Herbert Bayer, *A Glance into Life*, 1931
Museum Folkwang, Essen

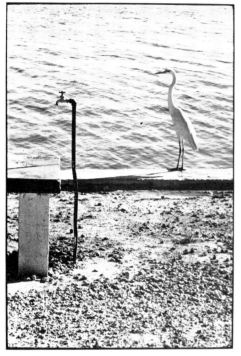

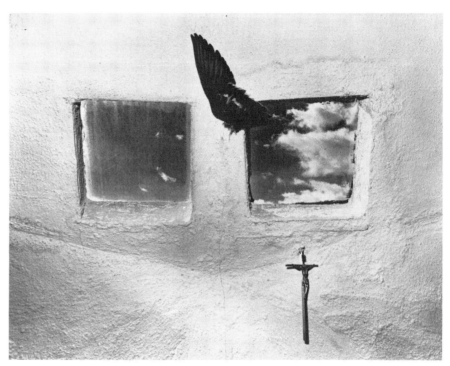

441   Elliot Erwitt, *New York*, 1946
      Bibliothèque Nationale, Paris

442   Ikko, *Sky through Twin Window*, no date
      The Nihon University of Art, Tokyo

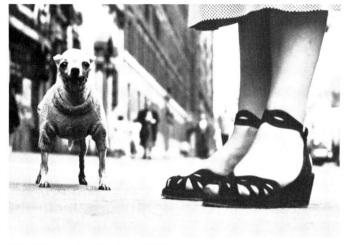

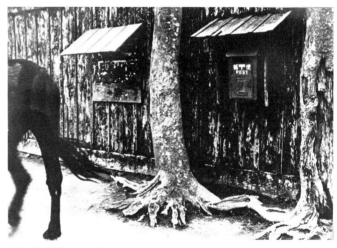

443   Elliot Erwitt, *New York*, 1953
      Bibliothèque Nationale, Paris

444   Ihei Kimura, *Horse*, no date
      The Nihon University of Art, Tokyo

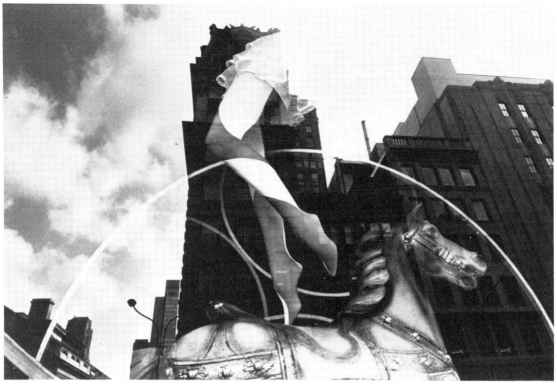

445 Takayuki Ogawa, *Display Window*, no date
The Nihon University of Art, Tokyo

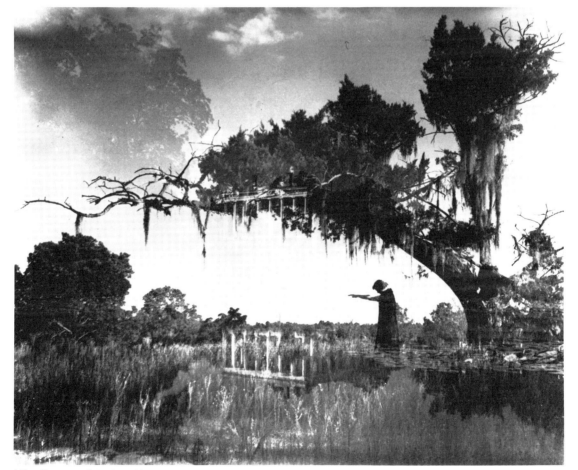

446 Clarence John Laughlin, *Elegy for Moss Land*, 1947
Gernsheim Collection, Austin

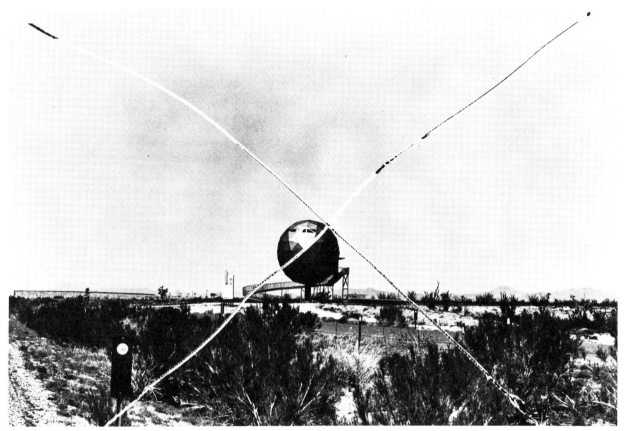

447 Thomas F. Barrow, *Dine Sphere*, 1974
San Francisco Museum of Modern Art

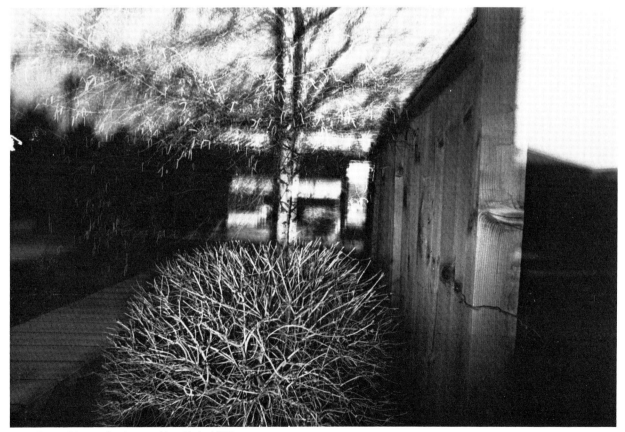

448 Roger Mertin, *Rochester, New York*, 1975
Art Museum, University of New Mexico, Albuquerque

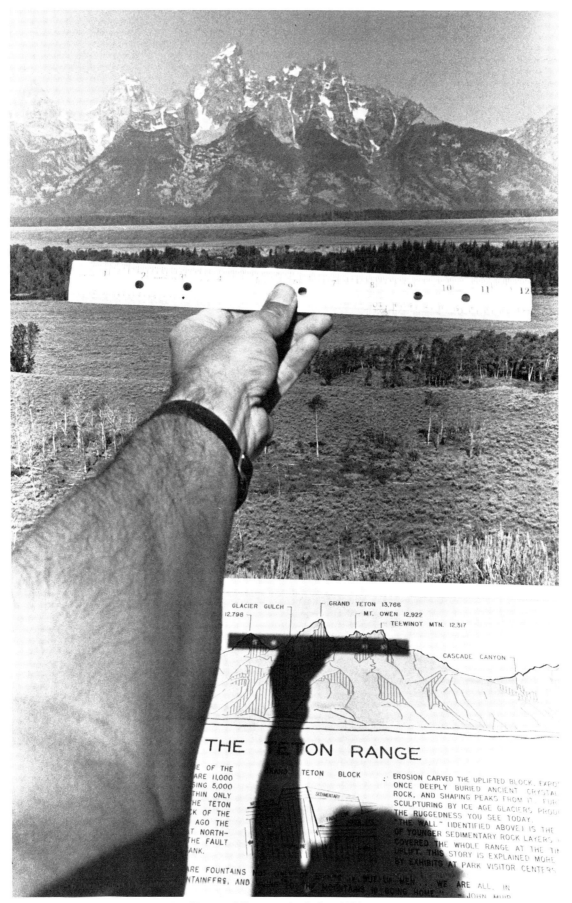

449 Kenneth Josephson, *Wyoming,* History of Photography Series, 1971
Fotografiska Museet, Stockholm

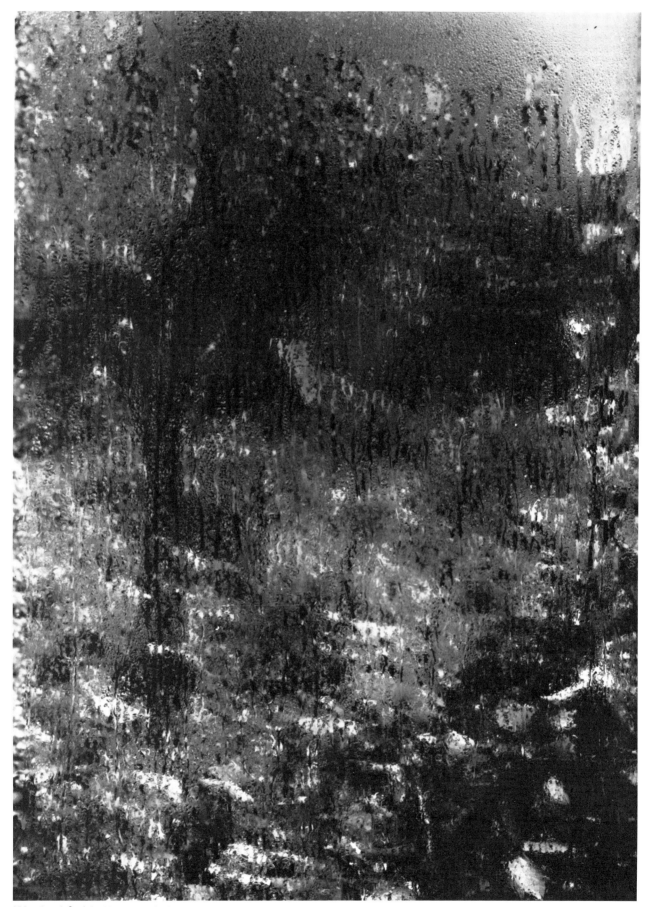

450   Josef Sudek, *Window*, 1944
Uměleckoprůmyslové Muzeum v Praze, Prague

AFTERWORD

Helmut Gernsheim

The trip I took in September 1980 to Cologne to look at my friend's photo-historical exhibit was filled with tense expectation—not without, however, a certain skepticism. Because I had already attended earlier, Photokina shows my recollection of them was, if not precisely of a commercially oriented enterprise, of exhibits that sought to use the various aspects of photography to appeal to a wide audience.

The Imaginary Photo Museum was divided into two sections: Chronology and Analogy. A selection of four hundred fifty vintage prints from thirty-four art museums around the world was displayed on two floors of the Cologne Kunsthalle. Compared to my own retrospective, the emphasis of which had been on the nineteenth century, the primary focus here was on the twentieth. I was impressed by the richness of the material, which came primarily from American collections, and by the organizational achievement of such an undertaking, not to mention the huge insurance sums that must have been involved. Twenty years ago I could have obtained all of this for nothing. If buyers existed at all, they wanted only old material. Most people put the right value on something only if the price is high, the Cologne City Council included. They wouldn't accept my collection as a gift—although it is today valued at 5 million dollars. So, perhaps the many visitors avidly discussing the exhibition were also thinking of the value of what they saw. For today such an exhibit has become every amateur's dream.

The Chronology section unrolled the history of photography as an art form using standard examples. Four large tablets with texts provided information and explanations of the visual experience for viewers.

The unorthodox juxtapositions in the seven subdivisions of the Analogy section provided a delightful as well as inspirational encounter between documentary and creative master-works. But was there a real need to separate Chronology from Analogy? I doubt it. Rather, it seems an admission to the German tendency to philosophize—a touch of complexity which in reality does not exist.

The restful manner in which the photos were displayed, mounted under glass with an invisible center line throughout, heightened the visual pleasure. Subliminally the viewer became aware that each of the rooms, with its palm trees and groups of chairs, was of a slightly different color. This helped prevent the notorious museum monotony.

To an expert the pictorial material was of course more than familiar. A few times I was taken aback when a famous classic seemed to have been intentionally excluded for the sake of a less well known, and perhaps less meaningful, photograph. For the great majority of visitors this material, largely from outside Germany or of emigrant origin, was inevitably unfamiliar. The first impression must have been overwhelming. I am quite certain that the Grubers' Photokina will continue to move people's minds for a long time to come, and it would not be uninteresting to discover why we had to wait twenty years for my Hundred Years of Photography exhibition to receive the affirmation of a second historical show.

Now it has happened and all participants deserve thanks.

Like all earlier and all future historical exhibits, The Imaginary Photo Museum is in every respect a real museum in time, and, according to André Malraux's dictum, this catalogue raisonné is elevated to an actual imaginary photo museum of its own. It maintains the sequence of the visual element and text commentary for everyone who has the ability to glean meaning, content, and joy from these master photographs of bygone times.

The Imaginary Photo Museum—A View of the Exhibition

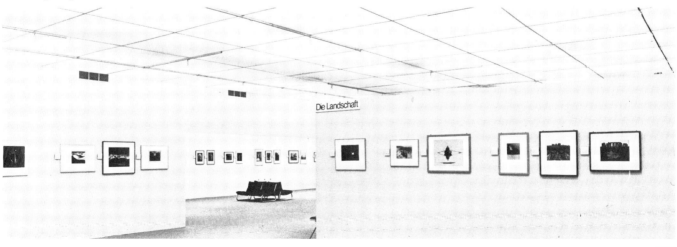

ABOUT THE PHOTOGRAPHERS

Jeane von Oppenheim

The following biographical data corresponds to the selection for the Imaginary Photo Museum exhibition. It contains (where known) the date of birth, other essential biographical information, as well as the photographer's habitats or place of death.

There follows the title of the photograph, the date of its creation (to the best of knowledge), the photographic method used (as supplied by each museum), the name of the lending institution, and a number reference to its reproduction in this book. The captions contain information supplied by the lending institution. In some cases we were able to supplement this information with data of our own.

There follow brief biographies, that is, biographical high points. The numerals therein refer to selected photo-historical publications (see list that follows) containing further information about the respective photographers. Following are designations (P) for photography book, (C) for selected catalogs, and (M) for the last-published monograph that will refer the interested reader to still further materials.

The reproductions in this volume, excepting only those few belonging to the authors, were made from reproductions which the lending institutions kindly made available to us. We therefore thank everyone who gave us permission to reproduce.

List of selected books:

1. **Wolfgang Baier,** Geschichte der Photographie. Munich: 1977
2. **Cecil Beaton and Gail Buckland,** The Magic Image. London: 1975
3. **André Jammes,** The First Century of Photography. Chicago: 1977
4. **Beaumont and Nancy Newhall,** Masters of Photography. New York: 1958
5. **Fritz Kempe,** Photographie. Hamburg: 1977
6. **Marilies von Brevern,** Künstlerische Photographie. Berlin: 1971
7. **Helmut Gernsheim,** Creative Photography. New York: 1960
8. **Ute Eskildsen/Jan-Christopher Horak,** Film und Foto. Stuttgart: 1979
9. **Peter Pollack,** Picture History of Photography. New York: 1977
10. **Valerie Lloyd,** Photography: The first eighty years. London: 1976
11. **Weston Naef,** The Collection of Alfred Stieglitz. New York: 1978
12. **Lee Witkin,** The Photograph Collector's Guide. New York: 1979
13. **Caude Nori,** La Photographie Française. Paris: 1978
14. **Margaret F. Harker,** The Linked Ring. London: 1979
15. **Bernard Marbot, Jean-Pierre Seguin, Weston J. Naef,** Regards sur la Photographie en France au XIXe Siècle. Paris and New York: 1980
16. **Beaumont Newhall,** Photography: Essays and Images. New York: 1980

Concerning special printing methods, pertinent information is contained in: Frank Heidtmann, Kunstphotographische Edeldruckverfahren Heute. Berlin: 1978.

Abbot, Berenice
1898 Springfield, Ohio—Abbotsville, Maine—

Murray Hill Hotel Spiral, 1935
The Art Institute of Chicago
Rep. 98

N.Y.C., Changing New York, 1937
The Art Institute of Chicago
Rep. 350

News Building, 1938
The Art Institute of Chicago
Rep. 371

Studies art in New York, Berlin, Paris—assistant to Man Ray—after 1926, her own portrait studio—acquaintance with Atget—in 1929, together with Julien Levy, brings Atget's estate to New York—documentaries about New York City (*Changing New York*, 1939)—teaching and book publications.

2, 8, 9, 12
P, M: New York 1970

Adam-Salomon, Antoine Samuel
1811—France—1881

Charles Garnier, 1865
Bibliothèque Nationale, Paris
Rep. 289

Sculptor—studies photography with Franz Hanfstaengl in Munich—portrait photographer since 1858—achieves international recognition with the Paris Exhibition of 1867—his portraits published in a portfolio of seven volumes (*Galerie des Contemporains*).

7, 15
C: Detroit 1963

Adams, Ansel
1902—San Francisco—Carmel, California—

Hulls, 1933
San Francisco Museum of Modern Art
Rep. 80

Lone Pine Peak, Mount Whitney, Sierra Nevada, California, 1944
George Eastman House, Rochester
Rep. 259

Moonrise over Hernandez, 1947
George Eastman House, Rochester
Rep. 101

House with Fence, 1948
San Francisco Museum of Modern Art
Rep. 247

Small House in Mountain, 1950
San Francisco Museum of Modern Art
Rep. 257

For more than fifty years taking the best known landscape photos of the American West—a master of lighting and development techniques—co-founder of the group f/64 (representatives of a new stylistic direction in 1932)—1946 founder of the first photography department of the California School of Fine Arts—conducts workshops for young photographers.

2, 4, 7, 9, 10, 11, 12, 16
P, M: London 1981

Albert, Josef
1825—Bavaria—1886

Ludwig II of Bavaria and his Bride, 1867
Münchner Stadtmuseum, Munich
Rep. 340

Bavarian court photographer—German inventor of the collotype process, 1867—color prints, 1870.

1
M: Munich 1977

Alinari, Giuseppe and Leopoldo
1836—Florence—1890
?—Florence—1865

Album of Flowers and Fruit, containing 106 photographs showing various techniques, 1861
Fondazione Fratelli Alinari, Florence
Rep. 5, 6

Founders of family business—active as professional photographers—their architectural photos and portraits constitute the largest photo documentation of the nineteenth century in Italy.

M: London 1878

Andriesse, Emmy
1914—The Hague—Amsterdam 1953

Juliet Greco, 1950
Stedelijk Museum, Amsterdam
Rep. 281

Negroes, 1950
Stedelijk Museum, Amsterdam
Rep. 400

Studies with Schuitema and Kiljan 1932–1937—freelance after 1937—becomes well known with her photographs of the 1947 winter of famine in Holland.

Arbus, Diane
1925—New York—1971

A Young Man in Curlers at Home on West 20th Street New York, 1956
San Francisco Museum of Modern Art
Rep. 123

Christmas Tree, 1962
San Francisco Museum of Modern Art
Rep. 376

Patriotic Boy with Straw Hat, Button and Flag, Waiting to March in a Pro-War-Parade, N.Y.C., 1967
San Francisco Museum of Modern Art
Rep. 316

Studies photography with Lisette Model—works with her husband as a fashion photographer in a department store—in the 1950s starts to photograph figures leading marginal existences in New York City—commits suicide in 1971—photos exhibited posthumously at The Museum of Modern Art, New York, start of worldwide recognition.

2, 9, 12
M: Millerton 1972

Atget, Eugène
1857 Libourne near Bordeaux, France—Paris 1927

Gif—Old Farmhouse, 1924
The Museum of Modern Art, New York
Rep. 84

Avenue des Gobelins, 1925
The Museum of Modern Art, New York
Rep. 82

Saint Cloud, 1926
The Museum of Modern Art, New York
Rep. 83

Sells photographs as models for artists—complete documentation of Paris (architectural sights, parks, monuments, display windows, streets)—posthumously gains recognition, due to efforts of photographer Berenice Abbott and the American collector Julien Levy.

1, 2, 3, 4, 7, 8, 9, 12, 15, 16
P, M: New York and London 1980

Avedon, Richard
1923 New York—

Brigitte Bardot, 1959
Museum Ludwig, Cologne
Rep. 339

John Ford, 1972
Museum für Kunst und Gewerbe, Hamburg
Rep. 136

Self-taught—during World War II takes identity card photos for the navy—studies with Alexey Brodovitch—makes his career with magazines as fashion photographer first at *Harper's Bazaar*, then at *Vogue*—recently exhibits and publishes portraits of famous personalities.

2, 9, 12
P, M: New York 1980

Babbit, Platt D.
?—U.S.A.—ca. 1870

Group at Niagara Falls, ca. 1855
Daguerreotype
George Eastman House, Rochester
Rep. 3

Made daguerreotypes of tourists—working on the American side of Niagara Falls.

7

Baldus, Edouard-Denis
1820 Westphalia—France 1882

Marseille, ca. 1858
Albumen print
Gernsheim Collection, Austin
Rep. 34

Paris, Le Louvre, 1860
Albumen print
Bibliothèque Nationale, Paris
Rep. 346

Painter—commissioned by the Comité des Monuments Historiques to photograph architecture in France (the Louvre and the city of Arles, first industrial landscapes—railroad

lines, bridges)—co-founder of the Société Héliographique.

3, 7, 10, 12, 15

Baltz, Lewis
1945—Newport Beach, California—

South Wall PlastX, 350 Lear, Costa Mesa, 1974 (on permanent loan to the Art Museum, University of New Mexico, Albuquerque, New Mexico)
Art Museum, University of New Mexico, Albuquerque
Rep. 364

Studies art at the San Francisco Art Institute—scholarships for photography from 1973 to 1976—teaching—publications in photography books and portfolios.

12
P, C: Lincoln, Nebraska 1967
M: New York 1980

Barnard, George N.
1819—Onondaga, New York—1902

Buen-Ventura, Savannah, Georgia, 1865
Albumen print
The Library of Congress, Washington, D.C.
Rep. 262

Ruins in Columbia, South Carolina, 1865
Albumen print
The Library of Congress, Washington, D.C.
Rep. 40

Ruins of Pickney Mansion, Charleston, South Carolina, 1865
Albumen print
The Library of Congress, Washington, D.C.
Rep. 353

Assistant to Mathew Brady—publishes photos of General Sherman's march during the American Civil War—becomes known also as a daguerreotypist.

9, 10, 12
M: New York 1977

Barrow, Thomas F.
1928 Kansas City, Missouri—

Dine Sphere, from the series entitled *Cancellations*, 1974
San Francisco Museum of Modern Art
Rep. 447

Studies life drawing and film—after 1965 student of Aaron Siskind—former curator and assistant director of the George Eastman House—professor of photography at the University of New Mexico.

12
M: Lincoln, Nebraska 1977

Bauret, Jean-François
1932—France—Paris—

Woman and Child (nudes), 1971
Bibliothèque Nationale, Paris
Rep. 216

Advertising photographer—particular interest in photographing the nude as a sociological study.

13

Bayard, Hippolyte
1801 Breteuil-sur-Noye—Nemours 1887

Hippolyte Bayard in His Garden, 1845–1847
Calotype-negative
Société Française de Photographie, Paris
Rep. 4

Photographic experiments before 1839—makes the first negative, then positives on paper, exhibited in June 1839.

1, 2, 3, 7, 12
M: Lucerne 1976

Bayer, Herbert
1900—Haag, Austria—Montecito, California—

A Glance into Life, 1931
Photomontage
Museum Folkwang, Essen
Rep. 440

Lonely City Dweller, 1932
Photomontage
Museum Folkwang, Essen
Rep. 70

Monument, 1932
Photomontage
Museum Folkwang, Essen
Rep. 435

Self-portrait, 1932
Photomontage

Museum Folkwang, Essen
Rep. 318

Student and teacher of Bauhaus—active in many artistic fields, especially in typography, advertising graphics, photomontage—works on the exhibition *Deutscher Werkbund*, Paris, 1930—emigrates to America in the 1930s—active in many aspects of advertising, graphics, and architecture.

8
P, C: Los Angeles 1977
M: Ravensburg 1967

Beato, Felice A.
?—Venice 1885

Bragière Sikhs, 1857
Det kongelige Bibliotek, Copenhagen
Rep. 298

The Sphinx and Pyramid of Cheops in Distance, 1865
Albumen print
Gernsheim Collection, Austin
Rep. 27

British citizen—in partnership with James Robertson—publishes photos of foreign countries in 1852—active in Russia, India, Palestine, China, Japan.

2, 3, 7, 10, 12

Beaton, Sir Cecil
1904 London—Salisbury, England 1979

Nana Beaton, ca. 1925
Museum Ludwig, Cologne
Rep. 303

Lady Oxford, 1927
Victoria and Albert Museum, London
Rep. 73

Salvador Dali, 1935
Museum Ludwig, Cologne
Rep. 319

Dr. Roy Strong, no date
National Portrait Gallery, London
Rep. 336

Multifaceted artist, stage and costume designer (*My Fair Lady*)—fashion photographer (*Vogue* magazine) and photographer (World War II)—does portraits of the British royal family, of society and artistic personalities.

2, 7, 8, 9, 12
P, M: New York 1972

Becher, Bernd and Hilla
1931—Siegen—Düsseldorf—
1934—Potsdam, Düsseldorf, and New York—

Typology from the series *Half-timbered Buildings from the Industrial Region of Siegen, 1959–1974,* 1959
Museum Ludwig, Cologne
Rep. 135

Bernd Becher: Studies at the Kunstakademie Stuttgart and Düsseldorf—after 1976 professor of photography at the Staatlichen Kunstakademie, Düsseldorf.

Hilla Becher: Studies photography in Potsdam. Collaboration since 1959 in and outside Germany—known for her typologies (documentation of industrial and apartment buildings).

12
C: Eindhofen 1981
P, M: Munich 1977

Bedford, Francis
1816—England—1894

Prince of Wales, Karnak, 1862
Det kongelige Bibliotek, Copenhagen
Rep. 23

Publishes numerous photographic sights of cities and villages in England and Wales in the form of stereoscopic cards—co-founder of The Royal Photographic Society of Great Britain.

7, 10, 12
P, M: Munich 1977

Bellocq, E.J.
1873—U.S.A.—1949

Nude, ca. 1912
Het Sterckshof Museum, Antwerp
Rep. 232

Professional photographer in New Orleans, Louisiana (ca. 1895–1940)—glass negatives of the Storyville region of New Orleans discovered after his death—known for photographs of prostitutes.

12
M: New York 1970

Biermann, Änne
1898 Goch/Niederrhein—Gera 1933

Piano, no date
Kunstbibliothek Preussischer Kulturbesitz, Berlin
Rep. 78 a–c

Educated as a pianist—self-taught photographer known in Germany as representative of the new style—participates in the film and photo exhibition of 1929—approximately five thousand photos confiscated in Trieste in 1937 and considered lost—monograph written by Franz Roh in 1930.

6, 8

Bischof, Werner
1916 Zürich—Peru 1954

Hungary, 1947
Museum Ludwig, Cologne
Rep. 279

Bihar, India, 1951
Stiftung für die Photographie, Kunsthaus Zürich
Rep. 106

Studies photography with Hans Finsler at the Kunstgewerbeschule, Zürich—freelance photographer from 1936, experimental photography—founder-member of the Magnum-Photos group—photos in international journals, books, and exhibitions—pictorial reports about Europe, the Far East and America—accidental death on assignment in Peruvian Andes.

2, 7, 9
C: New York 1968
P, M: Lucerne 1973

Bisson, Louis-Auguste and Auguste-Rosalie
1814 France—1876
1826 France—1900

Savoie 44, The Crevice, ca. 1860
Bibliothèque Nationale, Paris
Rep. 33

Belltower, Pisa, ca. 1860
Albumen print
Gernsheim Collection, Austin
Rep. 357

Daguerreotypist until 1851, Paris—expert in wet collodion process—takes first photos of Alpine peaks.

2, 3, 7, 9, 10, 12, 15
P

Boubat, Edouard
1923 Paris—

Child with a Coat of Leaves, 1947
Museum Folkwang, Essen
Rep. 113

Madras, 1971
Museum Folkwang, Essen
Rep. 392

Typesetter, designer, and typographer—reproduction photographer 1942 to 1945—freelance photographer from 1945—photojournalism trips—organizes exhibitions.

2, 12
P, M: Paris 1981

Bourke-White, Margaret
1904 New York—Connecticut 1971

Life magazine's first cover, *Fort Peck Dam, Montana*, 1936
The Art Institute of Chicago
Rep. 97

Mahatma Gandhi, Spinning, 1946
The Art Institute of Chicago
Rep. 297

A Mile Underground, 1950
The Art Institute of Chicago
Rep. 401

Studies photography with Clarence H. White—industrial photos for *Fortune* magazine—photojournalist from 1936 until 1957 for *Life* magazine (the first cover photo, November 23, 1936)—pictorial reports from Europe, Asia, and America.

2, 9, 12
P, M: Greenwich 1972

Brady, Mathew B.
1823—New York—1896

Ruins of Richmond, 1865
Albumen print
The Museum of Modern Art, New York
Rep. 41

Daguerreotypist, student of Samuel Morse and John Draper—first publication in 1850 *(Gallery of Illustrious Americans)*—documentation about the American Civil War (uncertain, however, whether all photos are his or whether some made by colleagues Alexander Gardner and Timothy O'Sullivan).

1, 2, 5, 9, 12
C: Washington, D.C. 1961
M: New York 1977

Brandt, Bill
1904 London—

Looking for Coal, 1936
Museum Ludwig, Cologne
Rep. 94

Stonehenge, 1947
Museum Ludwig, Cologne
Rep. 270

Nude, 1953
New print
Fotografiska Museet, Stockholm
Rep. 129

Nude in a Room, 1961
Museum Ludwig, Cologne
Rep. 224

Self-taught—studies with Man Ray—during the 1930s photojournalism and portraits of all classes of British society—photographs of nudes from special perspectives.

2, 7, 9, 12
P, M: London and New York 1977

Brassaï (Gyula Halász)
1899 Brasso, Siebenbürgen—Paris—

Salvador Dali, 1932
Bibliothèque Nationale, Paris
Rep. 321

In Paris, 1933
Museum Ludwig, Cologne
Rep. 91

Nude, 1934
Bibliothèque Nationale, Paris
Rep. 227

Backstage at the Opera, 1938
Bibliothèque Nationale, Paris
Rep. 396

Woman with Dog, no date
Het Sterckshof Museum, Antwerp
Rep. 413

Studies painting in Budapest and Berlin—moves to Paris in 1923—photos of Paris night life first published in 1933.

2, 7, 9, 12, 16
P, M: Frankfurt 1977

Bravo, Manuel Alvarez
1902 Mexico City—

The Stooped, 1934
The Art Institute of Chicago
Rep. 95

A Good Reputation, 1938
Bibliothèque Nationale, Paris
Rep. 233

Studies painting and music—as freelance photographer specializes in the reproduction of works of art—particular interest in the Mexican people and their culture.

2, 12
C: Boston and Washington, D.C. 1978
M: London 1981

Bruguière, Francis
1880 San Francisco—1945 London

Daphne, 1915
The Library of Congress, Washington, D.C.
Rep. 213

Skyscrapers, 1920
Het Sterckshof Museum, Antwerp
Rep. 351

Studies painting in Europe—becomes acquainted with Alfred Stieglitz in New York—studies photography with Frank Eugene—member of Photo Secession—also active as a film producer in the 1920s—one of the first photographers to do abstract photography.

8, 12
P, M: New York 1977

Bullock, Wynn (Percy Wingfield Bullock)
1902—Chicago—1976

Child in Forest, 1954
San Francisco Museum of Modern Art
Rep. 222

Trains as a singer in New York—visits Europe from 1928 until 1931—active in a variety of professions until 1948—moves to Monterey, California, in 1945—active as freelance and commercial photographer until 1968—photographs nudes in natural surroundings.

2, 12
P, M: Millerton 1976

Burchartz, Max
1887 Wuppertal—1961 Essen

Rollmops, no date
Kunstbibliothek Preussischer Kulturbesitz, Berlin
Rep. 195

Studies art in Düsseldorf from 1906 until 1909—acquaintance with the Bauhaus, around 1921—professor of applied art at the Folkwangschule—teaches photography, typography, and advertising until 1933—in 1949 is called back to the Folkwangschule—publishes books on the teaching of art.

6
C: London 1978

Burri, René
1933 Zürich

Che Guevara, 1963
Stiftung für die Photographie, Kunsthaus Zürich
Rep. 313

Studies with Hans Fisler at the Kunstgewerbeschule, Zürich—works on films—exhibition—makes documentary films in 1952 with Walt Disney—since 1953 also active as a photojournalist—publications in international journals.

P, C: Teufen 1974

Callahan, Harry
1912 Detroit—

Weed against Sky, 1948
New print
Fotografiska Museet, Stockholm
Rep. 108

Eleanor, 1948
Museum of Fine Arts, Boston
Rep. 235

Studies engineering—self-taught photographer (after 1926)—teacher at the New Bauhaus, Chicago—professor of photography and department head at the Rhode Island School of Design until 1979.

2, 8, 12
M: New York 1980

Callis, Jo Ann
1940 Cincinnati—

Man at Table, 1977
San Francisco Museum of Modern Art
Rep. 168

Studies photography at the University of California, Los Angeles—exhibition 1978—teaches at the California Institute of the Arts—participates in international exhibitions.

C: Lincoln, Nebraska 1977

Cameron, Julia Margaret
1815—Calcutta—London—Ceylon 1879

Sir John Herschel, 1867
Kunstbibliotek Preussischer Kulturbesitz, Berlin
Rep. 310

Sir Henry Taylor, 1867
Albumen print
Gernsheim Collection, Austin
Rep. 25

The Mountain Nymph, Sweet Liberty, 1870
Albumen print
The Royal Photographic Society of Great Britain, Bath
Rep. 24

Pomona (Alice Liddell), ca. 1872
Albumen print
The Royal Photographic Society of Great Britain, Bath
Rep. 338

Untitled (Girl), no date
The Royal Photographic Society of Great Britain, Bath
Rep. 278

Takes first photos at age forty-eight—amateur photographer—makes portraits of well-known contemporaries in England—develops own style (influenced by Pre-Raphaelite paintings), preferring aesthetic effect to technical perfection.

1, 2, 3, 4, 5, 6, 7, 9, 10, 11, 12, 14, 16
P, M: Millerton 1975

Capa, Robert (Andrej Friedmann)
1913 Budapest—Paris—1954 Thai-Binh, Indochina

Falling Spanish Soldier, 1936
Stedelijk Museum, Amsterdam
Rep. 419

D-Day, 1944
Stedelijk Museum, Amsterdam
Rep. 102

D-Day, Plus One: The Dead on Normandy Beach, 1944
Stedelijk Museum, Amsterdam
Rep. 421

Studies in Berlin 1931—emigrates to Paris in 1933—war photojournalist from Spain, China, Europe, Southeast Asia—founder of Magnum Photos group—dies accidentally while covering the war in Indochina.

2, 9
M: New York 1974

Caponigro, Paul
1932 Boston, Massachusetts—Santa Fé, New Mexico—

Stonehenge, 1967
The Art Institute of Chicago
Rep. 272

Creek and Trees, 1968
San Francisco Museum of Modern Art
Rep. 124

Briefly studies medicine at Boston University ca. 1950—assistant to a commercial photographer 1953 until 1958—studies photography with Minor White, among others—teaching—guest lecturer at numerous American institutions—specializes in nature photography.

2, 9, 12, 15
M: Millerton 1972

Carjat, Etienne
1828 Fariens, France—Paris 1906

Giacomo Rossini, from *Galerie des Contemporains,* ca. 1870
Carbon print
Münchner Stadtmuseum, Munich
Rep. 19

Caricaturist and writer—portrays prominent personalities from 1855 until ca. 1875.

1, 2, 7, 9, 10, 12, 15

Carroll, Lewis, pseud. (Charles Lutwidge Dodgson)
1832 Cheshire—Guilford, England 1898

Alexandra (Xie) Kitchin, 1876
Gernsheim Collection, Austin
Rep. 275

Cleric, author of children's books (*Alice in Wonderland*), and amateur photographer, 1856 until 1880—chief interest: children's portraits.

2, 7, 9, 10, 12
P, M: New York 1976

Cartier-Bresson, Henri
1908 Chanteloup, France—Paris—

Lunch by the Marne, 1938
Museum Ludwig, Cologne
Rep. 96

Seine Bargeman, 1957
Museum Ludwig, Cologne
Rep. 416

China, 1958
Bibliothèque Nationale, Paris
Rep. 418

Studies painting 1927–1928—takes photographs after 1931 (photojournalism on Mexico, New York, Spain)—first exhibition with Julien Levy in New York in 1932—studies film with Paul Strand—works on films with Jean Renoir 1936 to 1939—documentary films and photojournalism of World War II—flees in 1943 from German prisoner-of-war camp—documents German occupation and retreat from France—co-founder of the Magnum Photos group in 1946—visits the Orient—in 1954, is the first Western photographer to receive permission to take photos in the Soviet Union—devotes most recent years to drawing.

2, 4, 7, 9, 12, 16
P, M: Lucerne 1981

Chargesheimer (Carl Heinz Hargesheimer)
1924—Cologne—1972

Konrad Adenauer, 1956
Museum Ludwig, Cologne
Rep. 121

August Sander, 1956
The Museum of Modern Art, New York
Rep. 295

Self-taught—works as a scenic designer and director in the theater—creates first surrealistic photomontages and light experiments without camera—took photographs of Cologne, the Rhineland and Ruhr region in the 1950s—publishes photography books—freelance photographer, well known for unusual portraits of artists and politicians.

P

Coburn, Alvin Langdon
1882 Boston—Colwyn Bay, Wales 1966

St. Paul's from the River, before 1910
Photogravure
The Royal Photographic Society of Great Britain, Bath
Rep. 361

Thames Embankment by Night, ca. 1905–1910
Photogravure
The Royal Photographic Society of Great Britain, Bath
Rep. 58

New York Ferry, 1910
Photogravure
The Royal Photographic Society of Great Britain, Bath
Rep. 362

Vortograph, 1917
George Eastman House, Rochester
Rep. 67

Studies art—in Europe in 1900—co-founder of Photo Secession in 1902—multi-talented photographer (abstractions, photogravures)—publishes photos in *Camera Work*—portraits of prominent English and French personalities in *Men of Mark*, 1913, and *More Men of Mark*, 1922—organizes exhibition of old masters of photography at the Albright Art Gallery, Buffalo, N.Y., 1916.

1, 2, 5, 6, 7, 9, 10, 12, 14, 16
P, M: Boston 1980

Cohen, Mark
1943 Wilkes-Barre, Pennsylvania—

Untitled, no date
Art Museum, University of New Mexico, Albuquerque
Rep. 269

University from 1961 until 1965—opens own commercial photo studio in 1969—teaching and exhibitions.

12

Cosindas, Marie
1925 Boston—

Sailors, Key West, 1965
Museum of Fine Arts, Boston
Rep. 170

Louise Nevelson, 1974
Museum of Fine Arts, Boston
Rep. 171

Studies art in Boston—starts to take photographs at the end of the 1950s—specialization in portraits and still lifes with instamatic color photography.

2, 9, 12
P, M: Boston 1978

Cunningham, Imogen
1883 Portland, Oregon—San Francisco 1976

Nude, 1928
Museum Folkwang, Essen
Rep. 225

Martha Graham, 1931
San Francisco Museum of Modern Art
Rep. 307

Two Callas, ca. 1948
The Art Institute of Chicago
Rep. 111

The Unmade Bed, 1954
Museum Folkwang, Essen
Rep. 183

First photographs 1901—learns fine printing under Edward Curtis (1907 to 1909)—after attending university in Germany opens a portrait studio in Seattle, Washington, in 1910—moves to San Francisco in 1917—specializes in photographing plants from 1922 until 1929—member of the group f/64, 1932—receives Guggenheim fellowship in 1970—one of the longest and most influential careers in the history of American photography.

2, 8, 12, 16
M: Boston 1979

Curtis, Edward Sheriff
1868 Wisconsin—Los Angeles 1952

Lahla (Willow) Taos, 1905
Photogravure
Art Museum, University of New Mexico, Albuquerque
Rep. 327

Chaiwa-Tewa-Profile, 1921
Photogravure
Art Museum, University of New Mexico, Albuquerque
Rep. 59

Moves to Seattle, 1887—opens a photo studio there—in 1896 begins his North American Indian tribes documentation—financing by J. Pierpont Morgan makes possible the publication of his entire work in 1930, including both text volumes and volumes containing 2200 photogravures.

2, 10, 12
P, M: Washington 1980

Davidson, Bruce
1933 Oak Park, Illinois—Paris—New York—

Untitled (Man and Boy), no date
The Art Institute of Chicago
Rep. 118

London Life, 1964
The Art Institute of Chicago
Rep. 415

Studies photogravure at Rochester Institute of Technology 1953–1956—active as a freelance photographer in Paris and New York.

2, 9, 12
P, M: New York 1980

Davison, George
1856 London—Antibes 1930

Group at Ferry House, 1888
Kodak Museum, Harrow
Rep. 44

Near Portmadoc, 1920
Kodak Museum, Harrow
Rep. 252

Civil and amateur photographer—co-founder of the Linked Ring (1892)—leading director with Kodak, Ltd. (1889 to 1912)—later active in the British anarchist movement.

1, 2, 7, 11, 14

Day, F. Holland
1864—Norwood, Massachusetts—1933

Mother and Child, ca. 1905
Platinum print
The Library of Congress, Washington, D.C.
Rep. 324

Young Man in Checkered Cap, no date
Offset
The Library of Congress, Washington, D.C.
Rep. 332

Nude Youth, no date
Platinum print
The Library of Congress, Washington, D.C.
Rep. 240

Well-educated, eccentric artist—founds his own publishing house—spends time in Europe with Coburn—supports art photography at the start of the American Photo Secession—member of the Linked Ring, London 1896—organizes exhibition of American photography at The Royal Photographic Society, London 1900 (a third of it his own work).

2, 11, 12, 14
C: Boston 1981

De Meyer, Baron Adolf Gayne (Adolf Meyer)
1868 Dresden—London—Hollywood, California 1949

Woman and Lilies, no date
Platinum print
The Library of Congress, Washington, D.C.
Rep. 286

Marriage to the Prince of Wales' illegitimate daughter—afterward calls himself Baron A. de Meyer-Watson—member of the Linked Ring—publications in *Camera Work*—exhibits in Stieglitz's Photo Secession gallery—fashion photographer.

2, 5, 10, 12, 14
M: Paris 1980

Demachy, Robert
1859 St. Germain-en-Lye/Paris—Hennequeville, France 1936

Study (The Letter), no date
Oil print
The Royal Photographic Society of Great Britain, Bath
Rep. 53

Untitled, ca. 1900
Société Française de Photographie, Paris
Rep. 328

Untitled (Nude), ca. 1900
Oil print
Société Française de Photographie, Paris
Rep. 214

Perplexity, 1906
Oil print
The Royal Photographic Society of Great Britain, Bath
Rep. 229

Photographer since 1892—publishes in *Camera Work* on technical and esthetic aspects—representative of French art photography.

2, 5, 7, 9, 10, 11, 12, 14
P, M: Paris 1981

Divola, John M.
1949 Santa Monica, California—

From the *Zuma Series, No. 3,* 1977
San Francisco Museum of Modern Art
Rep. 164

Attends university in California—teaches after 1972—specializes in color photography.

Doisneau, Robert
1912 Gentilly, France—Paris—

Coalman and Newlyweds, 1948
Bibliothèque Nationale, Paris
Rep. 103

Monsieur and Madame Garafino, Clochards, 1952
Bibliothèque Nationale, Paris
Rep. 405

The Windowshopper, no date
Het Sterckshof Museum, Antwerp
Rep. 397

Trained lithographer and painter—industrial and advertising photographer—photojournalism in leading international newspapers after the end of World War II.

2, 9, 12
P, M: Paris 1981

Domon, Ken
1909 Yamagata, Japan—

Miyawaki Fan Shop, 1960
Shadai Gallery, Tokyo
Rep. 162

Waterfall, 1967
Shadai Gallery, Tokyo
Rep. 143

Katsura Rikyu, Kyoto, 1974
Shadai Gallery, Tokyo
Rep. 161

Photojournalism on Japanese life.

P, C: New York 1974

D'Ora, Madame (Dora Kallmus)
1881 Vienna—France 1963

Anna Pavlova, 1913
Museum für Kunst und Gewerbe, Hamburg
Rep. 301

Student of Nicola Perscheid in Berlin—society
photographer in Vienna in the 1920s and
1930s.

5
M: (with Benda and Perscheid) Hamburg 1980

Drtikol, Frantisek
1883 Pribram—Prague 1961

Nude, 1929
Pigment print
Uměleckoprůmyslové Muzeum v Praze,
Prague
Rep. 236

The Imaginary Photograph, no date
Uměleckoprůmyslové Muzeum v Praze,
Prague
Rep. 220

Studies at the Lehr und Versuchsanstalt für
Photographie in Munich—teaches in Czechoslovakia—specializes in photos of nudes, light
abstractions, and portraits of artists—painter
since 1935.

2
P

Dührkoop, Rudolf
1848—Hamburg—1918

*Elena Luksch-Makowsky with Her Children,
Peter and Andreas*, ca. 1910
Pigment print

Museum für Kunst und Gewerbe, Hamburg
Rep. 50

Self-taught—opens a photo studio in Hamburg
in 1883—master of photogravure—representative of art photography.

5, 6, 14

Eggleston, William
1941 Memphis, Tennessee—

Sumner, Mississippi, 1969–1970
Dye transfer
The Museum of Modern Art, New York
Rep. 173

Memphis, 1969–1970
Dye transfer
The Museum of Modern Art, New York
Rep. 157

Representative of the new American color realism—photographs in the American South.

12
P, M: New York 1976

Eisenstaedt, Alfred
1898 Dirschau, West Prussia—New York
City—

Toscanini in Bayreuth, 1932
Münchner Stadtmuseum, Munich
Rep. 90

Grows up in Berlin—one of the pioneers of
photojournalism in Germany at the end of the
1920s (*Berliner Illustrirte*)—emigrates to New
York in 1935, works for *Life* magazine from
1936.

2, 9, 12
P, M: London and Washington 1980

Elsken, Ed van der
1925 Amsterdam—Edam—

Africa, 1957
Stedelijk Museum, Amsterdam
Rep. 402

St. Germain, ca. 1952
Stedelijk Museum, Amsterdam
Rep. 122

International photojournalism and films of social criticism.

9
P

Emerson, Peter Henry
1856 Cuba—London 1936

Gathering Waterlilies, 1885
Platinum print
George Eastman House, Rochester
Rep. 273

A Stiff Pull, 1890
Platinum print
Kodak Museum, Harrow
Rep. 43

Doctor and writer—acclaimed as photographer since 1885—works in platinum prints or
photogravure (English country life in Norfolk
Broadland)—in 1887 he gives Stieglitz his first
international prize—his 1889 publication *Naturalistic Photography* creates a considerable
stir.

1, 2, 4, 7, 9, 10, 12, 14, 16
P, M: Millerton 1975

Erfurth, Hugo
1874 Halle—Dresden—Cologne—Gaienhov-
en/Bodensee 1948

Mother Ey, 1934
Agfa-Gevaert Foto-Historama, Leverkusen
Rep. 86

Käthe Kollwitz, 1935
Deutsche Gesellschaft für Photographie,
Cologne
Rep. 309

Fritz Schumacher, no date
Agfa-Gevaert Foto-Historama, Leverkusen
Rep. 290

Studies photography in Dresden—founder of
the Gesellschaft Deutscher Lichtbildner in
1919—moves to Cologne in 1934—leading
portrait photographer of intellectual and artistic
personalities—specialist in fine printing methods.

1, 2, 3, 5, 7, 8
M: Seebruck 1977

Erwitt, Elliott
1928 Paris—New York—

New York, 1946
Bibliothèque Nationale, Paris
Rep. 441

New York, 1953
Bibliothèque Nationale, Paris
Rep. 443

Grows up in California—lives in New York after 1948—specializes in photojournalism, advertising photography, and photographs of architecture.

2, 9, 12
P, M: New York 1978

Eugene, Frank (Smith)
1865—New York—Germany 1936

Hortense, no date
The Art Institute of Chicago
Rep. 51

Portrait of Woman, no date
Platinum print
The Art Institute of Chicago
Rep. 325

Studies art in New York and Munich—moves to Germany in 1906—well-known art nouveau painter—founding member of Photo Secession—publications in *Camera Work*—is named professor of art photography at the Kunstakademie Leipzig in 1913.

2, 5, 9, 11, 12, 14

Evans, Frederick H.
1853—London—1943

Aubrey Beardsley, ca. 1895
National Portrait Gallery, London
Rep. 292

A Sea of Steps, 1903
Museum für Kunst und Gewerbe, Hamburg
Rep. 360

Ancient crypt cellars in Provins, France, 1910
Platinum print
The Library of Congress, Washington, D.C.
Rep. 57

Amateur photographer—bookshop owner until 1898—portraits of artists and writers—(pursuing interest in microphotography)—photos of cathedrals (York Minster, 1894, one of the earliest photos of a British cathedral)—member of the Linked Ring—publications in *Camera Work.*

1, 2, 5, 6, 7, 9, 10, 11, 12, 14
C: Reinbek 1980
M: Millerton 1973

Evans, Walker
1903 St. Louis, Missouri—New Haven, Connecticut 1975

42nd Street, 1929
The Art Institute of Chicago
Rep. 92

Bed and Stove, 1931
San Francisco Museum of Modern Art
Rep. 373

Citizen in Downtown Havana, 1932
The Art Institute of Chicago
Rep. 409

West Virginia Coal Miner's House, 1936
The Art Institute of Chicago
Rep. 375

Tenant Farmer's Wife, 1936
San Francisco Museum of Modern Art
Rep. 330

Studies at the most important American institutes—professional photographer after 1928—artistic and professional stylistic iconoclast—co-author of *Let Us Now Praise Famous Men* with James Agee, documenting with photographs the life of the poor sharecroppers in the American South—professor at Yale University 1945–1965.

2, 4, 7, 9, 12, 16
P, C: Boston 1978
M: New York 1978

Fenton, Roger
1819 Heywood, Lancashire—London 1869

Sir John Campbell, ca. 1855
Det kongelige Bibliotek, Copenhagen
Rep. 21

Furness Abbey, The Transepts from the Northwest, ca. 1856
Albumen print
The Royal Photographic Society of Great Britain, Bath
Rep. 352

Still Life (Fruit and Flowers), ca. 1860
Albumen print
The Royal Photographic Society of Great Britain, Bath
Rep. 200

Studied art with Paul Delaroche in Paris—amateur colotypist—co-founder and first president of The Royal Photographic Society—Crimean War photojournalist—photographer at the British Court (family life under Queen Victoria)—distinguished still lifes and photos of architecture.

1, 2, 3, 7, 9, 10, 12
M: Boston 1976

Fink, Larry
1941 New York—

Studio 54, 1977
Museum of Fine Arts, Boston
Rep. 408

University studies—student of Lisette Model and Alexey Brodovitch—teaching—critical documentations of New York society life.

Finsler, Hans
1891 Zürich—1972

Fabric, ca. 1930
Kunstbibliothek Preussischer Kulturbesitz, Berlin
Rep. 187

Studies art history and architecture in Munich—1922–1932 teaches in Halle—in 1932 founds the photographic department of the Kunstgewerbeschule in Zürich—influential teacher and librarian.

2, 8
P, C: Teufen 1974
M: Rapperswill 1971

Fontana, Franco
1933 Modena, Italy—

Landscape, 1974
Stedelijk Museum, Amsterdam
Rep. 147

Landscape, 1974
Stedelijk Museum, Amsterdam
Rep. 148

Self-taught photographer (after 1961)—specialization in color landscapes—illustrated volumes (among others, on Modena, Venice).

M: Modena 1978

Frank, Robert
1924 Zürich—New York—Mabou County, Canada

U.S. 1, South Carolina, 1955
New print
Stiftung für die Photographie, Kunsthaus Zürich
Rep. 377

Indianapolis, 1955
New print
Stiftung für die Photographie, Kunsthaus Zürich
Rep. 398

Long Beach, California, 1955
New print
Stiftung für die Photographie, Kunsthaus Zürich
Rep. 182

U.S. 285, New Mexico, 1958
The Art Institute of Chicago
Rep. 256

St. Petersburg, Florida, 1958
The Art Institute of Chicago
Rep. 116

Studies photography in Switzerland—moves to New York—first works as a fashion photographer—freelance after 1948—revolutionary photographer of the younger generation of the 1950s.

2, 9, 12
P, M: Millerton 1978

———

Friedlander, Lee
1934 Aberdeen, Washington—New York—

Child on TV, 1962
San Francisco Museum of Modern Art
Rep. 378

Self-portrait, Woman with Shadow, 1973
San Francisco Museum of Modern Art
Rep. 134

Begins to take photographs at age fourteen—documents city people for leading American newspapers—discovers E.J. Bellocq—publishes *Storyville Portraits* (1970)—makes new prints from Bellocq's old negatives.

2, 12
P, M: New York 1981

Frith, Francis
1822 Derbyshire—Reigate, England 1898

The Pyramids of Dahshoor, from the Southwest, 1857–1858
Albumen print
Fotografiska Museet, Stockholm
Rep. 245

Egypt, 1858
Det kongelige Bibliotek, Copenhagen
Rep. 370

Osiride Pillars and Great Fallen Colossos, 1858
Albumen print
The Art Institute of Chicago
Rep. 29

Starts a printshop in 1859—takes photographs in Egypt, Greece, Turkey, and Tibet using the wet collodion method—publishes numerous books between 1858 and 1865.

2, 7, 9, 10, 12, 16
P, M: New York 1980

Funke, Jaromir
1896 Skutec, Bohemia—Prague 1945

Shadows, 1927
Uměleckoprůmyslové Muzeum v Praze, Prague
Rep. 429

Corners, no date
Uměleckoprůmyslové Muzeum v Praze, Prague
Rep. 432

Co-founder of the Czech Photographic Society 1924—publishes ideas on the esthetic aspect of photography in his own journal.

C: Bochum 1976

Gardner, Alexander
1821 Paisley, Scotland—Washington, D.C. 1882

Ruins of Paper Mill, Richmond, Virginia, 1865
Albumen print
Museum of Fine Arts, Boston
Rep. 39

Studies physics and chemistry—emigrates to America 1856—employed by Mathew Brady to take documentary photographs of the American Civil War—publishes *Gardner's Photographic Sketch Book of the War* in 1866.

2, 4, 7, 9, 10, 12
M: New York 1959

Gelpke, André
1947 Beienrode Kr. Giffhorn—Essen—

Carneval, 1978
Museum Folkwang, Essen
Rep. 133

Studies photography with Otto Steinert at the Folkwangschule in Essen—active as photo-journalist—works appear in publications and journals all over the world—freelance since 1978.

Genthe, Arnold
1869 Berlin—New Milford, Connecticut, 1942

Last Portrait of Eleonora Duse, no date
Museum of Fine Arts, Boston
Rep. 308

Photojournalism of Chinatown in San Francisco, 1896–1906—photographs San Francisco earthquake and fire—portraits of famous personalities.

2, 5, 7, 9, 11, 12
P, M: New York 1937

Ghirri, Luigi
1943 Scandiano—Modena, Italy—

Modena, 1973
Università di Parma
Rep. 150

Vignola, 1974
Università di Parma
Rep. 151

The Spina Lido, 1978
Università di Parma
Rep. 149

Begins to photograph in 1971—interested in the ambivalence between reality and photography—publications in photojournals and in his own publishing house.

M: Parma 1979

Giacomelli, Mario
1925 Senigallia, Italy—

From *The Earth*, 1955–1968
Università di Parma
Rep. 427

Scanno, 1963
Università di Parma
Rep. 305

Photographs after 1954—becomes well known for landscape photos of graphic quality.

2
P, C: Parma 1980

Gibson, Ralph
1939 Los Angeles, California—New York—

Maurine, ca. 1972
Stedelijk Museum, Amsterdam
Rep. 132

Untitled, 1974
Fotografiska Museet, Stockholm
Rep. 304

Studies photography at the San Francisco Art Institute—1962 assistant of Dorothea Lange—lives in New York after 1969—self publications—participates in workshops and symposia in Europe and America.

12
P, M: London 1980

Gorny, Hein
1904 Witten an der Ruhr—Hannover 1967

Pages of a Book, no date
Kunstbibliothek Preussischer Kulturbesitz, Berlin
Rep. 206

Advertising photographer after 1929—between 1935 and 1942 publishes photography books.

P

Grainer, Franz
1871—Munich—1948

Nude, no date
Münchner Stadtmuseum, Munich
Rep. 211

Co-founder of the *Gesellschaft Deutscher Lichtbildner*—portraits of the court and of society.

1

Güler, Ara
1928 Istanbul—

Turkey, Edirne, 1956
Bibliothèque Nationale, Paris
Rep. 428

Studies agriculture and journalism at the University of Istanbul—international photojournalism.

C: Lincoln, Nebraska 1977

Guidalevitch, Victor
1892—Antwerp—1962

Still Life, no date
Het Sterckshof Museum, Antwerp
Rep. 201

Engineer—particular interest in miniature photography—sheds new light on familiar subjects by using unusual placements.

Haas, Ernst
1921—Vienna—New York—

Corner of 38th Street, New York, 1952
Dye transfer
The Museum of Modern Art, New York
Rep. 154

New York (Sunset Silhouette), 1952
Dye transfer
The Museum of Modern Art, New York
Rep. 155

New York (Blurred Skyscrapers), 1952
Dye transfer
The Museum of Modern Art, New York
Rep. 153

Pioneer of modern color photography and photojournalism—publishes in international journals after 1946.

2, 9
P, M: Düsseldorf 1978

Hajek-Halke, Heinz
1898 Berlin—

Nude, no date
Museum Folkwang, Essen
Rep. 437

Lightgraphic, no date
Deutsche Gesellschaft für Photographie, Cologne
Rep. 426

Studies art at the Akademie der Bildenden Künste, Berlin—representative of experimental photography—publishes first book, *Experimentelle Fotografie,* in 1955.

P, M: Hannover 1978

Halsman, Philippe
1906 Riga, Latvia—New York 1979

Albert Einstein, 1947

The Royal Photographic Society of Great Britain, Bath
Rep. 311

Alfred Hitchcock, before 1958
The Royal Photographic Society of Great Britain, Bath
Rep. 312

The Duke and Duchess of Windsor, before 1958
The Royal Photographic Society of Great Britain, Bath
Rep. 341

Studies at the Technischen Hochschule, Dresden—from 1928 until 1931 works as a portrait and fashion photographer in his own studio in Paris—emigrates to New York, 1941—takes more than one hundred covers for *Life* magazine.

2, 9, 12
C: New York 1979
P, M: New York 1972

Hamaya, Hiroshi
1915 Tokyo—Oiso—

Toyama, Japan, 1955
Museum Ludwig, Cologne
Rep. 114

Snowcountries Children, 1956
Museum Ludwig, Cologne
Rep. 386

Leading Japanese photojournalist—main subjects: Japanese folklore, and landscape photos—photos from Manchuria, China, Europe, and America.

2, 9
P, C: New York 1974
M: Tokyo 1971

Hanfstaengl, Franz
1804 Bayernrain near Tölz—Munich 1877

Untitled, 1855
Münchner Stadtmuseum, Munich
Rep. 234

Successful portrait lithographer—in 1853 turns to photography—international recognition through the publication of the portfolio work *Album der Zeitgenossen (Album of my Contemporaries),* 1860.

M: Munich 1975

Hauron, Louis Ducos du
1837—France—1920

The Angoulême Countryside, 1877
Heliochromy on wood—the photographer's
own process
Société Française de Photographie, Paris
Rep. 139

Tekmni District: Algiers, 1884
Collography
Société Française de Photographie, Paris
Rep. 138

One of the inventors of the three-color system
(basic principle of color photography)—first
experiments in 1865—communicates his process in writing to the Société Française de
Photographie in 1868—publications on technical developments, 1868 to 1900.

1, 2, 9

Hege, Walter
1893 Naumburg—Weimar 1955

Propyläen, East Wing, ca. 1928
Museum Folkwang, Essen
Rep. 348

Photographs of the architecture and sculpture
of Germany's most important cathedrals—photographs the Acropolis for the Metropolitan
Museum of Art, New York.

B

Henneberg, Hugo
1863—Vienna—1918

Poplar Alley, no date
Two-color gum print
Kunstbibliothek Preussischer Kulturbesitz,
Berlin
Rep. 146

Representative of art photography in Austria—
collaborates with Watzek and Kühn (called the
three-leaf clover)—participates in the development of the color offset process.

1, 5, 6, 11

Henri, Florence
1895 New York—Paris—Bellival, Picardy—

Portrait, 1930
Museum Folkwang, Essen
Rep. 322

Reflecting Ball, 1930
Museum Folkwang, Essen
Rep. 178

Studies art at the Bauhaus, Dessau—portrait,
fashion, and advertising photographer in Paris.

8
C: Baden-Baden 1976
M: Genova

Hill, David Octavius, and **Adamson,** Robert
1802 Perth—Newington Lodge, Scotland 1870
1821 St. Andrews—1848

Self-portrait (D.O. Hill), ca. 1843
Calotype
Museum Ludwig, Cologne
Rep. 17

A Minnow Pool, the Finlay Children, 1843–
1848
Calotype
Museum Ludwig, Cologne
Rep. 276

Portrait of a Lady, no date
Calotype
Museum Folkwang, Essen
Rep. 285

D.O. Hill: landscape painter and lithographer—founds the Royal Scottish Academy in
1830—collaborates with the portrait photographer Robert Adamson from 1843 until 1847—
their collaboration consists of roughly 1500
calotypes.

1, 2, 3, 4, 5, 6, 7, 8, 9, 10, 11, 12
M: New York 1940

Hine, Lewis
1874 Oshkosh, Wisconsin—Hastings-on-Hud-
son, New York 1940

Bowery Mission Bread Line, 2 A.M., New York,
1907
The Library of Congress, Washington, D.C.
Rep. 389

Girl Working in a Cotton Mill, 1908
The Art Institute of Chicago
Rep. 62

First Work in America, 1910
The Art Institute of Chicago
Rep. 414

Studies sociology—self-taught—main photography subjects: emigrants from Europe after
1905 and their social conditions, child labor,

slums—photojournalism, commissioned by numerous official organizations.

2, 7, 9, 12
P, C: Basel 1980
M: New York 1981

Hoepffner, Maria
1912 Pirmasens—Kressbronn/Bodensee—1979

Still Life with Wine Bottle, 1945

Agfa-Gevaert Foto-Historama, Leverkusen
Rep. 190

Studies with Willi Baumeister from 1929 until
1933—photo studio in Frankfurt from 1934 until
1944—founds the Foto-Privat school in 1949.

P, C

Hofmeister, Theodor and Oskar
1868—Hamburg—1943
1871—Hamburg—1937

Swampflowers, 1897
Gum print
Museum für Kunst und Gewerbe, Hamburg
Rep. 142

Cypress Alley, 1903
Pigment print
Museum für Kunst und Gewerbe, Hamburg
Rep. 251

Dutch Canal, 1909
Multicolored gum print
Museum für Kunst und Gewerbe, Hamburg
Rep. 140

Amateur photographers specializing in large-
size offset prints—exhibitions and publications
from 1895 until 1914—the majority of negatives
and prints were destroyed in a bombing attack
in 1943.

1, 5, 6, 7, 11, 14

Höpker, Thomas
1936 Munich—New York—

Leprosy in Ethiopia, 1964
Museum für Kunst und Gewerbe, Hamburg
Rep. 403

Studies art history and archeology—freelance
photographer after 1960—widely traveled photojournalist and specialist in large color subjects—photo editor.

Hoppé, Emil Otto
1878 Munich—London 1972

Romance of Steel, 1911
Bibliothèque Nationale, Paris
Rep. 65

Lady Lavery, 1914
Bibliothèque Nationale, Paris
Rep. 326

Triangles, Magic, 1926
Bibliothèque Nationale, Paris
Rep. 406

Works as a banker until 1907—learns photography in London—co-founder of the London Salon of Photography—preferred portrait photographer of famous personalities until the 1920s—after 1930 takes photos during world travel—numerous book publications in England and Germany.

2, 7, 12
P

Horvat, Frank
1929 Italy—France—

Two Little Boys, 1961
Bibliothèque Nationale, Paris
Rep. 274

Photojournalist and fashion photographer—reports from India, Rome, Paris—fashion photographs regularly in *Elle, Jardin des Modes,* and *Vogue* magazines—color photos of trees.

Hosoe, Eikoh
1933 Yamagata-ken—Tokyo—

Nude, no date
The Nihon University of Art, Tokyo
Rep. 221

Photography school in Tokyo, 1954—founder of a photography circle, 1959—numerous photobooks—photography professor at Tokyo's Kogei University.

12
C: Bologna 1980
M: Japan

Howlett, Robert
1830—London—1858

J. Stevenson, 1857

Victoria and Albert Museum, London
Rep. 22

Professional photographer—in 1857 documents the launching of the steamer "Great Eastern"—portraits of soldiers in the Crimean War.

7

Ikko (Narahara Ikko)
1931 Fukuoka—Tokyo—

Sky Through Twin Window, no date
The Nihon University of Art, Tokyo
Rep. 442

Studies art history at the University of Waseda—lives in Europe from 1962 until 1965—New York 1970 to 1974.

C: New York 1974

Jacobs, Roel
1943 Antwerp—Brussels—

Nude, 1978
Het Sterckshof Museum, Antwerp
Rep. 175

Learns advertising photography in Holland, Germany, and London—freelance after 1974—publication of photos in European photojournals.

Johnston, Alfred Cheney
1893—America—1971

Gloria Swanson, 1920
Museum Ludwig, Cologne
Rep. 300

Studies painting—successful portrait photographer of stage and screen stars in the 1920s and 1930s—known for his elegant photos of the *Ziegfeld Follies.*

2

Josephson, Kenneth
1932 Detroit, Michigan—Chicago, Illinois—

Polapan, 1973
The Art Institute of Chicago
Rep. 439

Wyoming, History of Photography Series, 1971
Fotograficka Mucoot, Stockholm
Rep. 449

Studies at the Rochester Institute of Technology and Institute of Design, Chicago, until 1960—professor at The Art Institute of Chicago—book publications in 1960 and 1973—exhibitions in America and abroad.

P, C: Kassel 1978

Käsebier, Gertrude
1852 Des Moines, Iowa—New York 1934

Blessed Art Thou among Women, 1899
Platinum print
The Museum of Modern Art, New York
Rep. 48

The Picture Book, 1905
Gum print
The Library of Congress, Washington, D.C.
Rep. 282

Studies portrait painting in New York—visits Europe in 1893—learns photographic technique in Germany—first woman member of the Linked Ring in 1900—member of Photo Secession since 1902—leaves in 1910 because of differences of opinion with Stieglitz—publications in *Camera Work*—together with H.C. White and A.L. Coburn founds the Pictorial Photographers of America.

2, 5, 6, 9, 10, 11, 12, 14
C: Brooklyn, N.Y. 1979

Karsh, Yousuf
1908 Armenia—Ottawa—

George Bernard Shaw, 1934
Sepia print
Museum Ludwig, Cologne
Rep. 294

Studies portrait photography in Boston with John Garo—has his own portrait studio in Ottawa after 1932—international recognition for his photo of Winston Churchill which appeared on the cover of *Life* magazine in 1941.

2, 9, 12
P, M: Toronto 1978

Kertész, André
1894 Budapest—Paris—New York—

Satiric Dancer, 1926
New print

Fotografiska Museet, Stockholm
Rep. 345

The Fork, 1928
Kunstbibliothek Preussischer Kulturbesitz, Berlin
Rep. 76

Dew, no date
Kunstbibliothek Preussischer Kulturbesitz, Berlin
Rep. 184

Son of a banking family—studies economics in Budapest—works at the stock exchange, 1912—takes first photographs during World War I—moves to Paris in 1925—works for international journals as a freelancer—moves to New York in 1936—becomes an American citizen in 1944—under contract to Condé Nast until 1962—numerous book publications and exhibitions.

2, 6, 8, 9, 12
P, M: Boston 1981

Kiljan, Gerardus
1891—Hoorn—Amsterdam—The Hague—Voorburg—Leidschendam, Holland 1968

Barstool, ca. 1930
Haags Gemeente Museum, The Hague
Rep. 430

Graphic artist, designer and draftsman—learns lithography—teaches at the academies of The Hague and Rotterdam.

Kimura, Ihei
1901—Japan—1979

Horse, no date
The Nihon University of Art, Tokyo
Rep. 444

Photojournalist—documentations about Japan in the post World War II period—representative of an uncompromisingly realistic style—primarily landscape photography and photos of Asia, Europe, and America.

P, C: Bologna 1980

Klein, William
1928 New York City—Paris—

Lunch on the Grass, Rome, 1956
Museum Ludwig, Cologne
Rep. 119

Rome (Looks), 1956
Bibliothèque Nationale, Paris
Rep. 411

Studies social science in New York—self-taught, also a painter—works for *Vogue* magazine from 1957 until 1967—international recognition for unusual photography books.

2
P, M: Millerton 1980

Koppitz, Rudolf
1884—Austria—1936

Motion Study, 1926
Carbon print
The Royal Photographic Society of Great Britain, Bath
Rep. 219

Photography professor at the Graphischen Lehr- und Versuchsanstalt, Vienna—specialist in fine photo-printing methods.

1, 2

Koudelka, Josef
1938 Boskovice, Czechoslovakia—England—

Gypsy Children, 1964
Stiftung für die Photographie, Kunsthaus Zürich
Rep. 382

Gypsy in Eastern Slovakia, 1965
Stiftung für die Photographie, Kunsthaus Zürich
Rep. 374

Studies at the Technical University in Prague—active as flight engineer and theater photographer—freelance after 1967—documents gypsy life in Europe—scholarships—publications in international journals—prize for his book *Gitanes—La Fin du Voyage*.

2, 12
P, M: Millerton 1977

Krone, Hermann
1827 Breslau—Laubegast b. Dresden 1916

Album, 1874
Museum Folkwang, Essen
Rep. 35

Studies the natural sciences—active collaboration in the development of photography in Germany—teaches photography at the Polytechnikum in Dresden.

1

Kühn, Heinrich
1866 Dresden—Birgitz near Innsbruck 1944

Still Life with Oranges, 1903
Bromoil print
Museum Folkwang, Essen
Rep. 203

Alfred Stieglitz, 1904
Offset
Museum Folkwang, Essen
Rep. 288

Portrait of a Girl, 1905–1906
Offset
Museum Folkwang, Essen
Rep. 54

Studies medicine in Innsbruck—collaboration with Hans Watzek and Hugo Henneberg—member of the Vienna Camera Club, 1896—interest in fine printing processes—photos shown in the Munich Photo Secession exhibition 1898—publications in *Camera Work*—scientific dissertation published in 1921 on the technique of photography, Kühn later endorses straight photography.

1, 2, 5, 6, 7, 10, 11, 12
C: Essen 1978
M: Innsbruck 1978

Lange, Dorothea
1895 Hoboken, New Jersey—San Francisco, California 1965

Once a Missouri Farmer, Now a Migratory Farm Worker in California, 1936
The Library of Congress, Washington, D.C.
Rep. 317

Ex-tenant Farmer on Relief Grant in the Imperial Valley, California, 1937

The Library of Congress, Washington, D.C.
Rep. 93

Studies to become a teacher in New York 1914–1917—studies photography with Clarence H. White at Columbia University—moves to San Francisco—commissions for the Farm Security Administration and other American government organizations—photojournalism for *Life* magazine.

2, 4, 7, 9, 12, 16

Lartigue, Jacques Henri
1894 Courbevoie near Paris—Paris—

One Page from the Album, 1921
Ministère de la Culture, Paris
Association des amis de Jacques Henri Lartigue, Paris
Rep. 174

Paris, Florette, 1944
Bibliothèque Nationale, Paris
Rep. 305

Son of a banker family—at age twelve begins photographing the life of the Belle Epoque—studies painting—keeps photographic journals for decades—has his own museum in the Grand Palais, Paris.

2, 8, 12
P, M: Paris 1980

Laughlin, Clarence John
1905 Lake Charles, Louisiana—New Orleans—

Elegy for Moss Land, 1947
Gernsheim Collection, Austin
Rep. 446

Takes photographs in the southern United States from 1934—publications about disintegrating mansions on Mississippi plantations, among others.

12
P, C: Lincoln, Nebraska 1977
M: New York 1973

Lebeck, Robert
1929 Hamburg—

Kennedy's Burial, 1968
Museum Folkwang, Essen
Rep. 381

Studies in Zurich and New York—publishes first photographs in 1952—active as photojournalist with several German journals—in New York from 1966 until 1970—editor-in-chief of *Geo* magazine from 1970 until 1979.

Le Gray, Gustave
1820—Villiers le Bel near Paris—Cairo 1862

Study of Trees, ca. 1851
Victoria and Albert Museum, London
Rep. 32

Seascape of Sète, ca. 1857
Victoria and Albert Museum, London
Rep. 26

Seascape, ca. 1857
Victoria and Albert Museum, London
Rep. 264

A Picture Taken at Camp de Chalon, 1857
Société Française de Photographie
Rep. 417

Painter and Photographer—studies with Delaroche in Paris—professional photographer specializing in combining negatives of cloud formations and seascapes—inventor of a wax paper process especially suitable for landscapes and architecture (1851).

1, 2, 3, 7, 10, 12
M: California 1977

Lendvai-Dircksen, Erna
1883—Coburg—1962

Miner from Upper Silesia, no date
Agfa-Gevaert Foto-Historama, Leverkusen
Rep. 333

Nude, 1921
Kunstbibliothek Preussischer Kulturbesitz, Berlin
Rep. 212

Portraits/documentations from different German regions and neighboring countries.

1, 6

Lerski, Helmar
1871 Strassbourg—Israel—Zürich 1956

Self-portrait, 1912
Silver print
Museum für Kunst und Gewerbe, Hamburg
Rep. 60

Typist, before 1931
Silver print
Museum für Kunst und Gewerbe, Hamburg
Rep. 334

Lives in America from 1893 until 1914—actor in the German theater—learns photography from his wife—works in a Berlin film studio from 1915 until 1929—serial photographs in *Close up, Stil,* and *Köpfe des Alltags* journals—1931 until 1948 photojournalist and film maker in Palestine.

1, 2, 6, 7, 8
P

Lichtsteiner, Rudolf
1938 Zürich—

Moment, Self-portrait, 1972
Stiftung für die Photographie, Kunsthaus Zürich
Rep. 434

Scholarship student in Switzerland from 1958 to 1961—own studio in Basel—publishes portfolios in 1972—photography teacher at the Kunstgewerbeschule in Zürich after 1976.

C: Zürich 1980

List, Herbert
1903 Hamburg—Munich 1970

Hamburg, 1931
Museum Folkwang, Essen
Rep. 71

Munich, 1945
Museum Folkwang, Essen
Rep. 354

Professional photographer after 1931—poetic realism—work published in international cultural journals.

2
P, M: Munich and New York 1980

Löcherer, Alois
1815—Munich 1862

Montage of the Bavaria, 1850
Münchner Stadtmuseum, Munich
Rep. 388

Munich pharmacist and photographer—publishes *Photographisches Album der Zeitgenossen (Photographic Album of my Contemporaries)*—publications on photographic technique.

1, 7

Lynes, George Platt
1907 New Jersey—New York 1955

Male Nude, Legs Lifted, no date
The Art Institute of Chicago
Rep. 241

Nude in a Room, no date
Museum Ludwig, Cologne
Rep. 238

Jean Cocteau, 1930
Museum Ludwig, Cologne
Rep. 320

Self-taught—professional photographer after ca. 1925 (*Harper's Bazaar* and *Vogue* magazines)—specializes in nude and portrait photography as well as surrealist scenes.

2, 12
M: New Jersey 1977

Man, Felix H. (Hans Baumann)
1893 Freiburg—London—Rome—

Maxim Gorki, Sorrento, 1932
New print
Fotografiska Museet, Stockholm
Rep. 87

Studies art in Munich and Berlin—one of the leading photojournalists after 1928 (*Berliner Illustrirte Zeitung, Münchner Illustrierte Presse*)—moves to England in 1934—founds the journal *Weekly Illustrated* in London—commissions for *Picture Post* 1938–1951.

2, 7
C: Bielefeld 1978
M: New York 1977

Meatyard, Ralph Eugene
1925 Norma, Illinois—Lexington, Kentucky 1972

Untitled, no date
Art Museum, University of New Mexico, Albuquerque
Rep. 117

Untitled, ca. 1960
Art Museum, University of New Mexico, Albuquerque
Rep. 372

Optometrist—studies photography with Van Deren Coke, Henry H. Smith, and Minor White—surrealist photographs influenced by Zen Buddhism.

2, 12
P, M: Illinois 1976

Mertin, Roger
1942 Bridgeport, Connecticut—

Breast and Hair (After E.W.), Rochester, 1973
Art Museum, University of New Mexico, Albuquerque
Rep. 130

Rochester, New York, 1975
Art Museum, University of New Mexico, Albuquerque
Rep. 448

Studies at the Rochester Institute of Technology with Minor White—teacher at the Visual Studies Workshop, Rochester.

12
C: Lincoln, Nebraska 1977
M: Chicago 1978

Metzker, Ray K.
1931 Milwaukee, Wisconsin—

Untitled, 1972
Art Museum, University of New Mexico, Albuquerque
Rep. 365

Studies in Chicago at the Institute of Design with Harry Callahan—teaches photography at the Philadelphia College of Art—large format picture compositions and photo experiments in black-and-white.

12
C: Lincoln, Nebraska 1977
M: Millerton 1979

Meyerowitz, Joel
1938 New York—

New Jersey Home, 1966
Museum of Fine Arts, Boston
Rep. 438

Studies painting and drawing in Ohio—schol-

arships and commissions 1970–1978—specializes in color photography.

12
C: Amsterdam 1980
M: Cambridge 1980

Michals, Duane
1932 McKeesport, Pennsylvania—New York—

Things are Queer, Sequence of nine photos, no date
Stedelijk Museum, Amsterdam
Rep. 137

Ray Barry, 1963 and 1977
The Art Institute of Chicago
Rep. 314, 315

Works as a freelance photographer in New York—known for his sequences of several connected photographs, which are influenced by surrealism—also combines painting, text, or drawing with photography.

2, 12
P, C: Apeldoorn 1981
M: New Hampshire 1978

Migliori, Antonio
1926 Bologna, Italy—

From *The Cemeteries*, 1952
Università di Parma
Rep. 436

Photographer after 1948—experimentation with expressionistic possibilities of photography, especially with abstract darkroom formations.

C: Parma 1980

Misonne, Léonard
1870—Gilly, Belgium—1943

Gilly, 1898
Agfa-Gevaert Foto-Historama, Leverkusen
Rep. 45

Amateur photographer—romantic landscape portraits, uses his own filter construction—exhibits works from 1898 to 1939.

1, 5, 6, 7

Misrach, Richard
1949—Los Angeles—Emeryville, California—

Boojum II, 1977
San Francisco Museum of Modern Art
Rep. 267

Teacher at the University of California, Berkeley, 1972 to 1977—receives several scholarships between 1973 and 1978—specializes in color photography.

Moholy, Lucia
1900 Prague—Weimar—Berlin—London—Zollikon near Zürich—

Bauhaus, 1925–1926
New print
Museum Ludwig, Cologne
Rep. 356

Freelance photographer at the Bauhaus, Weimar, and Dessau—moves to London 1933—portraits and cityscapes—publishes *The History of Photography 1839–1939.*

Moholy-Nagy, László
1895 Bácborsód, Hungary—Weimar—Berlin—Chicago, 1946

Self-portrait, ca. 1922
Photogram
Museum Folkwang, Essen
Rep. 68

Untitled, no date
The Art Institute of Chicago
Rep. 358

Two Nudes, 1927/29
Museum Folkwang, Essen
Rep. 244

Nude, ca. 1935
Negative print
Gernsheim Collection, Austin
Rep. 243

Develops increasing interest in art, particularly painting, while studying law in Budapest—Russian P.O.W. during World War I—1920–1923 Berlin and marriage to Lucia Schultz—asked to join the Bauhaus in Weimar and Dessau—photography experiments—leaves Germany in 1934—emigrates via Holland and London to America—head of the New Bauhaus and co-founds the Institute of Design in Chicago.

1, 2, 6, 7, 8, 9, 12
P, M: Giessen 1980

Muncacsi (Munkacsi), Martin
1896 Kolozsvar, Hungary—Berlin—New York
—1963

Torso, no date
Museum Ludwig, Cologne
Rep. 237

Active as photojournalist in Budapest and then in Berlin (*Berliner Illustrirte*)—emigrates to America—one of the most successful photographers of the 1940s—publications in numerous journals.

2
P, C: Düsseldorf 1980

Mulas, Ugo
1928 Pozzolengo—Milan 1973

Roy Lichtenstein, 1964
Università di Parma
Rep. 335

Breaks off study of law and devotes himself to photography after 1954—voluminous documentation of artists and activities of the Biennale, Venice.

M: Parma 1973

Muybridge, Eadweard (Edward James Muggeridge)
1830 Kingston-on-Thames—America—Kingston-on-Thames 1904

Animal Locomotion, Philadelphia, Album, 1887
Twenty-one photographed tables (calotype)
Animal Locomotion. An electrophotographic investigation of consecutive phases of animal movements 1872–1885
Fotografiska Museet, Stockholm
Rep. 7

Inventor of motion photography and innovator in cinematography—first photo sequences.

1, 2, 7, 9, 10, 12
P, M: Milan 1981

Nadar (Gaspard-Félix Tournachon)
1820—Paris—1910

Jean François Millet, 1858
Agfa-Gevaert Foto-Historama, Leverkusen
Rep. 18

Santos Dumont, ca. 1906
Bibliothèque Nationale, Paris
Rep. 296

Studies medicine—active in the French Revolution (1848)—opens the first studio in Paris in 1853 and photographs famous contemporaries—also becomes known as a writer and caricaturist—first aerial photographs from a balloon in 1858—patents a method for color photography in 1858—takes first photos with artificial light (1860)—in 1886 his son Paul takes over the photographic work in the studio.

1, 2, 3, 4, 7, 9, 10, 12, 15, 16
P, M: Milan 1979

Nègre, Charles
1820 Grasse—1880

Arles, the Ramparts, 1852
Het Sterckshof Museum, Antwerp
Rep. 30

Woman of Arles, 1852
Het Sterckshof Museum, Antwerp
Rep. 287

Studies painting with Delaroche and Ingres—in 1850 turns to photography—specializes in photos of architecture and everyday scenes—co-founder of the Société Française de Photographie.

1, 2, 3, 7, 12, 15
M: Ottawa 1976

Newman, Arnold
1918 New York—

Igor Stravinsky, 1946
New print
Fotografiska Museet, Stockholm
Rep. 110

Early interest in art and painting—enrolls at the University of Miami—first works in a commercial studio—helped by Alfred Stieglitz and Beaumont Newhall—opens his own portrait studio in New York in 1946—concentrates on portraits of artists—after 1947 commissions from *Life* magazine and other journals, numerous covers.

2, 9, 12
P, M: London 1981

Nishayama, Kiyoshi
1893 Tokyo—

Grapes, no date
The Nihon University of Art, Tokyo
Rep. 193

Amateur photographer—specializes in still lifes and landscapes—his prewar photos disappear during bombing attacks on Tokyo.

M: Tokyo 1979 (No. 21)

Nooijer, Paul de
1943 Eindhoven, Holland—

Self-portrait, 1976
Hand-colored
Stedelijk Museum, Amsterdam
Rep. 172

Studies at the Akademie für Industriele Vormgeving in Eindhoven 1960–1965—self-taught photographer—active in advertising and film—first one-man show, 1973.

P

Ogawa, Takayuki
1936 Tokyo—

Display Window, no date
The Nihon University of Art, Tokyo
Rep. 445

Studies photography at Nihon University—freelance after 1964—one-man shows in Japan.

Ollman, Arthur
1947 Milwaukee, Wisconsin—

Untitled, 1976
San Francisco Museum of Modern Art
Rep. 158

Representative of modern color photography of the American West—teaches at the San Francisco Art Institute.

O'Sullivan, Timothy H.
1840 New York City—1882

Battlefield of Gettysburg, Bodies of Dead Federal Soldiers on the Field of the First Day's Battle, July 1863
Albumen print
The Library of Congress, Washington, D.C.
Rep. 42

Dead Confederate Soldier in Trenches of Fort Mahone in Front of Petersburg, Virginia, April 3, 1865
Albumen print
The Library of Congress, Washington, D.C.
Rep. 420

Canyon de Chelle, New Mexico, 1873
Museum für Kunst und Gewerbe, Hamburg
Rep. 249

Learns photography with Mathew Brady in New York—works in Washington, in Brady's studio, headed by Alexander Gardner—photographs the battlefields of the American Civil War—after 1866 expeditions to the West on commission for the government.

2, 4, 5, 7, 9, 10, 12
M: New York 1966

Outerbridge, Paul, Jr.
1906—New York City 1958

Fruit in a Majolica Dish, 1921
The Library of Congress, Washington, D.C.
Rep. 191

Torso, 1923
Museum of Fine Arts, Boston
Rep. 218

Piano, 1924
The Library of Congress, Washington, D.C.
Rep. 205

Consciousness, 1931
The Art Institute of Chicago
Rep. 75

Studies art and photography in New York at the Clarence White School of Photography—teaches at the same school—advertising photographer in Paris and New York in the 1920s—acquaintance with Man Ray—specializes in the three-color carbon technique for color photography—a large part of his oeuvre published posthumously.

8, 12
P, C: Los Angeles 1977
M: Munich 1981

Owens, Bill
1938—San José—Livermore, California—

"Our house is built with the living room in the back, so in the evenings we sit out front of the garage and watch the traffic go by," 1972
Fotografiska Museet, Stockholm
Rep. 131

Photographer for a California newspaper—documentation of middle-class American life—publisher of photography books.

12
P, M: New Hampshire 1978

Pabel, Hilmar
1910 Rawitsch—Umratshausen/Chiemsee—

Volunteers in Bolivia, 1975
Museum Folkwang, Essen
Rep. 383

Photojournalist known for his postwar photos—photographs for *Terre des Hommes* and the German Red Cross, especially children's portraits for the purpose of reuniting families after World War II.

Parks, Gordon
1912 Fort Scott, Kansas—New York—

Red Jackson, 1948
Museum Ludwig, Cologne
Rep. 331

Active for *Life* magazine 1949 to 1970—especially interested in the problems of his black compatriots—filmmaker, writer, and composer.

2, 9
P, M: New York 1975

Penn, Irving
1917 Plainfield, New Jersey—New York—

American Ballet Theatre, 1947
Platinum print 1968
Museum für Kunst und Gewerbe, Hamburg
Rep. 299

Yellow Rose and Skyscraper, 1950
Dye-transfer
The Museum of Modern Art, New York
Rep. 166

Rowboat on the Seine, 1951
Museum Ludwig, Cologne
Rep. 141

Trees Along French Canal, 1951
Dye-transfer
The Museum of Modern Art, New York
Rep. 152

Pablo Picasso, 1957
Museum Ludwig, Cologne
Rep. 120

Truman Capote, 1965
Platinum print 1968
Fotografiska Museet, Stockholm
Rep. 128

Studies art at the Philadelphia Museum School of Industrial Art with Alexey Brodovitch—visits Mexico to paint in 1942—cover designer with *Vogue* magazine—leading fashion photographer in the 1950s—portraits of famous contemporaries, artisans, and workers, still lifes, and color photographs—blows up his most important photos as platinum prints on deckle-edged paper.

2, 9, 12
P, M: New York 1977

Perscheid, Nicola
1864 Leipzig—Berlin 1930

Young Girl, no date
Kunstbibliothek Preussischer Kulturbesitz, Berlin
Rep. 283

Society photographer of the 1920s—invents and builds the Perscheid Lens in 1925—master of the bromoil printing process for color.

1, 5, 6
M: Hamburg, 1980

Ponti, Carlo
1821 Sagno, Tessin—Venice 1893

Piazza San Marco, Belltower, Venice, ca. 1860
Albumen print
Gernsheim Collection, Austin
Rep. 31

Manufacturer of optic instruments—leading Italian photographer of the nineteenth century—specializes in architectural photos of Venice, Padua, and Verona—appointed the personal optician of King Victor Emmanuel II in 1866.

7, 9, 12

Porter, Eliot
1901 Winnetka, Illinois—Santa Fé, New Mexico—

Woodland Stream, Pittsburgh, New Hampshire, 1965
Art Museum, University of New Mexico, Albuquerque
Rep. 144

Bush and Yellow Grass, Adirondacks, 1965
Art Museum, University of New Mexico, Albuquerque
Rep. 145

Student of engineering and medicine at Harvard University—research and teaching in bacteriology and biochemistry—acquaintance with Alfred Stieglitz around 1936—gives up scientific activity in 1939 to become a photographer—specializes in color photos of birds and landscapes.

2, 11, 12
P, M: London and Munich 1981

Puyo, Emile Joachim Constant
1857—France—1933

Woman with Sunshade by the Waterside, ca. 1896
Société Française de Photographie, Paris
Rep. 46

Woman, ca. 1896
Société Française de Photographie, Paris
Rep. 284

Artillery officer in the French army—amateur photographer—member of the Photo Club de Paris—starts a photographic salon with Demachy, Le Bègue, and Bucquet—exhibitions in America, 1906 with Alfred Stieglitz and 1910 in Buffalo, New York.

1, 2, 5, 11, 12

Ray, Man
1890 Philadelphia, Pennsylvania—Paris 1976

Woman, 1929
Negative print
Bibliothèque Nationale, Paris
Rep. 69

Woman, 1930
Bibliothèque Nationale, Paris
Rep. 291

Rayograph no date
Her Sterckshof Museum, Antwerp
Rep. 425

Lee Miller, 1930
Museum Ludwig, Cologne
Rep. 302

The Lovers, no date
Museum Ludwig, Cologne
Rep. 72

Solarization, 1932
Museum Ludwig, Cologne
Rep. 306

Studies art in New York from 1908 until 1912—becomes familiar with all artistic media—member of the New York Dada group—moves to Paris in 1921—works as a fashion and portrait photographer—photographs his circle of friends (Picasso, Duchamp, Tzara, Max Ernst, Cocteau)—interest in photo and film experiments—returns to America in 1940—lives in Hollywood as painter, fashion photographer, and teacher until 1950—moves to Paris, where he devotes himself to photography and painting until the end of his life.

1, 2, 7, 8, 9, 12, 16
P, M: Paris 1980

Rejlander, Oscar Gustave
1813 Sweden—London 1875

The Two Ways of Life, 1858
Albumen print
The Royal Photographic Society of Great Britain, Bath
Rep. 36

Out of Work, ca. 1860
Platinum print
The Royal Photographic Society of Great Britain, Bath
Rep. 38

Portrait painter—learns photography in 1853—one of the pioneers of art photography in England—becomes known for his composed photos with allegorical themes which consist of several joined negatives.

1, 2, 7, 9, 10, 12
M: Connecticut 1973

Renger-Patzsch, Albert
1897 Würzburg—Wamel bei Soest—1966

The Copper Beech, 1925
Kunstbibliothek Preussischer Kulturbesitz, Berlin
Rep. 266

Street in Essen, 1932
Kunstbibliothek Preussischer Kulturbesitz, Berlin
Rep. 355

Street, no date
Kunstbibliothek Preussischer Kulturbesitz, Berlin
Rep. 254

Still Life with Utensils, no date
Kunstbibliothek Preussischer Kulturbesitz, Berlin
Rep. 77

Studies chemistry in Dresden—head of the picture sections of the Folkwang archive after 1922 and freelance photographer—representative of an objective style exemplified in numerous subjects (close-ups of animals and plants, landscapes, industrial photos).

1, 2, 6, 7, 8, 9, 12, 16
P, C: Bonn 1977

Riboud, Marc
1923 Lyon—Paris—

Radjastan, India, 1956
Bibliothèque Nationale, Paris
Rep. 115

Neger Barroros, 1963
Bibliothèque Nationale, Paris
Rep. 399

Photojournalist after 1952—numerous photographs from China, Russia, Vietnam, India, and Africa—publications in international journals.

2, 9
P, M: New York 1981

Riis, Jacob August
1849 Ribe, Denmark—New York—Barre, Massachusetts 1914

Ludlow Street, New York, ca. 1890
Münchner Stadtmuseum
Rep. 63

Carpenter—emigrates in 1870 to America—after years of poverty he becomes a reporter with a New York newspaper—as of 1887, with the discovery of lycopodium powder, he photographs the slums in New York and thus becomes the first American photojournalist—book publications in 1890 and 1892.

2, 7, 9, 12, 16
P, M: Millerton 1974

Robinson, Henry Peach
1830 Ludlow, England—Tunbridge Wells, England 1901

Fading Away, 1858
Albumen print
The Royal Photographic Society of Great Britain, Bath
Rep. 37

Amateur painter—interest in photography after 1852—opens his own portrait studio in 1857—like Rejlander he is one of the pioneers of art photography—recognition through prizes and exhibitions at The Royal Photographic Society of Great Britain—co-founder of the Linked Ring 1892.

1, 2, 6, 7, 9, 10, 12, 14
M: New York 1973

Rössler, Jaroslav
1902 Smilov, Bohemia—Paris—Prague

Glass, 1923
Uměleckoprůmyslové Muzeum v Praze, Prague
Rep. 189

Cigarette, 1929
Uměleckoprůmyslové Muzeum v Praze, Prague
Rep. 431

Student of Drtikol—stays in Paris from 1924 to 1926 and from 1927 to 1935—specializes in advertising and industrial photography—also well known as a documentary photographer in Prague.

Rubinstein, Eva
1933 Argentina—New York—

New York, 1972
New print
Fotografiska Museet, Stockholm
Rep. 209

Old Man on Steps, 1973
Bibliothèque Nationale, Paris
Rep. 359

Trained as a dancer and actress—photographer after 1967—teaches at various institutes from 1972 to 1975—international exhibitions after 1970.

12
M: New York 1976

Salomon, Erich
1886 Berlin—The Hague—Auschwitz 1944

Aristide Briand, 1929
Stiftung für Photographie, Kunsthaus Zürich
Rep. 74

The King of Indiscretion (There He Is!), 1931
Museum Folkwang, Essen
Rep. 380

Self-portrait, no date
Museum Folkwang, Essen
Rep. 337

Son of a Berlin banker—studies law in Munich—prisoner during World War I—employed by the publisher Ullstein—begins a successful career as freelance photojournalist in 1928 (*Berliner Illustrirte*)—visits to England and America in 1929 and 1930—photographs extremely important historical events and well-known politicians (*Berühmte Zeitgenossen in umbewachten Augenblicken—Famous Contemporaries in Unguarded Moments*, 1931)—emigrates to Holland in 1934—dies in 1944 in Auschwitz with his wife and one of their sons.

2, 5, 7, 9, 12
P, M: New York 1978

Sander, August
1876 Herdorf, Siegerland—Cologne 1964

Parliamentarian, 1928
Museum Ludwig, Cologne
Rep. 88

Jockey, 1932
Museum Ludwig, Cologne
Rep. 342

Unemployed, 1932
Museum Ludwig, Cologne
Rep. 344

Siebengebirge, ca. 1936
Museum Ludwig, Cologne
Rep. 261

Takes his first photos at age sixteen—while in the service near Trier he is encouraged by a local photographer—after studying briefly at the Kunstakademie Dresden he opens a photo studio in Linz, Austria, together with a friend, in 1902—takes first color photos in 1904—moves to Cologne in 1910—opens his own portrait studio—after World War I, portraits of people from all walks of life—first publication: *Antlitz der Zeit* in 1929—his project *Menschen des 20. Jahrhundert* is stopped by the Nazis after 1936, landscape photos (Cologne cityscapes, Rhineland, Westerwald).

1, 2, 5, 9, 12
P, M: Munich 1981

Sannes, Sanne
1937 Groningen, Holland—Bergen (N.H.) 1967

Nude Back, no date
Stedelijk Museum, Amsterdam
Rep. 230

Studies photography and graphics in Groningen—interest in experimental photography and film—participates in numerous international exhibitions.

Sarony, Napoleon
1821—New York—1886

Oscar Wilde, ca. 1882
National Portrait Gallery, London
Rep. 20

Trained lithographer—starts his own institute in New York in 1846—studies painting in Europe—visits his brother in England and learns of photography in 1856—opens his own studio—two years later returns to New York—becomes a successful New York portrait photographer (more than forty thousand photographs, particularly of actors).

2, 5, 9, 12
M: Ohio 1978

Saudek, Jan
1935 Prague—

Man and Baby, no date
Stedelijk Museum, Amsterdam
Rep. 215

Female Torso, no date
Stedelijk Museum, Amsterdam
Rep. 217

Student of photography from 1950 until 1953—first exhibition in Prague in 1963—trip to Amer-

ica in 1969—finances his photography by working in a factory—participates in exhibitions in Chicago, Melbourne, Sidney, and Prague.

Schad, Christian
1894 Miesbach—Zürich—Italy-Berlin—Keilberg im Spessart—1982

Schadography, 1918
The Museum of Modern Art, New York
Rep. 66

Studies art at the Münchner Akademie 1913—painter and graphic artist—member of the Dada group in Zürich 1915–1920—interest in photo abstractions after 1918, called Schadographies (photographs without camera)—more than seven years in Italy—transition to the *"neu-sachlichen"* (new objectivity) style in painting.

7, 9

Schuitema, Paul
1897 Groningen, Holland—Wassenaar 1973

Lampshades, 1929
Haags Gemeente Museum, The Hague
Rep. 192

Typographical consultant—photographs as of 1926—professor at the Royal Academy for Art in The Hague 1930–1963.

8

Schulthess, Emil
1913 Zürich—

Sunset of the Rolling Icebreaker, 1958
New print
Stiftung für die Photographie, Kunsthaus Zürich
Rep. 176

Graphic artist, art director—specialization in geographic photographs—expeditions to Africa, America, and China, which result in large books.

Senn, Paul
1901—Switzerland—1953

Volcanic Landscape, Mexico, 1951
New print
Stiftung für die Photographie, Kunsthaus Zürich
Rep. 265

Hog Traders, Mexico, 1951
New print
Stiftung für die Photographie, Kunsthaus Zürich
Rep. 391

One of the first Swiss photojournalists in the 1930s—photographs from Europe, America, and Mexico after World War II.

C: Zürich 1974
M: Bern 1981

Shahn, Ben
1898 Kaunas, Lithuania—New York 1969

Destitute, 1935
San Francisco Museum of Modern Art
Rep. 89

Urbana, 1938
San Francisco Museum of Modern Art
Rep. 410

Well-known American painter and graphic artist—inspired by his friend Walker Evans to become a photographer—committed to social reforms, particularly evident in his gripping photo documentations for the Farm Security Administration, from 1935 to 1938.

2, 9, 12
M: Massachusetts 1975

Sheeler, Charles
1883 Philadelphia—New York 1965

Fuel Tanks, Wisconsin, no date
The Library of Congress, Washington, D.C.
Rep. 180

United Nations Building, ca. 1950
The Library of Congress, Washington, D.C.
Rep. 125

Uses photography to finance his study of painting—friend of Stieglitz, Strand, and Steichen in New York—representative of a distinct, objective style in his photos of architecture and industry—devotes himself exclusively to painting after 1945.

2, 8, 9, 11, 12
P, M: New York 1975

Shinoyama, Kishin
1940 Tokyo—

Nude, no date
The Nihon University of Art, Tokyo
Rep. 226

Studies photography at Nihon University—freelance after 1968—advertising and nude photographer of post World War II in Japan.

P, C: Bologna 1980
M: Shuisha 1971

Shirakawa, Yoshikazu
1935 Ehime-ken, Japan—

Landscape, no date
The Nihon Art University, Tokyo
Rep. 260

Studies photography at Nihon University—active in radio and television—leading nature photographer specializing in photos of mountains.

P, C: Bologna 1980
M: New York 1971

Shore, Stephen
1947 New York—

El Paso Street, El Paso Texas, 1975
Type C—Print
The Museum of Modern Art, New York
Rep. 159

Green County Court House, 1976
The Art Institute of Chicago
Rep. 169

Fort Lauderdale Yankee Stadium, Fort Lauderdale, Florida, 1978
Type C—Print
The Museum of Modern Art, New York
Rep. 160

Interested in photography since childhood—studies photography with Minor White—exhibition at the Metropolitan Museum, New York, 1970—representative of the new American color realism—specialization in cityscapes.

12
C: Lincoln, Nebraska 1977
M: New York 1978

Sieff, Jean-Loup
1933 Paris—

Jetty in the Reeds, no date

Het Sterckshof Museum, Antwerp
Rep. 250

Homage to Seurat, 1965
Bibliothèque Nationale, Paris
Rep. 208

Fashion photographer—develops a personal style using the wide-angle lens for landscape and nude photography.

2
P

Siegel, Arthur
1913 Detroit—1978

France, 1953
The Art Institute of Chicago
Rep. 156

Photojournalist for the U.S. Farm Security Administration from 1935 to 1943—in 1946 he founds, with László Moholy-Nagy, the photography section of the Institute of Design in Chicago—organizes a symposium with lectures and exhibitions of well-known photographers such as Berenice Abbott, Paul Strand, Beaumont Newhall, Weegee, and Moholy-Nagy.

Siskind, Aaron
1903 New York—

Martha's Vineyard, Seaweed, 1944
San Francisco Museum of Modern Art
Rep. 109

Gloucester I, 1944
San Francisco Museum of Modern Art
Rep. 185

Wedged Rock, 1954
San Francisco Museum of Modern Art
Rep. 181

Documentary photographer in New York—photographs of structural surfaces resulting in the effect of abstract compositions—teacher at the Institute of Design in Chicago—head of the photography section.

2, 9, 12
P, M: Oxford 1979

Smith, W. Eugene
1918 Wichita, Kansas—New York—Tucson, Arizona 1979

Albert Schweitzer, 1949
Museum Ludwig, Cologne
Rep. 105

Pride Street, no date
Museum Ludwig, Cologne
Rep. 387

First job as photographer at age fifteen with a newspaper—photojournalist for *Life*, *Newsweek*, *Harper's Bazaar*, and other magazines—war correspondent during World War II—photographs wounded at Okinawa—becomes well known in the postwar period—one of his photos (two children holding hands) becomes the key picture of the exhibition entitled Family of Man.

2, 9, 12, 16
P, M: New York 1969

Sorce, Wayne
1946 Chicago—New York—

Dr. Soter's Pink Couch, 1976
The Art Institute of Chicago
Rep. 167

Dr. Soter's Drape in Living Room, 1976
The Art Institute of Chicago
Rep. 163

Studies at The Art Institute of Chicago—freelance after 1970—specialization in color.

Sougez, Emmanuel
1889 Bordeaux—Paris 1972

Linens, 1935
Bibliothèque Nationale, Paris
Rep. 79

The White Quill, 1939
Bibliothèque Nationale, Paris
Rep. 207

Masks, no date
Museum Folkwang, Essen
Rep. 186

Studies painting—photographs all over Europe before World War I—representative of the *neusachlichen* (new objectivity) style in France (during the 1920s and 1930s)—photos used in archeology books—co-author of *History of Photography*, 1945.

2
B

Stefani, Bruno
1901 Forli, Italy—Milan 1980

The Galeria, Milan, 1930
Università di Parma
Rep. 366

Milan, 1938
Università di Parma
Rep. 367

Photographs from the mid-twenties until ca. 1960—a chronicle of the city of Milan and surroundings, especially the changing architecture and street scene.

C: Parma 1976

Steichen, Edward (Eduard Jean Steichen)
1879 Luxembourg—West Redding, Connecticut 1973

The Photographer's Best Model: George Bernard Shaw, 1907
Platinum-pigment print
The Museum of Modern Art, New York
Rep. 293

Nocturne—Orangerie Staircase, Versailles, ca. 1910
Bichromate gum print
The Museum of Modern Art, New York
Rep. 55

Heavy Roses, Voulangis, France, 1914
The Museum of Modern Art, New York
Rep. 56

Athens, 1921
George Eastman House, Rochester
Rep. 349

Dolor, ca. 1922
Kunstbibliothek Preussischer Kulturbesitz, Berlin
Rep. 228

George Washington Bridge, New York, 1931
George Eastman House, Rochester
Rep. 368

Primo Carnera, 1933
George Eastman House, Rochester
Rep. 99

Family emigrates to America in 1881—lithography apprentice with the American Fine Art Company—first photographs taken in 1895—participates in exhibitions supported by Clarence H. White and Alfred Stieglitz—Paris 1901–1902—acquainted with Rodin—portraits of artists—moves to New York—interest in all fine printing methods—co-founder of Photo Secession 1902—marries in 1903—lives in Paris from 1906 to 1914—arranges exhibitions for Stieglitz's Photo Secession galleries—publications in *Camera Work,* 1903–1917, represented by seventy-one photographs—wartime service in France—second marriage—establishes himself as the most successful advertising and portrait photographer in the United States—wartime service, 1942–1945—heads the aerial photography section of the U.S. Navy—after World War II heads the photographic section of The Museum of Modern Art, New York—organizes the world famous exhibition entitled Family of Man at The Museum of Modern Art (503 photos from 68 countries) 1955—last marriage in 1960.

1, 2, 3, 4, 5, 6, 7, 8, 9, 10, 11, 12, 14, 16
P, M: New York 1981

Steinert, Otto
1915 Saarbrücken—Essen 1978

Walking on One Foot, 1950
Museum Folkwang, Essen
Rep. 112

Landscape 2, 1953
Deutsche Gesellschaft für Photographie, Cologne
Rep. 246

Still Life with Fish, 1958
Deutsche Gesellschaft für Photographie, Cologne
Rep. 188

Studies medicine in Berlin 1939—first portraits taken in 1947—member of the fotoform group—proponent of subjective photography—teacher and then head of the Staatlichen Schule für Kunst und Handwerk in Saarbrücken, which produced numerous young well-known photographers—teacher at the Folkwang Schule, Universität Essen—organizer of exhibitions on the history of photography—collector and publicist.

2, 7
P

Stelzner, Carl Ferdinand
1805 Flensburg—Hamburg 1894

Burned-out Ruin and the Nicolai Church, 1842
Daguerreotype
Museum für Kunst und Gewerbe, Hamburg
Rep. 1

Burned-out Ruin with the New Stock Exchange, 1842
Daguerreotype
Museum für Kunst und Gewerbe, Hamburg
Rep. 2

First a painter—trained as daguerreotypist in Paris—photographs the great fire of Hamburg in 1842—regarded as the first photojournalist in Germany.

1, 2, 5, 7

Stieglitz, Alfred
1864 Hoboken, New Jersey—1946 New York City

The Terminal, 1893
The Art Institute of Chicago
Rep. 407

A Wet Day, Paris, 1897
The Art Institute of Chicago
Rep. 47

The Steerage, 1907
Photogravure
George Eastman House, Rochester
Rep. 61

Georgia O'Keeffe, 1918
The Art Institute of Chicago
Rep. 329

Equivalents, 1930
The Art Institute of Chicago
Rep. 85a–c

Later Lake George, 1935
The Art Institute of Chicago
Rep. 177

Studies photography with Hermann Vogel, Berlin—devotes his life to the recognition of photography as an artistic medium—documents New York over a forty-year period—rediscovery of the important photographers Hill and Cameron—support of young unknowns such as C.H. White, Steichen, Coburn, and others—publisher of *Camera Notes* and *Camera Work* (50 volumes, 1903–1917)—founder of Photo Secession—organizer of exhibitions of contemporary international artists and photographers in the Photo Secession galleries (291 Fifth Avenue, New York) (1905–1917)—marries American painter Georgia O'Keeffe

1924—after 1929 discovery and support of the newest stylists, such as Strand, Adams, Porter—realizes his life's goal in 1933 by making a gift of his photographic collection to the Metropolitan Museum of Art, New York (*The Collection of Alfred Stieglitz*. Catalog, New York: 1978).

1, 2, 4, 5, 7, 9, 10, 12, 14, 16
P, M: New York 1978

Strache, Wolf
1910 Greifswald, Germany—Berlin—Stuttgart—

Journey into the Past, ca. 1945
Museum Folkwang, Essen
Rep. 379

Studies economics at the universities of Cologne and Münich—works as a freelance photojournalist in Berlin as of 1934—war reporter with the German Air Force 1942 to 1945—founds a publishing house in Stuttgart and publishes his own series of photography books—publisher of the annual *Das Deutsche Lichtbild,* 1955 to 1980.

Strand, Paul
1890 New York—Paris 1976

New York, 1916
Gernsheim Collection, Austin
Rep. 64

Iris, Georgetown Island, Maine, 1928
Museum of Fine Arts, Boston
Rep. 196

White Horse, 1932
San Francisco Museum of Modern Art
Rep. 268

Barns and Sheds, 1936
San Francisco Museum of Modern Art
Rep. 363

Vermont Church, 1944
Museum of Fine Arts, Boston
Rep. 107

Tailor's Apprentice, Luzzara, Italy, 1953
Museum of Fine Arts, Boston
Rep. 280

Student of Lewis Hine in New York—first works as professional photographer around 1912, in

the "artistic style"—first abstract photos in 1915—is heavily supported by Alfred Stieglitz (one-man shows and publications in the last two numbers of *Camera Work*)—main subjects after 1919, the city and nature—works for the Mexican government from 1932 until 1934 as the head of the photo and film section of the Ministry of Education—documentations for American government organizations from 1937 until 1943—a key figure straddling two eras of American photography.

2, 4, 5, 7, 9, 11, 12
P, M: Millerton 1977

Strelow, Liselotte
1908 Hamburg—Berlin—Düsseldorf—Hamburg 1981

Oskar Fritz Schuh, 1955
Deutsche Gesellschaft für Photographie, Cologne
Rep. 343

Portrait photographer—photos of famous personalities—participates in international exhibitions—author of books.

C: Bonn 1977

Sudek, Josef
1896 Kolin nad Labem, Czechoslovakia—Prague 1976

Window, 1944
Uměleckoprůmyslové Muzeum v Praze, Prague
Rep. 450

Roses, 1956
Uměleckoprůmyslové Muzeum v Praze, Prague
Rep. 199

Leaves, 1970
Uměleckoprůmyslové Muzeum v Praze, Prague
Rep. 197

Aerial Remembrances, for Dr. Brumlik, 1971
Uměleckoprůmyslové Muzeum v Praze, Prague
Rep. 198

Loses his right arm during World War I—studies photography at the State School of Graphic Arts in Prague from 1922 until 1924—cofounder of the Czech Society of Photography in 1924—first book publications in 1928—receives high acclaim in his homeland during lifetime.

2, 12
P, C: Aachen 1976
M: New York 1978

Sutcliffe, Frank Meadow
1853 Headingly, Leeds—Whitby, England 1941

Natives of these Isles, 1885
Carbon print
The Royal Photographic Society of Great Britain, Bath
Rep. 385

Stern Realities, 1900
Albumen print
The Royal Photographic Society of Great Britain, Bath
Rep. 423

Hawksfield, no date
Albumen print
The Royal Photographic Society of Great Britain, Bath
Rep. 390

Professional portrait photographer—participates in international exhibitions between 1881 and 1905—main subject: landscapes from his environs—forerunner of naturalistic photography as developed by Emerson—co-founder of the Linked Ring 1892.

2, 7, 9, 12
M: Whitby 1978

Talbot, William Henry Fox
1800 Dorsetshire, England—Lacock Abbey, Wiltshire 1877

Photogenic Drawing of a Leaf, negative; *Photogenic drawing of a leaf,* positive, ca. 1836–1839
The Fox Talbot Museum, Lacock
Reps. 9, 10

The Fruit Sellers—Group Portrait Taken in Cloister Courtyard of Lacock Abbey, ca. 1842
The Fox Talbot Museum, Lacock
Rep. 394

Portrait of Claudet (sitting on the right), no date
Calotype
The Fox Talbot Museum, Lacock
Rep. 8

The Bust of Patroclus, Plate 5 from *The Pencil of Nature,* August 9, 1843
The Fox Talbot Museum, Lacock
Rep. 15

Avenue des Capucines, ca. 1843
The Fox Talbot Museum, Lacock
Rep. 16

The Ladder, Plate 14 from *The Pencil of Nature*, ca. 1844
The Fox Talbot Museum, Lacock
Rep. 393

A Fruit Piece, Plate 24 from *The Pencil of Nature*, ca. 1844
The Fox Talbot Museum, Lacock
Rep. 202

Loch Katrine from *Sun Pictures in Scotland*, ca. 1845
The Fox Talbot Museum, Lacock
Rep. 263

The Reverend Calvert Jones Sitting in the Cloisters at Lacock Abbey, no date
The Fox Talbot Museum, Lacock
Rep. 13

Articles of China, Plate 3 from *The Pencil of Nature*, no date
The Fox Talbot Museum, Lacock
Rep. 11

Elm Tree at Lacock, no date
The Fox Talbot Museum, Lacock
Rep. 14

Man with a Telescope from the Battlements of Mount Edgecomb, Plymouth, no date
The Fox Talbot Museum, Lacock
Rep. 12

Studies at Cambridge University—Member of the British Parliament from 1833 to 1834—first photographic experiments in 1834—first exhibition and publication of *The Art of Photogenic Drawing* in 1839—inventor of calotype, also Talbotype (photographing on paper)—publishes the world's first photography books: *The Pencil of Nature*, 1844–1846, and *Sun Pictures from Scotland*, 1845.

1, 2, 3, 7, 9, 12, 16
P, M: England 1977

Tas, Filip
1918 London—Antwerp—

Long Avenue without Leentjie (Little Helen), from *Portfolio 1979*, 1979
Het Sterckshof Museum, Antwerp
Rep. 255

Think alone House, from *Portfolio, 1979*, 1979
Rep. 347

Studies at the Academy of Fine Arts, Antwerp—participates in international exhibitions—professional photographer and professor at the National Hoger Instituut voor Bouwkunde in Stedebouw, Antwerp.

Teynard, Félix
1817 Grenoble, France—1892

Karnak, ca. 1850
Det kongelige Bibliothek, Copenhagen
Rep. 369

Theben, Médinet Habou, Second Courtyard, Southeast Gallery, ca. 1851
Det kongelige Bibliothek, Copenhagen
Rep. 28

Engineer—travels to Egypt and photographs there from 1851 to 1852—photographs published in an expensive book (1853 to 1858), a rarity in his time.

3, 15

Tice, George A.
1938 Newark, New Jersey—

Cemetery Gates, 1965
The Art Institute of Chicago
Rep. 248

Specialization in platinum print method—photojournalism from the northeastern United States.

12
P, C: Lincoln, Nebraska
M: Danbury 1977

Tuggener, Jakob
1904 Zürich—

Lathe in the Oerlikon Engineering Works, 1935
Stiftung für die Photographie, Kunsthaus Zürich
Rep. 179

Ticinesi Ball, Grand Hotel Dolder, Zürich, 1948
Rep. 412

Self-taught—photo essays on special themes—particularly the world of the worker and social events in Switzerland.

C: Zürich 1974

Ueda, Shoji
1913 Tottori-ken, Japan—

Procession, no date
The Nihon University of Art, Tokyo
Rep. 422

Numerous publications after 1930 in photographic journals—professor at the Kyushu Sangyo University.

M: Tokyo 1978 (No. 11)

Uelsmann, Jerry N.
1934 Detroit, Michigan—

Ritual Ground, 1964
The Royal Photographic Society of Great Britain, Bath
Rep. 126

Equivalent, 1964
The Royal Photographic Society of Great Britain, Bath
Rep. 223

Untitled, 1971
The Art Institute of Chicago
Rep. 271

Studies at the Rochester Institute of Technology and at Indiana University beginning in 1960 teaching photography at the University of Florida—specializes in the Sandwich method (combination of several negatives).

2, 12
P, M: New York 1975

Veronesi, Luigi
1908 Milan, Italy—

Photogram on Motion Picture Film, 1936
Università di Parma
Rep. 424

Photography, 1938
Università di Parma
Rep. 433

Interest in several artistic media, especially experimental photography (photograms, solarization, light-abstractions).

C: Parma 1975

Vishniac, Roman
1897 Parlosk, Russia—New York—

Jewish Child, 1938
Münchner Stadtmuseum, Munich
Rep. 384

Documents with more than five thousand photos Jewish life in East European ghettos from 1933 to 1939—emigrates to New York in 1940—interest in micro-photography and scientific photography.

2, 12
P, M

Vogt, Christian
1946 Basel—

Male Nude, 1969
Stiftung für die Photographie, Kunsthaus Zürich
Rep. 242

Freelance photographer after 1970—photo series of trips to the Far East, New York—participation in international exhibitions.

C: Zürich 1974
M: Geneva 1980

Watzek, Josef
1848 Vienna—1903

Wineglass with Apple, 1896
Three-color gum print
Kunstbibliothek Preussischer Kulturbesitz, Berlin
Rep. 165

Studies at the academies of art in Leipzig and Munich—teaches drawing—photographs after 1890—member of the Vienna Camera club—collaborates with Hugo Henneberg and Heinrich Kühn (after 1895) on the improvement of the offset method—produces the first multicolor print in 1896.

1, 5, 7, 11

Weegee (Arthur Fellig)
1899 Zloczew, Poland—New York 1968

Man Killed in Accident, 1945
Bibliothèque Nationale, Paris
Rep. 104

A Couple Driven Out, 1945
Bibliothèque Nationale, Paris
Rep. 404

Emigrates to America in 1909—at first, street photographer and newspaper assistant—police photographer from 1935 to 1945—publishes documentation of city catastrophes in 1945—portrait distortions of well-known personalities after 1950—signs his photos, "Weegee the Famous."

2, 7, 9, 12
P, M: Munich 1978

Weston, Edward
1886 Highland Park, Illinois—Carmel, California 1958

Ruth Shaw, 1922
The Art Institute of Chicago
Rep. 323

Shell, 1927
San Francisco Museum of Modern Art
Rep. 81

Nude, 1927
San Francisco Museum of Modern Art
Rep. 231

Nude on Sand, 1936
The Royal Photographic Society of Great Britain, Bath
Rep. 100

Powerlines and Telephone Poles, 1939
San Francisco Museum of Modern Art
Rep. 253

Leading representative of straight photography from 1922—co-founder of the group f/64 with Ansel Adams and Willard Van Dyke—technical perfectionist—main subjects: formalistic studies of nature, man, and landscape.

2, 4, 7, 8, 9, 12
P, M: New York 1980

White, Clarence H.
1871 East Carlisle, Ohio—Mexico City 1925

Ring Toss, 1899
Platinum print
The Library of Congress, Washington, D.C.
Rep. 277

In the Orchard, 1900
Palladium print
The Library of Congress, Washington, D.C.
Rep. 49

Nude (collaboration with Stieglitz), no date
Platinum print
The Royal Photographic Society of Great Britain, Bath
Rep. 210

The Kiss, 1904
Platinum print
The Library of Congress, Washington, D.C.
Rep. 52

Amateur photographer after 1894—founder of the Camera Club of Newark, Ohio, 1898 and organizes exhibitions of the Photo Secession artists Day, Käsebier, Stieglitz, and others—shows his own work in New York, Boston, and London in 1899—co-founder of the New York Photo Secession 1902—moves to New York in 1906—teaches—publications in *Camera Work* from 1903 until 1910—conflict with Stieglitz—founder of the Clarence White School of Photography 1914—co-founder and first president of Pictorial Photographers of America.

White, Minor
1908 Minneapolis, Minnesota—Arlington, Massachusetts 1976

Peeled Paint, 1959
San Francisco Museum of Modern Art
Rep. 127

Three Tides, 1959
San Francisco Museum of Modern Art
Rep. 258

A very influential photographer and theoretician in America—teaches for years at the best-known institutions and workshops—co-founder of the magazine *Aperture*—active as editor and publisher until 1975.

2, 9, 12, 16
P, M: Millerton 1978

Winogrand, Garry
1928 New York—

Party, Norman Mailer's Fiftieth Birthday, New York, 1973
The Museum of Modern Art, New York
(Not shown. The photo was in the exhibition but permission to reproduce it had not been received when this book went to press.)

Studies painting in New York—studies photojournalism with Alexey Brodovitch at the New School for Social Research 1951—advertising photographer at first—teaches at the University of Texas after 1973—photographs of social criticism.

2, 12
P, C: Lincoln, Nebraska 1977
M: New York and Boston 1977

Winquist, Rolf
1910 Göteborg, Sweden—Stockholm 1968

Feather, 1950
Fotografiska Museet, Stockholm
Rep. 204

Fashion and advertising photographer—also known for his portraits of artists—pictures of Swedish women.

7

Yokosuka, Noriaki
1937 Yokohama—

Male Nude, no date
The Nihon University of Art, Tokyo
Rep. 239

Studies photography at Nihon University—publishes first book in 1972.

_____

Zwart, Piet
1885 Zaandijk—Wassenaar, Holland 1977

Cabbage with Hoarfrost, 1930
Haags Gemeente Museum, The Hague
Rep. 194

Teaches drawing and art history from 1908 until 1913—after studying at the Technical Institute in Delft, he works with typography and in advertising—takes first photographs in 1929—guest lecturer at the Bauhaus, 1931.

8
C: The Hague 1973

ACKNOWLEDGMENTS

Photokina and Dumont Publishers
thank the following persons
for their invaluable assistance:

Hans Christian Adam, Göttingen
Lanfranco Colombo, Milan
Michelle Dumas, Paris
Ger and Marejke Fiolet, Amsterdam
Charles E. Fraser, London
Rolf D. Fricke, Rochester, New York
Pierre Gassmann, Paris
F. C. Gundlach, Hamburg
Manfred Heiting, Amsterdam
Fritz Kempe, Hamburg

Rudolf Kicken, Cologne
Elisabeth Kraemer, Bonn
Goro Kuramochi, Tokyo
Norman C. Lipton, New York
Bernd Lohse, Leverkusen
Harry Lunn, Jr., Washington, D.C.
Peter McGill, New York
Antonia Mulas, Milan
Weston J. Naef, New York
Mrs. John A. Pope, Washington, D.C.
Allan Porter, Lucerne
Dr. Pier Paolo Preti, Milan
Howard Read III, New York
Dr. Laurent Roosens, Antwerp
Christine and Gerd Sander, Washington, D.C.
Gunther Sander, Rottach-Egern
Dr. Karl Steinorth, Stuttgart
Eelco Wolf, Cambridge, Massachusetts

LENDING MUSEUMS AND INSTITUTIONS

Fotografiska Museet, Stockholm
Åke Sidwall, Director
Leif Wigh, Associate Curator
Ulla Bergmann, Librarian

Det kongelige Bibliotek,
Copenhagen
Bjørn Ochsner, Curator a. D.
Hans Berggreen
Hendrik Dupont
John Lorenzen
Bodil Østergaard

The Fox Talbot Museum, Lacock
Anthony Burnett Brown, Owner
of the Fox Talbot Collection
Robert E. Lassam, Curator

National Portrait Gallery, London
Colin Ford, Keeper of Film and
Photography
Terence Pepper
Kate Poole

Victoria and Albert Museum,
London
Mark Haworth-Booth, Assistant
Keeper of Photographs

The Royal Photographic Society
of Great Britain, Bath
Kenneth R. Warr, BA FSAE, FSIM
Secretary
Valerie Lloyd, Curator of
Photographs

Kodak Museum, Harrow
Brian Coe, Curator

Stedelijk Museum, Amsterdam
E.E.L. de Wilde, Director
Els Barents, Division of Applied
Art—Photography
Petra Blaisse

Haags Gemeente-Museum,
The Hague
Dr. Th. van Velzen, Director
Kees Broos, Curator
Slip Book, Curator

Het Sterckshof Museum,
Antwerp
Jan Walgrave, Director
Roger Coenen, Director of
Photography

Museum für Kunst und Gewerbe,
Hamburg
Prof. Dr. Axel von Saldern,
Director
Dr. Heinz Spielmann,
Chief Curator
Fritz Kempe, Honorary
Director of Photo Collection
Ernst Kaphengst, Official Expert
of Photo Collection

Kunstbibliothek Preussischer
Kulturbesitz, Berlin
Prof. Dr. Ekhart Berckenhagen,
Director of Art Library
Dr. Klaus Popitz, Director of
Commercial Art
Collection of Art Library

Photography Collection,
Museum Folkwang, Essen
Dr. Paul Vogt, Director
Ute Eskildsen, Curator

Museum Ludwig, Cologne
Prof. Karl Ruhrberg, Director
Dr. Evelyn Weiss, Senior Curator
Dr. Christoph Brockhaus,
Director of Graphics Collection,
Photography Collection
Dr. Reinhold Misselbeck,
Learned Assistant,
Photography Collection

Deutsche Gesellschaft für
Photographie, Cologne
Dr. Hans Friderichs,
President
Assistant Gert Koshofer,
General Secretariat

Agfa-Gevaert Foto-Historama,
Leverkusen
Klaus op ten Höfel, Director

Münchner Stadtmuseum-
Fotomuseum München
Ditmar Albert, Director of
Photography Museum

Stiftung für die Photographie im
Kunsthaus Zürich, Zürich
Walter Binder, Director
Rosellina Burri Bischof

Centro studi e archivio della
communicazione, Università
di Parma, Parma
Prof. Arturo Carlo Quintavalle,
Director

Fondazione Fratelli Alinari,
Florence
Dr. Filippo Zevi, President

Uměleckoprůmyslové Muzeum v
Praze, Prague
Ph Dr. Dagmar Hejdová, Director
Ph Dr. Zdeněk Kirschner

Ministère de la Culture, Paris
Agnès de Gouvion Saint Cyr,
Service de la Photographie
Association des Amis de Jacques
Henri Lartigue, Grand Palais
Isabelle Jammes, Curator

Bibliothèque Nationale, Paris
Georges Le Rider,
General Administrator
Jean-Pierre Seguin,
Chief Curator
Jean Claude Lemagny,
Curator
Bernard Marbot,
Curator
G. Lassalle, Chief Curator
in Charge of Loans

Société Française de
Photographie, Paris
Pr. J. J. Trillat, President
Jean Prissette, President
Christiane Roger, General
Administrator in
Charge of Collections

Museum of Fine Arts, Boston,
Massachusetts
Dr. Jan Fontain, Director
Cliff Ackley, Curator
Eleanor Sayre, Curator
Jane S. Larsen

International Museum of Photog-
raphy at George Eastman
House, Rochester, New York
Robert A. Mayer,
Director

EDITORS AND CONTRIBUTORS

Professor L. Fritz Gruber (b. 1908) is generally known as the head of the Photokina photography and film shows in Cologne, West Germany. Between 1950 and 1980 he conceived and mounted more than three hundred exhibitions. He has written a number of books and television programs about photography and was the owner of a photography collection which is now with the Ludwig Museum in Cologne. He has received awards both in and outside Germany for the significant role he has played in the world of photography since 1950.

Renate Gruber (b. 1936) has been her husband's closest associate for more than twenty years, and during this time she has cared for the Gruber collection.

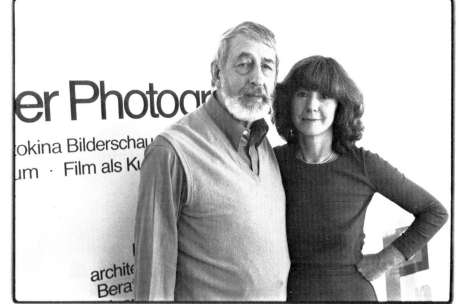

Professor Helmut Gernsheim (b. 1913) is the most important European historian and photography collector. He has written numerous works on the history and esthetics of photography as well as monographs on the early pioneers of photography. In 1959 he received the Culture Prize of the German Society for Photography.

Gernsheim rediscovered many of the world's first photographs, including many Victorian ones. His comprehensive exhibit entitled One Hundred Years of Photography, which traveled through Europe and America from 1951 through 1963, included more than six hundred important vintage prints from 1826 to 1938, all from the Gernsheim collection.

This exhibit was an important trailblazer for the worldwide renaissance of interest in photography and served to provide impetus for the eventual creation of a European photography museum. The Gernsheim Collection, with thirty-four thousand photographs, four thousand books, and cameras, has been at the University of Texas, Austin, since 1964.

Professor Beaumont Newhall (b. 1908) is *the* senior photography historian. Thanks to him, museums collect, curate, and exhibit photographs. That is why he was asked to describe this development from his personal perspective.

He studied art history at Harvard University and after receiving his degree became librarian at The Museum of Modern Art in New York and later director of the newly founded department of photography at that museum. Subsequently, he worked as curator and then director of the International Museum of Photography at the George Eastman House in Rochester, New York, where he remained until 1971. Since that time he has devoted himself to further studies and publications and taught at the University of Rochester and the State University of New York at Buffalo. He lives in Santa Fe, New Mexico, where he also lectures at the state university. Newhall is the author of numerous standard works on photography. He has received the most coveted international awards as well as the Culture Prize of the German Society of Pho-

tography (1970). In 1978 his alma mater, Harvard, awarded him an honorary Doctor of Arts.

Jeane von Oppenheim (b. 1941) studied art history at Connecticut College for Women. After practical training at a New York advertising agency, she married in 1962 and has lived in Paris, London, and, since 1964, in Cologne. As of 1974 her interest in art has concentrated particularly on photography. When the Wallraf-Richartz Museum/Museum Ludwig took over the Gruber collection in 1977 Jeane von Oppenheim was the first curator. Since 1980 she has been a member of the board of the German Society for Photography.

CREDITS

The photographs in the present volume appear with the kind consent of the lending institutions, their heirs, or the rightful owners listed below. The numbers in the acknowledgments that follow refer to the numbers of the respective pictures in the body of the book.

98, 350, 371 © Berenice Abbott, Abbot Village; 80, 101, 247, 257, 259 © Ansel Adams, Carmel; 281, 400 © Lydia Oorthuis, Amsterdam, and Joost Elffers, Amsterdam; 123, 316, 376 © The Estate of Diane Arbus, New York; 136, 339 © Richard Avedon, New York; 364 © Lewis Baltz, Castelli, New York; 447 © Thomas F. Barrow, Albuquerque; 216 © Jean François Bauret, Paris; 70, 318, 435, 440 © Herbert Bayer, Montecito; 73, 303, 319, 336 © Sotheby's Belgravia, London; 135 © Bernhard and Hilla Becher, Düsseldorf; 106, 279 © Rosellina Burri-Bischof, Zürich; 113, 392 © Edouard Boubat, Paris; 97, 297, 401 © Time-Life Picture Service, New York; 94, 129, 224, 270 © Bill Brandt, London; 91, 227, 321, 396, 413 © Brassaï, Paris; 95, 233 © Manuel Alvarez Bravo, Coyoacan; 213, 351 © Francis Bruguière Jr., Reston; 222 © Edna Bullock, Monterey; 195 © Lotte Burchartz, Essen; 313 © René Burri, Zürich; 108, 235 © Harry Callahan, Providence; 167 © Jo Ann Callis, Culver City; 102, 419, 421 © The Estate of Robert Capa, New York; 124, 272 © Paul Caponigro, Santa Fe; 96, 416, 418 © Henri Cartier-Bresson, Paris; 121, 295 © Fritz Redlin, Langen; 58, 67, 361, 362 © George Eastman House, Rochester; 269 © Mark Cohen, Wilkes-Barre; 170, 171 © Marie Cosindas, Boston; 111, 183, 225, 307 © The Imogen Cunningham Trust, Berkeley; 118, 415 © Bruce Davidson, New York; 53, 214, 229, 328 © Société Française de Photographie, Paris; 164 © John M. Divola, Venice; 103, 397, 405 © Robert Doisneau, Paris; 143, 161, 162 © Ken Domon, Tokyo; 301 © Fritz Kempe, Hamburg; 220, 236 © Ervina Boková, Podebrady; 157, 173 © William Eggleston, Washington, D.C.; 90 © 1932 Alfred Eisenstaedt, New York; 122, 402 © Ed van der Elsken, Edam; 86, 290, 309 © Gottfried Erfurth, Gaienhofen; 441, 443 © Elliott Erwitt, New York; 92, 330, 373, 375, 409 © John T. Hill, Bethany; 408 © Larry Fink, Martins Creek; 186 © Regula Lips-Finsler, Zollikerberg; 147, 148 © Franco Fontana, Modena; 116, 182, 256, 377, 398 © Robert Frank,

Mabou; 134, 232, 378 © Lee Friedlander, New York City; 133 © André Gelpke, Essen; 149, 150, 151 © Luigi Ghirri, Modena; 395, 427 © Mario Giacomelli, Senigallia; 132, 304 © Ralph Gibson, New York; 428 © Ara Güler, Istanbul; 301 © J. Guidalevitch, Wilryk; 153, 154, 155 © Ernst Haas, New York; 426, 437 © Heinz Hajek-Halke, Berlin; 311, 341 © Philippe Halsman, Yvonne Halsman, New York; 114, 386 © Hiroshi Hamaya, Kanagawa-Ken; 348 © Ursula Dörmann, Bochum; 178, 322 © Martini & Ronchetti, Rome; 190 © Marta Hoepffner, Kressbronn; 403 © Thomas Höpker, Bildagentur Hamann, Munich; 274 © Frank Horvat, Boulogne; 221 © Eiko Hosoe, Tokyo; 175 © Roel Jacobs, Mortsel; 442 © Ikko Narahara, Tokyo; 439, 449 © Kenneth Josephson, Chicago; 294 © Yousuf Karsh, Ottawa; 76, 184, 345 © André Kertész, New York; 430 © M. Wagner, Leusden; 444 © Ihei Kimura; 119, 411 © William Klein, Paris; 219 © Höhere Graphische Bundeslehr- und Versuchsanstalt, Wien; 374, 382 © Josef Koudelka, Paris; 174, 305 © Association des Amis de Jacques Henri Lartigue, Paris; 446 © Clarence John Laughlin, New Orleans; 381 © Robert Lebeck, Hamburg; 60, 334 © Renata Mertens, Zürich; 434 © Rudolf Lichtsteiner, Zürich; 71, 354 © Max Scheler, Hamburg; 238, 241, 320 © Bernard Perlin, New York; 87 © Felix H. Man, Rome; 117, 372 © Ralph Eugene Meatyard, Lexington; 130, 448 © Roger Mertin, Rochester; 365 © Ray K. Metzker, Philadelphia; 438 © Joel Meyerowitz, New York; 137, 314, 315 © Duane Michals, New York; 436 © Antonio Migliori, Bologna; 45 © L. Biernaux, Brussels; 267 © Richard Misrach, Emeryville; 356 © Lucia Moholy, Zollikon; 68, 243, 244, 358 © Hattula Moholy-Nagy, Ann Arbor; 335 © Antonia Mulas, Mailand; 237 © Joan Munkacsi, New York; 110 © Arnold Newman, New York; 193 © Kiyoshi Nishiyama; 172 © Paul de Nooijer, Eindhoven; 445 © Takayuki Ogawa, Tokyo; 158 © Arthur Ollman, Oakland; 75, 191, 205, 218 © G. Ray Hawkins Gallery, Los Angeles; 131 © Bill Owens, Livermore; 283 © Hilmar Pabel, Umratshausen; 331 © Gordon Parks, New York; 166 courtesy Vogue, © 1950 (renewed 1978) by the Condé Nast Publications Inc.; 152 courtesy Vogue, © 1953 Irving Penn, New York; 120, 128, 141, 299 © The Condé Nast Publications Inc. and © Irving Penn, New York; 144, 145 © Eliot Porter, Santa Fe; 46, 284 © Société Française de Photographie, Paris; 69, 72, 291, 302, 306, 425 © Juliet Man Ray, Paris; 77, 254, 266, 355 © Ernst Renger-

Patzsch, Cologne; 115, 399 © Marc Riboud, Paris; 189, 431 © Jaroslav Rössler, Prague; 209, 359 © Eva Rubinstein, New York; 74, 337, 380 © Berlinische Galerie, Berlin; 88, 261, 342, 344 © Gunther Sander, Rottach-Egern; 230 © Galerie Fiolet, Amsterdam; 215, 217 © Jan Saudek, Prague; 66 © Christian Schad, Keilberg; 192 © E. Schuiteman, Wassenaar; 176 © Emil Schulthess, Zürich; 265, 391 © Joa Marti, Bern; 89, 410 © The Estate of Ben Shahn; 226 © Kishin Shinoyama, Tokyo; 260 © Yoshikazu Shirakawa, Tokyo; 159, 160, 169 © Stephen Shore; 169 © Seagram County Court House Archives, Library of Congress, Washington; 208, 249 © Jeanloup Sieff, Paris; 156 © Irene Siegel, Chicago; 109, 181, 185 © Aaron Siskind, Providence; 105, 387 © John Morris, New York; 163, 168 © Wayne Sorce, Brooklyn Heights; 79, 187, 207 © Bibliothèque Nationale, Paris; 366, 367 © Università di Parma; 55, 56, 99, 228, 293, 349, 368 © Joanna T. Steichen, New York; 112, 188, 246 © Marlis Steinert, Genf; 47, 61, 85a–c, 177, 329, 407 © The Art Institute of Chicago; 379 © Wolf Strache, Stuttgart; 64 © The Paul Strand Foundation, Millerton; 107 © 1950, 1971, 1977 The Paul Strand Foundation, Millerton, as published in Paul Strand: Time in New England, Aperture, 1980; 196 © 1971, 1977 The Paul Strand Foundation, Millerton, as published in Paul Strand: Time in New England, Aperture, 1980; 268 © 1940, 1967, 1971 The Paul Strand Foundation, Millerton, as published in Paul Strand: A Retrospective Monograph, The Years 1915–1968, 2v., Aperture, 1971; 280 © 1955, 1971 The Paul Strand Foundation, Millerton, as published in Paul Strand: A Retrospective Monograph, The Years 1915–1968, 2v., Aperture, 1971; 363 © 1971 The Paul Strand Foundation, Millerton, as published in Paul Strand: A Retrospective Monograph, The Years 1915–1968, 2v., Aperture, 1971; 343 © Liselotte Strelow, Hamburg; 197, 198, 199, 450 © B. Sudkova, Prague; 255, 347 © Filip Tas, Antwerp; 248 © George A. Tice, Iselin; 179, 412 © Jakob Tuggener, Zürich; 422 © Shoji Ueda, Tokyo; 126, 223, 271 © Jerry Uelsmann, Gainesville; 424, 432 © Luigi Veronesi, Mailand; 384 © Roman Vishniac, New York; 242 © Christian Vogt, Basel; 104, 404 © Wilma Wilcox, New York; 81, 100, 231, 253, 323 © Cole Weston, Carmel; 204 © Raina Winquist, Stockholm; 127, 258 © The Trustees of Princeton University; 239 © Noriaki Yokosuka, Tokyo; 194 © C. Zwart, Wassenaar; 269 © Ulrich Tillmann, Cologne